NEW REALITIES
IN AUDIO

A PRACTICAL GUIDE FOR
VR, AR, MR, AND 360 VIDEO

New Realities in Audio

A Practical Guide for VR, AR, MR, and 360 Video

Stephan Schütze

with

Anna Irwin-Schütze

CRC Press
Taylor & Francis Group
Boca Raton London New York

CRC Press is an imprint of the
Taylor & Francis Group, an **informa** business

AN A K PETERS BOOK

CRC Press
Taylor & Francis Group
6000 Broken Sound Parkway NW, Suite 300
Boca Raton, FL 33487-2742

© 2018 by Taylor & Francis Group, LLC
CRC Press is an imprint of Taylor & Francis Group, an Informa business

Printed on acid-free paper

International Standard Book Number-13: 978-1-138-74081-5 (paperback)
978-1-138-74082-2 (hardback)

Library of Congress Cataloging-in-Publication Data

Names: Schutze, Stephan, author.
Title: Virtual sound : a practical guide to audio, dialogue and music in VR and AR / Stephan Schutze.
Description: Boca Raton : Taylor & Francis, a CRC title, part of the Taylor & Francis imprint, a member of the Taylor & Francis Group, the academic division of T&F Informa, plc, [2018]
Identifiers: LCCN 2017037804| ISBN 9781138740815 (pbk. :acid-free paper) | ISBN 9781138740822 (hardback : acid-free paper)
Subjects: LCSH: Sound in virtual reality. | Computer sound processing | Multimedia systems.
Classification: LCC TK7881.94 .S39 2018 | DDC 006.8--dc23
LC record available at https://lccn.loc.gov/2017037804

**Visit the Taylor & Francis Web site at
http://www.taylorandfrancis.com**

**and the CRC Press Web site at
http://www.crcpress.com**

Printed and bound in the United States of America by Sheridan

contents

acknowledgments xiii
authors.. xv
contributors..xix
photography xxv

1 new realities...1

    introduction 1
    why this book...5
    what's in this book 12
    references... 14

2 definitions and core concepts.................................... 15

    a critical distinction: thinking differently about spatial
    audio for the new realities 15
        Spatialization in Stereo.. 17
        Spatialization in Surround Sound 19
        Spatialization in the New Realities...............................20
        Spatial Audio in VR and 360 Video 23
    setting the stage: defining our terminology.......................24
    VR: virtual reality 25
        Replacing the World 25
        360 Video 25
    AR: alternate reality 27
    MR: mixed reality..28

core concepts and other terms 28
   Haptics 29
   Transfer Function 29
   Head-Related Transfer Function 29
   Interaural Time Difference 29
   IID or ILD 30
   Interaural Phase Difference 30
   Cone of Confusion 32
   Transcoding 33
   Flat Plane or Zero Plane 33
   Diegetic 34
   Formats 34
   Localization 35
   Channel-Based Audio 35
   Binaural 36
   Mid-Side (MS) Recording Format 36
      Ambisonics 37
further reading 49

3 why isn't this easy? The many challenges of the
new realities 51

the challenge of 3D audio 51
adapting to new formats 56
how and why we hear 56
   The Uncanny Valley 57
      Why the uncanny valley matters to the
      new realities 58
   Why What We Hear Matters 60
      Hearing versus listening 64
random or designed: the battle between order and chaos 65
choose your reality 68
   How Far Down the Rabbit Hole Do We Go? 68
      Example: wavefront curvature 69
   Challenges Common to All New Reality Formats 70
   Balancing Information and Entertainment 71
the triangulation challenge 73
   Localization and Spatialization: Defining the Issues 74
   The Human Problem 74
   Delivery 78
   Spatialization 78
   Physics Is Expensive 79

mixing for the new realities 81
unique format challenges 83
   Virtual Reality Challenges 83
   Head Tracking 85
why bother getting audio right? 86
   Aiding the Visual Experience 86
   360 Video 87
alternate reality challenges...89
   "Pardon?" AR Audibility 90
   Turn that Racket Down! 90
   Choose Wisely...91
   Frequency Range 92
mixed reality challenges...93
   MR: Contamination of Content..93
hyperreality (HR)...96

4 what we're doing now: analysis of existing projects..............99

VR project analysis..99
broadcast 100
   BBC Special Binaural Audio Broadcast *Doctor Who*
   Series 10, Episode 4, Knock 100
vive 102
   Earthlight...102
gear VR 105
   Dark Days..105
playstation VR...109
   How We Soar..109
   Environment..110
   World Objects..110
playstation VR...113
   Star Wars Battlefront: Episode One X-Wing Mission.........113
location-based experiences 120

5 creation and implementation: putting it into practice..........143

working with the new realities...143
   Placement...144
   Implementation..145
   Min and Max Distance Functions and
   Attenuation Curves..145
   Reverb 149

Breaking Our Sounds for Better Implementation........... 151
"Observation" of Audio 153
working analysis 158
Amplitude Drop-Off 159
creating a VR clock.. 164
The Actual Sound of a Clock 164
Accuracy and Detail 165
Sidebar 166
Physical Placement 168
Simulating Sound Wave Properties 168
Reverb.. 168
Smoke and mirrors 172
serious audio design for serious purposes 173
Simulating Survival... 175
the James Bond adventure in AR...................................... 176
Working with 360 Video... 181
What microphones should I use?.............................. 182
What format should my 360 video be in?................. 182
How do I encode my project and what is the
best delivery method?.. 184
Video file container.. 184
Codec.. 184
Frame rate 185
Bitrate... 185
Audio format 185
Attention focus... 187
content creation.. 190
New Realities: New Creation Approaches...................... 190
World Building with Audio 191
Building a weather system 191
Applications for immersive audio............................. 194
Getting the details right 194
Creating a Virtual Environment.................................... 195
Creating a forest... 196
Example: wind and water 199
Ocean waves 200
Footsteps...202
Noise Reduction 203
Near Field versus Far Field 205

6   sound? what sound? gathering assets for your project 207

gathering, designing, and creating your raw assets 207
   Cost, Time, and Quality..208
   Sound Libraries 208
      The good 210
      The bad.. 210
   Location Recording 210
      The good 214
      The bad.. 214
   Foley.. 214
      The good 216
      The bad.. 216
   Sound Creation.. 216
      The good 217
      The bad.. 217
   Generative or Procedural Audio................................. 217
microphones... 219
   Directional Microphones 219
      Sennheiser MKH60 220
      Rode NTG3.. 221
      Audio Technica stereo BP4029 221
      Sanken CS1e..222
   Dynamic Microphones 223
      Shure SM7B..224
      Shure SM57 224
      AKG D112...225
   Omnidirectional Microphones 226
      Lapel mics..226
      DPA 4061 227
   Binaural Microphones..228
      Binaural recording as a new realities
      audio technique...230
      DIY binaural dummy head 232
   Ambisonic Microphones 234
      Sennheiser Ambeo 235
      After testing 236
   Specific Purpose Microphones...................................239
      Aquarian H2a 239
   Portable Digital Recorders..240

7 music: how and why music in the new realties forces a
shift in perspective 243

blurring the line between diegetic and nondiegetic
"musical" content..244
    Where Is Our Music?..246
musical possibilities 247
musical risk: just because you have a thing does not
mean you should use it..249
    Don't Deafen Your Audience 250
how to utilize your space 251
    Depth and Parallax...251
    Conventional Linear Stereo Music 253
    Attention Focus and Music..254
let's go to extremes 255
generative music...256
    Basic Approach...257
    Taking Generative Music to Extremes 258
    Learning from Defect: Spaceship Destruction Kit..........258

8 working together: navigating the team project minefield 263

consistency of environment..264
    Communication with non-audio Team Members
    and Clients 269
    Emotional Mapping...270
    Team Workflow 273

9 platform considerations: how different platforms affect
what you can, can't, or shouldn't do 275

tools that enhance our workflow...275
user experience: the device conundrum..............................283
delivery platforms...284
    Mobile...284
    HoloLens..287
        Headphones, except not...288
        Both good and bad 289
        Cut your coat to suit your cloth 289
    Ossic Headphones..290
    Different Platforms, Different Solutions.........................292

remember the audience, our customers 294

    Comfort and Control 296

        A welcoming environment 296

        Setup 298

        Communication..299

        Use it wisely 300

    Fatigue 302

        Reality versus fun 306

    User Control: How Much Control Do We Give

    Our Players? 308

10 roadmap for the future: what do we do next? 311

we don't know what we don't know 311

    Learning a Whole New Vocabulary...............................313

    Research, Development, and Evolution 314

using the knowledge..319

    Research and Practice 319

    Endless Opportunities 320

    Dreamers and Doers...321

    Be Fearless, Be Reckless, Be a Little Crazy 322

references..322

index..323

acknowledgments

A book such as this seldom comes from the mind of a single individual. In the case of the new realities, this is such a new area of craft and so complex that I spent many months speaking with colleague, friends, and complete strangers about how we can best evolve this new creative format and how we can all grow together to develop a new form of media. To everyone who contributed a thought or an idea, I say thank you.

My wife, Anna Irwin-Schütze, has contributed to the production of this book in a very practical way as an editor and a mental wrangler of my thoughts, but beyond that she has always provided the inspiration and support that has allowed me the privilege to maintain a creative career, and for that I owe her a debt I can never repay.

This book also includes contributions from some of the leading craft persons in this new industry. While we are all learning and developing skills in this field there are some that are leading the way and inspiring us all with their creative minds. For each of the contributors I have asked them to provide a brief introduction so they can be acknowledged and their contributions to this new media form can be remembered.

authors

Stephan Schütze is a multitalented force in the video game audio world, having strengthened countless projects through his music and sound design. Most recently, he composed the score for the Prideful Sloth's critically acclaimed open-world video game *Yonder: The Cloud Catcher Chronicles*. To complement the enchanting, explorational tone of the game, Stephan created a score and sound design that was subtle, yet whimsical, and constantly beckoned the player to return for more. Showcasing his exceptional talents, Stephan crafted both the music and sound design, a rarity in the audio for the visual media world, which usually divides these tasks across multiple individuals.

Creating music for nearly every console generation of the new millennium, Stephan has scored projects from early 2000s mobile games, all the way to recent MMOs. He recently provided sound design for the acclaimed digital board game *Armello*, bolstering the tone for the game's strategic, high-fantasy battles. He won Best Audio at the Australian Game Developers Conference for his work on *Jurassic Park: Operation Genesis*, the first full orchestra game score recorded in Australia, and his work enlivening this franchise has been praised as the favorite of fans, second only to John Williams. Other fan-favorite franchises and brands Stephan has uplifted include *Star Trek: The Cold Enemy*, *Need For Speed: Underground*, *Nicktoons Unite*, and *Rugby League Live*. Many of the top developers and publishers in the space have entrusted Stephan with their project audio, as he has collaborated with companies including Ubisoft, THQ, Konami, and Universal Interactive. Whether utilizing a full orchestra, or a few live players, Stephan's scores and sound design consistently enrich the game worlds, and leave fans wanting more.

Stephan's compositional style is highly influenced by his time in Japan working for the renowned Tokyo anime studio, Studio Easter. While he enjoys the powerful sound of a large orchestra, the delicate touch inspired by the music of Ghibli is the unique quality he brought to the score for *Yonder: The Cloud Catcher Chronicles*. In an era of boisterous musical themes and massive walls of sound, Stephan uses subtlety to support character and narrative. Many years spent as a performing drummer also enhances the more dynamic material he creates.

A highly sought-after speaker, Stephan has been a featured presenter at GDC, Game Sound Con, Animfx, GCAP, and more. Recognized by his peers for his leadership and community building, Stephan was awarded the 2017 G.A.N.G. Distinguished Service Award. In his free time, he has also been a vocal analyst of sound in games media, writing for numerous sites including Polygon, Gamasutra, and Develop Magazine. Additionally, Stephan is considered a leading expert in the development of audio for VR/AR/MR and 360 video, having worked with Magic Leap, Oculus, and the Facebook Spatial Audio team.

Stephan is also an avid location recordist. He has channeled this passion into his company, Sound Librarian, for which he has created an extensive catalog of commercial sound effects libraries. These libraries are utilized by many of the world's top media producers such as Skywalker Sound, Disney, Warner Brothers, Activision, and EA. He has captured some of the rarest sound sources in the world such as classical military aircraft and historical technological equipment.

Stephan was born in Guildford, England, and moved to Australia as a child. He studied at both the Victorian College of the Arts and LaTrobe University, before spending five years in the Australian Army Band Melbourne as a horn player. He may also be one of the few people in the industry who likes *BioShock 2* more than the original.

 **Anna Irwin-Schütze** is the co-founder of Sound Librarian, narrative designer, and writer. Anna Irwin-Schütze has been in and around the games industry for nearly 10 years. After many years as a technical writer for tele-communications and financial services, Anna stepped into the games industry, helping to update and maintain technical manuals for Firelight Technologies and co-authoring the FMOD Studio training course and textbook.

Anna has a degree in linguistics and, working with Stephan Schütze, she helped design a procedurally generated language using audio engine FMOD Studio.

In 2015, Anna moved into narrative design and scriptwriting, working on *Yonder: The Cloud Catcher Chronicles*, *Singularity* (team VR experience), and a number of yet-to-be-released VR projects. Anna is currently working on *Ashen*, an action RPG multiplayer game being developed by Aurora44.

contributors

Martin Dufour is the chief technology officer at Audiokinetic. After a few years of hacking as part of the local Montreal BBS scene, he started his professional programming career while in high school. He worked at Softimage/Avid on the DS nonlinear editing and visual effects system from 1998 until old colleagues convinced him to join a game audio middleware start-up in 2004. Audiokinetic turned out to be a perfect match for his interests in sound, video games, and software development.

Simon Goodwin is principal audio programmer with DTS Inc, working on VR and AR tech. His game development career started in the 8-bit 1970s, latterly including a productive decade as principal programmer in the Central Technology Group at Codemasters Software Company, where he designed and implemented advanced ambisonic 3D audio technology in several multimillion-selling games, including six number 1 hits in the United Kingdom and major EU territories and two BAFTA award winners, *RaceDriver Grid* and *F1 2011*. He is expert in console, mobile, and PC audio and streaming system development, variously working as a sound designer, game audio programmer, and (most often) audio systems engineer. Simon lives and works in Warwick, UK. He has been granted five US and UK patents, advises on AHRC and EPSRC research programs, and gives talks at GDC, AES, and university conferences.

Sally-anne Kellaway is the creative director at OSSIC—the internal studio that develops content to showcase Ossic 3D audio smart headphones. This brings together some of Sal's favorite things—organizing, daydreaming, and audio design for VR.

As well as practicing audio design as a part of her day-to-day activities, Sally also communicates worldwide about the role of audio in virtual reality, diversity in STEM fields, and the virtual reality industry through speaking and writing. Sally has a cross-discipline history of working across games, VR, and middleware, with highlights including her time with SEGA Studios Australia, Firelight Technologies, and Zero Latency VR. She's also a well-read professional, having completed her masters in design science with a specialization in audio and acoustics, and developed her knowledge for spatial audio in direct application to HRTF technology for VR and AR.

Sally is still riding the VR hype train because she believes VR is the future of entertainment. She is enabling this future by advocating and supporting developers through the communities she has founded—the Virtual Reality Content Creators network for Australia (VRCC_AUS) and the IGDA Special Interest Group for Virtual, Augmented, and Mixed Realities. She has been named as one of MCV Pacific's Most Influential Women in Games, and in MCV Pacific's 30 Under 30 in 2017, as well as being named as IGDA's Most Valuable Person for 2017.

Viktor Phoenix is sound supervisor and senior technical sound designer for The Sound Lab at Technicolor in Los Angeles with expertise in sound design, 3D audio, mixing, and interactive audio for immersive media (http://www.technicolor.com/en/solutions-services/entertainment-services/sound-post-production/sound-lab-technicolor). Client projects include Passengers VR (MPC/Sony), Wonder Buffalo VR (ETC@USC), Major Crimes 360 video series (TNT), Giant VR (Milica Zec), The Click Effect (VRSE/New York Times), ADR1FT (Three One Zero/505), *The Gallery* (Cloudhead Games), and Insurgent VR (Kite & Lightning/Lionsgate).

Viktor has been focused on the intersection of creativity and technology for as long as he can remember; his passion for coaxing weird noises out of computers can be traced back to his experiments at the age of six. He began with altering software programs on his parents' TRS-80 computer and playing them back from the cassette tape drive, up to circuit bending Furbys in the late 1990s, and professional sound design at AAA game developers such as Pandemic Studios, Electronic Arts, Turtle Rock, and Robotoki.

Robert Rice is an interactive developer specialized in technical sound design and audio implementation for XR, games, and simulation. Born in Greensboro, North Carolina, in 1987, he was raised with a deep appreciation for music and the arts. His fondest childhood memories are sitting at the piano bench with his mother and playing video games after bedtime with (or without) his older siblings.

After a decade of experimental electronic music and video performance, he moved out of the south and dove head first into his dream of working in interactive sound design and game development. He embraced emerging VR technologies at a pinnacle time, and became a pioneer for real-time spatial audio techniques on some of the most ambitious teams in the industry.

His contribution to VR development spans from cutting-edge medical research to interplanetary space travel and major Hollywood IP. In addition to having shipped content on all consumer VR platforms, he has experienced working with custom-built hardware for show and corporate clientele. His work has been featured in many international trade shows, festivals, and conventions, including VRLA, GDC, SXSW, and SVVR, and made history with *Paranormal Activity* as the first video game ever featured in the 69th annual Cannes Film Festival.

Jay Steen is a software engineer and audio lead at Criterion Games, based in sunny Guildford, UK. He studied music technology at the University of Hertfordshire and computer games technology at City University, London. During the latter, he took part in Dare To Be Digital 2011 at Abertay University in Dundee. Since joining Criterion in 2012, he has worked on audio and online gameplay for the *Need for Speed* series, collaborated with DICE on *Star Wars: Battlefront and Battlefield 1*, and most recently was audio lead for the *Star Wars Battlefront: Rogue One X-Wing VR Mission*. When not making tea, he can be found playing action, adventure, indie, and racing games, and being passionate about audio and narrative in games.

Chanel Summers joined VRstudios in 2017 as its first vice president of Creative Development, where she is responsible for delivering the kind of breakthrough content experiences the industry has come to expect from the leading provider of VR-enabled attractions for location-based entertainment operators. A pioneer in the field of interactive audio, Chanel has been a respected game producer and designer, Microsoft's first audio technical evangelist, and a member of the original Xbox team. She helped to design and support the audio system for that groundbreaking console and creating the first ever support team for content creators. An accomplished touring drummer, Chanel also owns and runs her own audio production and design company, Syndicate 17, specializing in sound design, music production, and audio implementation for location-based attractions and virtual, augmented, and mixed reality products. Chanel serves as a technical consultant to a number of organizations and innovative technology companies, and lectures and educates around the world on subjects as diverse as the aesthetics of video game audio, world building, and secondary-level STEM education for young women.

Garry Taylor started his career as a bass guitarist and sound engineer, working for 10 years mainly in the United Kingdom and Europe. After taking a couple of years out in the mid-1990s to study astronomy and planetary science with the Open University, he joined Mythos Games as a sound designer working on PC titles *X-Com Apocalypse*, and *Magic and Mayhem*.

After 4 years at Mythos Games, he joined Sony's London Studio in 2001 as a sound designer, working on *This Is Football*, *The Getaway*, *Gran Turismo*, *Singstar*, and other Sony first-party franchises.

In 2006 he took over audio management for Sony's Cambridge Studio, before taking an audio director role with responsibility for audio development across London, Cambridge, and Evolution Studios.

In 2011 he cofounded Sony's Audio Standards Working Group, introducing loudness standards that have since been adopted by the wider games industry.

He is currently audio director for Sony Worldwide Studios' Creative Services Group, responsible for strategy and direction, working with audio development and R&D teams across the company.

photography

Photography

Anna Irwin-Schütze

Stephan Schütze

Models

Alex Orr

Anthony Clare

Blake Mizzi

Kathryn O'Brian

Sophia Van Leest

Stephan Schütze

new realities

---

introduction

Beginnings are important. Beginnings are when we establish trust and define much of how a relationship will progress. The new formats of virtual reality (VR), alternate reality (AR), and mixed reality (MR) are at a beginning. These new "realities" are at a delicate stage and I sincerely believe they will define a new era of communications and entertainment. There is a risk, however, that if they are not presented in the right way or form the right relationships, they could easily just become another tech fad, another grab for quick cash from some people wanting to take advantage of unwitting consumers looking for the next big thing. If this happens then these new formats are going to fail.

Let me begin, therefore, by stating I do not consider myself an expert in the new realities, not yet at least. I have spent the past few years exploring, discovering, and researching possibilities. I have worked for several leading companies specializing in the new realities and have participated in some very exciting projects. I am also incredibly passionate about the creative potential offered by these new formats. I believe that we have opened up an area that is so new to all of us, and potentially so very different to everything we have used up till now, that it would be unrealistic for anyone to claim to be an "expert" just yet.

I am quite sincere when I say I do not think we currently have the slightest idea of the true potential of where the new realities can take us. But I do think they are an entirely new approach to communication.

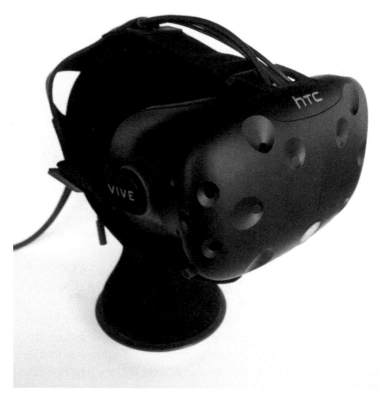

HTC Vive VR headset.

Our current media started with the still photograph hundreds of years ago; then through technology and brilliant minds we developed moving pictures (film) then radio added sound to the mix. Then we developed television, video games, and mobile devices. If we consider all of those to be evolutionary states along the same line, then I believe that the new reality is not the next step along that line.

While the new technologies owe much to our previous creative media, I think we are going to discover that they are the start of an entirely new branch of human communication and engagement. This is why it is so important that we develop the new realities carefully to allow them to reach their real potential. I also believe that we cannot even conceive of the types of experiences that will exist in 5–10 years' time. This both excites and terrifies me.

I have heard people refer to this early stage of the new realities as "the Wild West of technology," a time of discovery, of vague laws and rules where the shape of things is not yet determined. An opportunity for heroes to carve out reputations and become legends. This analogy works well, especially when you remember the Wild West was also a time of snake oil salesmen; people who made wild claims about their expertise and the wondrous abilities of their products. This is what we need to guard against the most if our use of new realities is to reach its true potential.

Microsoft HoloLens.

There is a conflict in this book that has been there since Day 1. My position has shifted back and forth as I have done research, as I have experienced different VR and AR projects and as I have drafted sections of this text. I think in many ways this conflict might be the subtext of the whole book because I think it is currently important to the evolution of this new format. The conflict is the science versus the creative process.

As you progress through this book, you will discover many references to the science and math that drives this technology. I am constantly amazed at the genius minds that allow us to work in virtual environments and create incredible and engaging visual and audio aspects of our experiences. The science is critical and core to this technology. However, I am also constantly amazed at how often very basic, age-old techniques such as those we have been using in theater for hundreds of years are not just still relevant, but in some ways, they are more relevant than ever.

The science allows us to flex our creative muscles and provide tools that enable us to create, but again and again I see that so many of our old methods of narration, presentation, and communication continue to serve us no matter how advanced our technology becomes. So there is conflict in this book as I cite the amazing capabilities of head-related transfer function (HRFT) spatial audio tools and at the same time suggest we adopt old-fashioned stagecraft to get the best results for our projects. There is conflict as we explore just how immersive a VR experience with amazing audio can be, but discover that there is a significant level of smoke and mirrors, that is, just as critical to the engagement as the technology that drives the delivery platforms. I do not think this conflict is a bad thing, in fact I think a mix of bleeding edge technology and established narrative techniques may be the best approach for many things, but I do think it is worthy of mention as this conflict is something that has come up again and again as I have progressed in writing this book.

In this book, I want to start a dialogue about what audio for VR, AR, and MR currently looks like, what it can be in the near future and what ultimately we might achieve when we have had time to become experts. So let me be your guide and suggest ways in which you can explore this Wild West frontier together.

I feel that sound is half the experience. Filmmakers should focus on making sure the soundtracks are really the best they can possibly be because in terms of an investment, sound is where you get the most bang for your buck

George Lucas 2004, Mixonline

George Lucas has consistently spoken about how important the sound is to a quality film. Game audio folk love to share this quote, to use it to give us more legitimacy. It helps us feel like we have some value. We tell developers, good quality audio is "nice" and will benefit their product.

For the new realities, the quality of the audio is not simply beneficial to your end result, or a "nice to have," it is absolutely critical. A VR/MR/AR experience will live or die based on how well you use and implement the audio. We will return to this point repeatedly throughout this book, as there are many different aspects of the new realities that reinforce this simple truth.

why this book

Because of the nature of the new technologies, I have invited others in the field to contribute their thoughts and approaches to working with VR/AR/MR. Some of these people have significant experience working with the new technologies and all of these people are brilliant at what they do. Their contribution to this industry and to this book is significant because we all benefit from the sharing of experience. Throughout this book you will find contributions from various creative minds writing about aspects of the new realities they are passionate about, and how they approached various challenges to producing content. It is important to me to acknowledge the people who are helping to build this industry through their hard work and clever thoughts.

As part of researching this book, I spoke with many of my industry colleagues in the games industry. I asked in particular about the use of obstruction and occlusion in video game projects. The technology to support these two features has existed for several years, but they are still not utilized as often as they could be. When I queried my colleagues I got a range of reasons. Often the computational resources needed for accurate occlusion were too high but one statement I felt cut right to the heart of the matter:

The trick for us (resource wise) was to create a 'difference' rather than go for absolute realism.

I have heard this comment or similar from many audio professionals. Our job is not to simulate reality for the sake of accuracy. Often, simulating reality is the first step and then from there we alter the content to make it more fun or more entertaining. Hollywood films are an excellent example of the world being significantly exaggerated from the audio point of view. So if a character moves from an outside space into a room we would apply some reverb. The change is what is important, the exact value of the reverb echoes and if they accurately match the room space exactly is not only less important, it probably borders on irrelevant to most of our audience.

The new realities will certainly need to utilize some important math and physics to assist in the creation of convincing and immersive content; there are brilliant engineers doing just that right now. The work they do with the math and science of manipulating audio allow those of us who work on the creative side to accomplish amazing results. But I am not an engineer and this book is aimed at composers and sound designers, artists, and creative producers. I will trust in the engineers to create amazing tools, and instead use this book to discuss our approach to getting the most out of them.

The advances in computer technology have been incredible over the last 20 years and graphics rendering has improved remarkably, but we can still usually tell the difference between CG and real-world footage. The same applies to audio creation. We can spatialize audio and utilize some incredible technology to create immersive experiences, but we are still many years from being able to simulate the real world precisely. Because of this there will be a continuing need to balance out the technology we have with techniques we use to produce convincing and exciting sonic content.

Right now, technology is advancing almost faster than we can keep up. In the last few weeks, as I write this book, there have been multiple spatial audio toolsets released and it is almost impossible to learn them all. We have more options than we have had before, but the craft of clever sound design is as important as ever and this book will discuss and compare the careful balancing act we must perform between these two elements.

The art of Foley is as important as ever.

There are so many aspects of creative media that are critical to its success and the new realities, if anything, add more challenges for the creator. But there are some core truths about creative content and why it is relevant to our audiences. Throughout this book we will investigate and discuss many of them. Viktor Phoenix provides a

The art of Foley is as important as ever.

wonderful insight and overview into one important aspect of the new realities: agency for the audience.

Agents of Change

Creating Presence through Real-Time Spatial Audio

Viktor Phoenix

All Great Stories Are about Change

Narrative elements move from one state to another. Gameplay state changes as players progress through games. Plots move forward, characters change their points of view, bison is hunted across cave walls, points are scored, battles are won, wars are lost, and heroes make journeys.

If a Story Doesn't Change, It's Dead in Its Tracks

There are many forms that those changes can take.

Time Domain

In interactive experiences, one way in which change happens is in the *time domain*—events transpire at different intervals during each playthrough and users can unlock narrative elements in a nonlinear order.

Frequency Domain

Another way that change happens is in the *frequency domain*—events that can be repeated might happen only once or they might happen once every 2 seconds.

Spatial Domain

In immersive experiences, change can also happen in the *spatial domain*—events and objects move in multiple directions and, when users have freedom to move through 3D space, at any distance.

Free to Be Me or Not

Allowing players to drive change is a large part of the appeal of video games. Applying that same level of interactivity to nongaming immersive experiences, to give users the freedom to decide how they can be a part of the narrative and give them the control they crave to truly be a part of the story, is a large part of determining the success of an immersive experience. That freedom is called *agency*.

What Is Agency?

Agency in an interactive immersive experience means that users have basic freedoms and the capability to make decisions. The degree of agency which a user can have depends on the experience, but the basic idea is that the user gets a sense that their actions affect the virtual environment or the narrative (or both!) in a meaningful way.

How Does Agency Change Perspective?

One measurement of agency is the degree to which a user has the freedom of movement through a virtual environment. The minimum amount of movement for fully immersive experiences is six degrees of freedom: when a user can move along three perpendicular axes (X, Y, and Z) and change orientation by rotating in three directions around those axes (pitch, yaw, and roll).

When we enter virtual environments using equipment that tracks our movement and position in the real world, our physicality is translated into 3D space. The virtual environment then needs to change relative to our movement and position in a way that tricks our brain into believing that we are actually there. When you look up, your field of view changes and the scene is rendered on the screens in our HMD so that your mind thinks that you're looking up within the scene.

When the virtual environment and the response to user movement is convincing enough, users are able to suspend their disbelief that they aren't actually in that environment. The more they are able to suspend their disbelief, the greater the sense of *presence* they will have.

Perspective Is as Critical to Story as Change

In the real world, sounds are changed by the environment that they travel through to reach our ears; they change based on our perspective to that sound. The perspectives that change based on choices users make within a virtual environment, within the limits of their agency, need to affect sound in a way that feels natural to the users.

How Do Changes in Perspective Affect Sound?

Time Domain

One way that sound changes is in the *time domain*—sound waves travel at a slower speed than light waves, so sounds at great distance appear to happen later than the visual aspect. Every grade school knows that you can calculate how far away a lightning strike is by using the flash-to-bang method (counting the time between seeing the flash of lightning and hearing the bang of thunder, then dividing by five).

Frequency Domain

Another way that sound changes is in the *frequency domain*—different frequencies are affected by absorption and reflections at different levels; frequencies have different energy levels and travel different distances.

Spatial Domain

In immersive experiences, one of the most important ways that sound changes is in the *spatial domain*—using real-time binaural rendering, sound changes as it moves through 3D space around us.

Environmental Propagation

Sounds are reflected, absorbed, refracted, diffused, and generally messed with as they move through environments. They tell us stories about the size, shape, and surfaces of the space around us and our position in that space. Put an ear close to a wall and see how the sounds around you change.

Distance

The closer a sound is to us, the more it reaches our ears directly. The further away we move from the sound (or it moves from us), the more we hear the affect the environment has on it and less direct it sounds.

Point of View

As characters evolve, their viewpoints change. We can experience those new emotional perspectives by changing how users see and hear the world.

Real-Time Rendering

Regardless of what changes in perspective affect sound, those changes have to be rendered real time in response to movements users make or we risk breaking presence. Doing so allows the user to change their physical perspective and still keep a coherent narrative perspective to the experience. It helps them to suspend disbelief.

This goes beyond rotating 360 degrees around the azimuth of the user or mixing different audio streams based on pitch, yaw, or roll. Any experience that allows for natural movement, such as room scale VR, requires that audio is processed and rendered in real time in response to any movements the user makes. We may not perceive the issues on a conscious level, but we sense it on an unconscious level. *It just won't feel right.*

Prerendering Locks the User into a Single Perspective

Audio with a prerendered perspective creates a cognitive dissonance in users. Anytime we force a perspective on the user, presence is diminished. When you don't notice it, when you don't think about it, when you're emotionally invested, deep within a virtual environment, when the sound is perfectly married to the visuals, and both respond to the choices that we make, that's when it's at its best—when it's simply part of a cohesive experience. That's when it's magical.

Presence and Interactivity

There are a number of factors contributing to presence, of which audio is but one. While we are multimodal sensory beings and all senses need to work together to create true states of presence, one of the most important aspects to creating presence is the level of interactivity in the content. *Interactive fidelity* can play a similar role as subjective quality (or *aesthetic fidelity*) and quantitative quality measurements (or *visual and audio fidelity*) in the success of an experience (McMahan et al. 2012).

Interactive 3D Audio Helps Finalize the Illusion of Presence

It's a two-way street: the virtual environment changes based on our input, but we also change our perspective based on the changes to elements in the environment. By prerendering perspective changes, we may gain creative control, but we can also rob the user of the chance to experience deep levels of presence. That doesn't mean that we don't have creative options when rendering audio at runtime. We can choose what rules we follow when generating audio.

Naturalistic

The audio can sound realistic within that environment regardless of where the player is in relation to that sound—above, below, behind, in front of, far away, etc. It can follow the exact laws of physics in the real world with little or no creative input from developers.

Magical

But audio can also break the laws of physics. Virtual environments can be as fantastical as our imagination allows and as long as we are consistent in following the rules that we define for the way sound propagates through that environment—or consistently break the rules if that fits the creative—users will have an understanding of that environment, as unreal as it may be.

We can also break the laws of nature when we need to bring a sound into focus, but it comes at a cost. Be aware of the risk of pulling the user out of the experience when doing so and weigh it against the creative goals.

The Future Sound of Entertainment

Let's take it one step further. We may have sound that renders in real time and feels natural in the virtual environments that we create, but how are those sounds generated? Today's standard for audio is to layer elements of recorded and designed sounds. Those sounds can be dynamic: footstep sounds that change based on the material characters walk on, for instance. Dialogue can branch based on rules designers set. Hundreds and sometimes thousands of sound files are streamed, mixed, and processed at runtime. It sounds great and feels dynamic, but it still limits the possibilities of change.

The future of interactive entertainment is procedural; entire world is generated and modified in real time using elements and rules that we, the storytellers, define. That future will require us—as artists, as storytellers, and as developers—to move out of our comfort zone of control over every nuance, of studio tools built for a different medium and way of thinking, and into a world of sounds—from the spoken word to music to designed sound effects and Foley—that will be built on the fly from rules and scripts and models that we craft.

While the goal of something akin to the Holodeck may be years off, we can lay the foundation today by focusing on dynamic content when developing our projects and using real-time rendering and procedurally generated audio as much as we can.

As we tell more and more stories in this new medium, the technology will continue to improve and soon enough storytellers will rely entirely on high quality, procedurally generated content, rendered in real time, to build interactive narrative structures, sound design, and music that are indistinguishable from prerendered content that currently takes minutes, hours, days, even weeks to compose, design, record, and render. Along the way, a language will develop around those changes.

what's in this book

A topic like this covers such a broad range of information, it would be a challenge at the best of times to cover it all. In this book, I will attempt to cover all the essential topics relevant to audio in the new realities. This will include advanced concepts and techniques aimed at experienced audio producers as well as more basic elements needed for a good grounding in the field.

The technology and software that power the new reality formats are still being developed and understood, with many software developers changing their approach and updating their applications too quickly for a book like this to remain relevant. Fortunately, there is a wealth of discussion to be had around the broader concepts and approaches to developing audio for the new realities. Developing a deep understanding of the field will give you the knowledge to remain relevant for years.

I will keep discussions of the technical "how to do" the different tasks mostly format-agnostic. Although specific examples of how to achieve an outcome with a particular software package are useful, we run the very real risk of that process being out of date before this book is even published, or soon after, which won't be of much use to you. I will use some examples from specific software to explain overall processes and techniques, but these examples are more to illustrate possibilities than to train you how to use that software.

This does not mean this book will not discuss current technologies, hardware equipment, and software. These are critical elements of production for AR, VR, and MR, but I won't usually drill down into tutorial-style demonstration of what button X does in software package Y.

What you will get out of this book is detailed, practical solutions to many of the issues you will encounter when creating audio for the new realities, through tutorials and examples. I have structured these to let you apply what you learn to your own preferred toolset. Knowing how to do something is important, but understanding *why* you should be doing it is far more valuable.

Chapter 1 introduces the topic and provides you with an overview of what to expect in the overall book.

In Chapter 2, I will introduce a range of concepts, formats, and definitions to help lay the foundations for the more detailed discussions in later chapters. Audio is a complex subject at the best of times, but the new formats are different enough that we must pay attention to elements that previously we may have been able to ignore or gloss over.

While this book will discuss some of the aspects of physics and math related to spatialized sound it will equally deal with the "smoke and mirrors" involved with creative media. Our stagecraft is about creating audio for an audience. Mostly this is designed to entertain through the creation of worlds and characters.

In the first few chapters, I will introduce the general concepts and terminology I will be using throughout this book. There are also a number of core concepts that apply to the nature of physics, sound design, and the technology we are working with. In any exploration of a topic such as this, everyone needs to be on the same page with what specific terms are referring to.

In Chapter 3, I will explore the challenges we face when creating audio for the new realities. This includes challenges common to all of the realities, as well as ones that are unique to each platform.

Chapter 4 takes an in-depth look at what we're doing now. I delve into a range of projects designed for different realities and platforms and look at what's working well and what isn't, and why.

In Chapter 5, I get into the meat of creation and implementation. Although we can use much of what we already know from developing audio for 3D games, the new realities have opened up a whole new can of worms around what we can and can't do, as well as what we should be doing.

Chapter 6 explores the challenge of sourcing, recording, and creating assets for your new reality project.

Chapter 7 looks into the way we approach music for the new realities; do we use diegetic or nondiegetic music? How much should the physics of the real world affect new reality music? This chapter almost deserves a book all on its own!

In Chapter 8, I tackle the challenge of teamwork. No audio person stands alone, and we need to understand the unique challenges of developing new reality content from not just our own perspective. Communication, workflow, and project planning are all important parts of getting it right.

Chapter 9 investigates the platform considerations that affect the planning, development process, workflow, and limitations around creating audio for your next project.

Chapter 10 brings it all together and looks at where we need to go next to develop true expertise in creating sound and music for the new realities as they stand now, and into the future.

references

Lucas, G. 2004. *Mixonline*. http://www.mixonline.com/news/profiles/ george-lucas/365460 (Accessed October 14, 2017).

McMahan, R.P., Brady, R.B., Zielinski, D.J. and Bowman, D.A. 2012. Evaluating Display Fidelity and Interaction Fidelity in a Virtual Reality Game. *CSDL Home IEEE Transactions on Visualization & Computer Graphics* 18(4): 626–633.

definitions and core concepts

a critical distinction: thinking differently about spatial audio for the new realities

When I was researching this book, I spent time on various social media channels that discussed spatial audio and audio specifically for the new formats. There have been a lot of people interested in the new formats and many people new to audio production as well as experienced veterans are experimenting with the possibilities. However, I noticed a common misunderstanding about exactly how these new formats work, which needs to be addressed before any other discussion can start. This misunderstanding goes right to the heart of the way spatial audio functions.

Many people started discussions about delivery formats, uses of low-frequency channels such as subwoofers and the best techniques for speaker routing. It is these discussion topics that rang some alarm bells for me. Ambisonic, binaural, and spherical surround can certainly be delivered through loudspeaker systems, but this is not likely to be the optimal delivery format for some very specific reasons.

Let's take a look at how audio is delivered in other formats, such as console games or PCs, and compare it to the spherical surround sound we encounter in the real world.

In the below figure, you have two examples of audio delivery: one of a loudspeaker and one of a tree in the real world. In both examples, the sound we hear will be exactly the same. The birds in the tree are chirping away as they normally would and the speaker is playing back an exact recording of those birds.

Where things differ is that the loudspeaker is a single source of sound waves. The speaker vibrates and generates the sounds of the birds in the tree, but all the sound emanates from the speaker, a single point source in space. In the real world, the tree and the birds within it have a much larger spread. The tree might be 4 m high and 2 m across, and the birds can be positioned anywhere within this

A speaker is a single source of sound; in the real world,
sounds come from many sources.

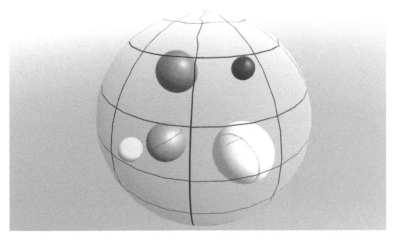

A volumetric sound may consist of an area with lots of point sources within it or where the sound source is everywhere within the volume (such as underwater).

area and even on the ground below and possibly in the air above it if they are flying. This means each bird is a sound source and the entire tree itself can generate sound as the leaves move in the wind and the branches creak. So the entire area occupied by the tree and the birds is a potential volumetric area from which sounds can emanate. If you were sitting on the tree you may hear the sounds coming from all around you. By comparison, the speaker will only ever be a single point from which sound will be generated. TV, computers, radio, and film all work with speakers as the source for generating sound waves.

Spatialization in Stereo

A stereo mix can provide a spectrum of positional information across the left and right speakers, so where a single speaker emits sounds from one location a stereo pair can create the sensation of a sound being located at any point between the two speakers by adjusting the output balance of the speakers. But the sound is essentially still "anchored" to a line between the speakers.

The below figure illustrates two speakers in a stereo pair. From the listener's point of view, sounds appear to come from either of the speaker positions or from anywhere along the line between the speakers. This positional illusion can be affected by the layout of the listening space and objects within the room as well as the listener's

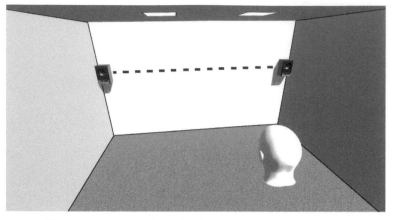

Stereo panning moves along a fixed path between the two speakers.

proximity to the speakers. The further away the listener is from the speakers, the less effective the stereo spatialization becomes. Stereo spatialization is far more effective than headphones, which also give a more convincing sense of depth. With headphones, the speakers are at a fixed distance to the listener's ears at all times even if they move. This means the listener is always in the "sweet spot" and there are no factors within the listening space to interfere with the effect.

If you listen to a rain shower recorded in stereo through a set of headphones, you will hear the rain in both your left and right ears. You can even get a sense of distance of different raindrops, near and far. Listening through speakers you can also get a sense of depth as long as you are positioned in a suitable sweet spot relative to the speakers. The main difference is that speaker output is directly affected by the environment of the room where you are listening. Reflections off walls, furniture, and other surfaces will affect the sound. In a purpose-built room such as a theater, we can improve the propagation of sound and enhance the spatial mixing. A well-designed acoustic space may enhance the sense of spatialization of sounds outputted through speakers, but in most household or communal spaces, the layout of the room often interferes with the sense of spatialization.

Whether the listening space is good or bad, you are still hearing the sound output within a world space and as such what you are hearing is colored by the room you are in. So if you are listening to a recording of music recorded in St Paul's Cathedral, you are not hearing a pure representation of the St Paul's Cathedral space, you are hearing St Paul's Cathedral modified by your own listening space. It is a little like looking at a picture through a window. If your window is dirty it filters everything you see through it.

Spatialization in Surround Sound

The below figure expands on the stereo layout with a seven-speaker system similar to many home theater systems. In this example, the spatial panning can now move along multiple axes and create a sensation of sound coming from all around you. But the sounds are still "locked" to the lines between the speakers. It is like there is a rail track running around the outside of the room. The sound can move back and forth along that track, but it can never leave it and sound closer to the listener. If a sound is played through three or more speakers, then we can achieve the illusion of envelopment. This sounds as though the listener is inside a sound source and is completely immersed in the sound. It can be an interesting effect but it does have limitations to its usefulness. Another key aspect to note is this system, along with mono and stereo, spatializes on a flat plane. There is no sense of elevation in what the listener hears.

If we take your average multichannel film, television program, or game, these have been produced and mixed to rout out of channels in fixed positions around the audience. When engaging in these media, the ideal position to be seated when watching a multispeaker

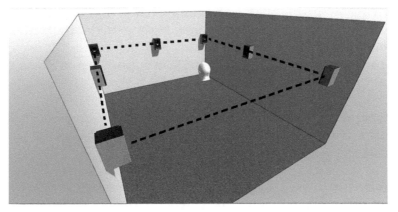

Surround system pans between multiple speakers but the path is still locked.

experience is in the very center, the sweet spot. The center of a speaker array is where you will hear the most balanced and even version of the audio. All the panning and spatialization should be exactly as the author intended. For a standard film experience, you cannot sit the entire audience all in the center of a theater; therefore, modern films are produced with as broad a sweet spot as possible. Even so, those sitting at the edges of the cinema will likely have a less than ideal experience. The same applies to a home theater setup. Sitting at right angles to the speaker system or off to one side is going to seriously color your audio experience.

> *VR, you step through the door; in MR, the door steps through you!*

> **Pdx Drescher**

Spatialization in the New Realities

Linear media such as film and television have a slightly different goal to what we have in the new realities. In linear media, we are peering at a world through a window. We get to see certain aspects of that world, those which are most critical to the narrative. The writer and director have carefully selected which elements are important to ensure the audience has the most entertaining view of that world.

In almost all instances, the role of audio is to support narrative. In film and television, this is done by focusing on key aspects of the world's audio environment. Interesting narrative elements, such as a car driving by, are highlighted by audio events. At other times, we are presented with lush audio environments that surround us and draw us into the world we are viewing.

Sound designer Sally-anne Kellaway provides an insightful observation about audio for linear media:

> *It is so much more about size and envelopment in a cinema though, like you only have one window into the world you're watching.*

Because we have this window into the narrative world, it is far more important to surround the listener with elements of this world to help the process of immersion. So the specific location of a sound at 86 degrees and 6 ft from the listener is not a critical aspect of these kinds of screen-based experiences.

The new technologies are significantly different from linear media, as the entire point of the experience is the sense of immersion and agency. When you're inside the virtual world, you feel a connection because you are within and can move around relative to that world. You have the choice to change your perception anytime simply by turning your head. Even slight movements change what you can see and what you should be able to hear. The most complex speaker array simply cannot provide this kind of responsive functionality.

New reality is generally experiences that involve wearing personal headsets, visors, and headphones. This is not only because of how the visual material is presented but because it can be the best way to experience 360 spatial audio via headphones. To truly experience a spherical audio experience without headphones, you would need to access a complex and expensive loudspeaker array. A design for a 22.2 channel speaker array does exist, and there are a handful of working installations in the world with this setup, which lets a single person sit in the optimal position to experience it. I imagine you can see a few challenges that might arise when setting this up in your average living space. The figure below shows a speaker array with only 16 speakers. Even then, there would be quite the complex setup for mounting, wiring, and signal routing.

Beyond the impracticality of setting up this kind of speaker system, there is another, more important element to consider. Using a

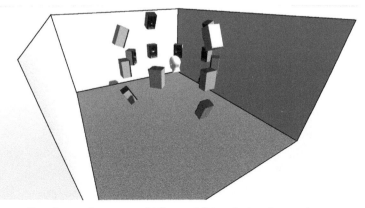

Complex speaker arrays exist for specialist projects and research.

virtual reality (VR) or alternate reality (AR) headset without head-phones risks a total disconnect between what the user sees and the accompanying audio. If the user turns their head, the visuals will change but the audio will be in a fixed position, no matter how many speakers you may be using.

In regard to low-frequency content such as subwoofer channels, humans utilize the entire frequency spectrum to localize sound so we may need those frequencies attached to objects in our spherical space. This means that routing low-frequency content in the way we might do for a 5.1 DVD movie risks causing confusion to the spatial panning, and undermining some of the aspects that make spatial audio more effective.

None of this is to say that the new reality cannot utilize external speaker systems or that combining loudspeaker arrays with head-sets or with headsets and headphones may not produce some inter-esting and engaging experiences. But it is important to understand the core design of how the new realities differ from traditional media presentation techniques and how these differences can be utilized to maximize the audience's experiences.

One of the primary advantages of producing audio content for headphones is that three-dimensional (3D) plugin technology allows content creators to utilize full spherical spatialization. So instead of panning between two or more fixed speakers, sound sources can be placed anywhere within the virtual space. This means the entire

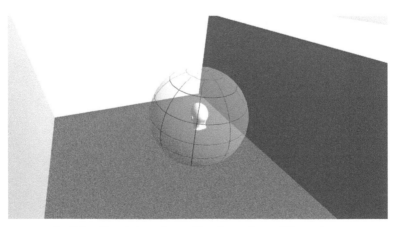

Spatial audio points can be positioned anywhere within a sphere.

volume of a sphere can be utilized. The above figure shows a relatively small sphere encompassing the listeners head, but the size of the sphere can be whatever suits the project.

I do believe it is important to understand the core concept of how the new realities differ from existing media presentation techniques and explore how these differences can be utilized to maximize your audience's experiences.

Spatial Audio in VR and 360 Video

VR content and 360 video works by replacing our real world with a visual representation of a virtual world. The VR headset covers your eyes and completely replaces your ability to see any aspect of the real world. If you only half position a VR headset on so you can still see any aspect of the real world, the sense of immersion is undermined or destroyed completely. The illusion of being inside a virtual world only works because at the exact point where our eyes start to receive a visual signal, we replace everything the eye can see with virtual content.

Audio for VR and 360 video is the same. At the exact point where our ears would capture sound waves, we block out the real world and replace that signal with virtual content. So we provide the audience with everything that they should hear in the virtual world: the spatial location of a sound source, the relevant room reflections for our virtual space, and behavioral factors of the virtual audio. Again, trying to utilize speakers to provide audio content for these formats is like presenting a VR experience on a standard computer monitor. Certainly, the audience can see the virtual world on the screen, but seeing that content is not the same as being "inside" that content. The sense of immersion and engagement relies on presenting all the content so that the audience's senses convince them that they really are in the virtual space. Any gaps in that sensory support lessen the impact of the experience.

An exception to this is room-based experiences. If an environment is set up and carefully curated to provide a specific experience to the audience that includes VR visuals with speaker-based output keyed to specific locations and directions, then engaging experiences can be created. As with all aspects of the new realities the blurry lines will always make clear definitions tricky, but those lines, even when

Zero latency location-based VR experience.
(From Zero Latency, Copyright Zero Latency 2017. Used with permission.)

blurry, allow us to compare differences and discuss various aspects of production in isolation.

setting the stage: defining our terminology

Before we get into much detail, we need to ensure that we are all on the same page with what we are talking about. For the sake of consistency and mutual understanding, I will outline the terms and definitions used in this book.

There are a number of ways we can refer to the new realities of VR/MR/AR. Collectively, I will use the term "new realities." I may also refer to them as "new technologies" or "new formats," even though some aspects of these have existed for some time. Currently, we do not know exactly what these new formats are capable of, and I suspect it will be years before we do. During that time, we will see new and innovative ways in which people present information to communicate, entertain, and inform. Take the definitions here as loose descriptions that serve the purpose of sharing ideas within this book. Do not let these definitions confine or restrict your thinking. The future for these new realties has unbelievable potential if we allow ourselves to think far beyond the current media formats.

VR: virtual reality

VR in one form or another has been around for many years and we have explored its potential in science fiction stories even longer. The idea of putting equipment on your head that transports you into a different world through your senses has been exciting us for generations. Even the early VR experiences, which were very basic, were still immersive due to the nature of the format. Let's take a deeper look at the defining features of virtual reality.

Replacing the World

In its current form, virtual reality aims to replace the user's world. Typically, the headset completely replaces direct and peripheral vision with a rendered world. This can be either a linear video or an interactive 3D space. Generally, the experience also includes headphones that mask all real world audio with virtual audio. Some multiplayer experiences do blend in microphone signals from fellow players, which technically means an aspect of the real world is blended into the virtual experience. Even so, as a general rule we are presented with a crafted environment in which to experience a variety of things. Audio, visuals, narrative elements, and haptic feedback are all common aspects of VR media.

Because of the "complete" nature of a VR experience, the design and implementation of the audio is critical to create the immersion that people expect. It does not matter how good the visuals are and how convincingly the movement mechanics simulate a particular experience, poor audio design and implementation can easily shatter the sense of immersion. Even now, numerous reviews of early VR games comment on how poor audio has affected the entire experience and pulled the player out of the virtual world.

Audio in VR does more than simply support a narrative and accompany the visuals. Audio affects how our brains place objects in the real world. Understanding what audio needs to do in a VR environment helps us better approach the challenge of creating VR audio.

360 Video

The 360 video system will usually utilize a VR headset to view, but it is a rapidly growing format and deserves its own definition. In this book, 360 video will often share techniques with VR

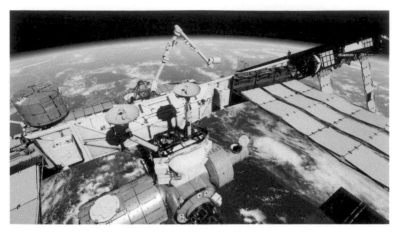

Earthlight VR experience created by Opaque Media.
(From Opaque Media, Copyright Opaque Media 2017. Used with permission.)

production. Generally, 360 video is a linear experience that can utilize spatial audio. The experience is most effective when viewed through a VR headset with headphones, and this is why I consider it linked to VR. There are tools that allow for the capture of 360 video and audio content and many of the major online video channels are already supporting this format. Because it can be viewed on mobile devices with the headset peripherals, this format has the greatest potential for rapid consumer growth. Anyone can watch a 360 video with an inexpensive headset adaptor for their mobile device.

A 360 camera still image.

AR: alternate reality

The term "AR" can be applied to many types of experience. From chasing Pokemon on your mobile device to wearing the technology as part of a device such as Microsoft's HoloLens or Magic Leap's Sensoryware, AR is a format that is still very much searching for an identity as the possibilities and opportunities are only just being explored. AR has the potential to redefine how we do many things, from education to medical diagnosis and vehicle control. It really is going to be an incredible technology.

AR technology generally blends real world with virtual content. In games like *Pokemon Go*, you see the world through your phone camera on the phone screen and the game renders Pokemon creatures into your real-world view. HoloLens does the same thing except you look at the world through glasses and it adds the virtual objects into your view. This can be effective for placing virtual objects into your world space in a convincing way. The real world is not replaced, but it is enhanced by the addition of the virtual objects to create entertaining situations or useful applications. Like VR, we have been exploring the potential of AR for years. Think of the cool virtual computer interfaces we see in *The Avenger* films, or the heads-up display in *The Terminator* or even the holographic chess game in *Star Wars* *(let the Wookie win!)*.

Creating audio for AR brings challenges that are different to what we encounter with VR. In the same way that AR visuals blend with real-world vision, AR audio needs to blend with what you can hear in the real world. Devices have speakers that can play audio, but unlike VR headsets they do not try to block the audio from the real world. This means the audio has to be projected at a level to be audible to the user without being too loud for everyone else around them. It also means the audio needs to sync with virtual objects without clashing with real-world elements. AR devices have significant challenges with reproducing a full frequency range as well as issues of amplitude and blending with the real world that you would not get with standard headphone audio.

AR experiences may include practical communication applications as well as military uses, emergency services, entertainment, education, and things not yet thought of. Therefore, how the audio will be addressed for all these purposes is food for thought and a lengthy, in-depth discussion.

MR: mixed reality

Exactly what MR will be and how it will work is a bit like asking how long is a piece of string. MR can be anything that combines aspects of VR or AR but does not exactly fit neatly within either technology. A likely format will be AR devices combined with external speakers and screens. The challenges here will be syncing output devices so that a wearable device blends seamlessly with environmental sound sources. The possibilities for these kinds of experiences are fascinating, especially because they will create a whole new series of challenges to be overcome. In many ways, MR will be a case of, "think of the craziest idea for combining media formats and figure out how we can actually achieve it."

While MR is difficult to clearly define in a paragraph, it serves a useful purpose as a catch-all term to capture all the space between projects that are not VR or AR but live somewhere in-between.

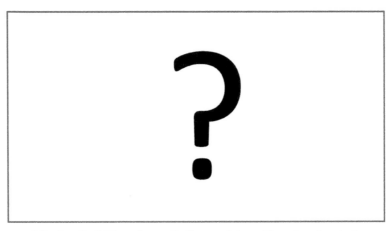

Mixed reality (MR) can be practically any mixture of formats and content.

core concepts and other terms

Beyond the core definitions of format types, there is a cascade of interrelated terms that are important to the topic. With a list like this, sometimes the challenge is knowing exactly the best order in which to explain them without getting into a circular definition tangle.

Term A may be reliant on understanding Term B and vice versa. Even so, I'll take a stab at it. Here is my list of important terminologies, hopefully in an order that works for you.

Haptics

Haptics is any form of feedback that involves touch (such as vibrating controllers, pressure pads, or other physical feedback).

Transfer Function

Before we describe head-related transfer function (HRTF), it helps if you start by defining what a transfer function is. Essentially, it is a way of describing a relationship between an input and an output. Transfer functions can be used for a variety of purposes; but in relation to HRTFs, they refer to information about frequency response and time response.

Head-Related Transfer Function

An HRTF describes how an ear receives sound from a specific location in space. A pair of HRTFs is required to simulate binaural hearing. Humans have only two ears and yet we can localize or triangulate a sound in 3D space. There are limitations to our ability to track sounds and many animals are far more efficient at localizing sounds than humans, but we are still relatively effective at detecting the location of a sound in our environment.

So while we may understand how the ear receives sound waves through the air, it is more relevant how humans process the subtle differences between how a sound is received by our two ears and how that allows us to locate the source of the sound in 3D space.

With two eyes, sight gives us stereo vision and provides us with a sense of depth as we navigate the world. Binaural hearing does a similar thing with hearing. Someone who is deaf in one ear would struggle to accurately localize sounds.

Interaural Time Difference

Interaural time difference (ITD) is the delay in time that a sound takes to reach both ears. A centered sound will reach both ears at

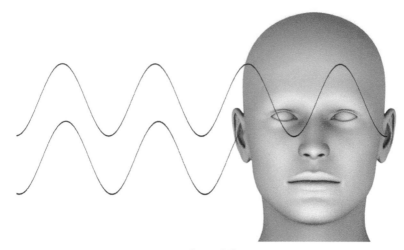

Interaural time difference.

the same time where a sound that is positioned to our left side will reach the left ear sooner than it reaches the right ear. This delay is part of the information the brain uses to tell us that the sound is positioned to our left.

IID or ILD

Interaural intensity difference (IID) or interaural loudness difference (ILD) refers to the difference in amplitude between your ears. A sound positioned to one side or the other will display an ITD as it takes longer to reach the furthest ear; however, because of the shape and makeup of our head, the sound will often also be quieter to the ear that is furthest away.

Interaural Phase Difference

Interaural phase difference (IPD) is the difference in the phase of a sound wave that reaches each ear. This depends on the frequency content of the sound we hear and the ITD. For example, in the case of a sine wave of 1000 Hz, the length of the sound wave means if this sound reaches one ear 0.5 ms before it reaches the other ear, there will be a 180-degree phase difference between what

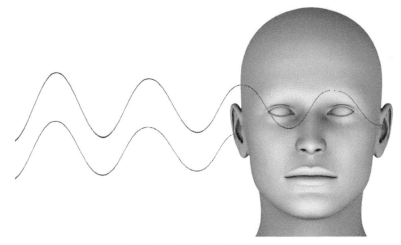

Interaural loudness difference.

each ear hears. Although it's nearly impossible to actively notice a difference in the sound reaching each ear, our brain can detect the difference and use the information to locate the sound source.

Humans can detect phase differences as small as 3 degrees; therefore, IPD is important for both spatial localization and determining the frequency content of the sound we are hearing.

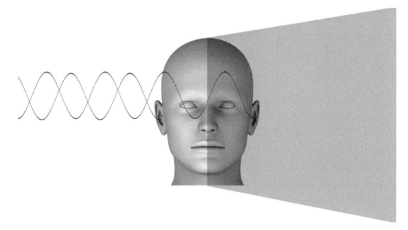

Interaural phase difference.

Cone of Confusion

One of the weaknesses of human hearing is referred to as the cone of confusion. A sound that occurs at 45 degrees to the front and left of a listener will result in the same ITD and IID as a sound that occurs to 45 degrees to the rear and left. The same applies to elevation. A sound that is 45 degrees to the left and above will be perceived as the same as 45 degrees to the left and below. As a general rule, higher frequency content makes localization easier and so can reduce the cone of confusion effect. Humans tend to rotate their heads to assist further in sound localization; this is particularly useful for lower frequency content and also for reducing the effect of the cone of confusion. Moving the head also helps detect changes in elevation. Frequency content below 1,000 Hz is mainly detected through ITD and content above 1,500 Hz is mainly detected through IID.

The shape of the outer ear affects sound waves as they travel to the inner ear. The spectral characteristics of different frequencies change depending on the direction of origin. We get into trouble with creating HRTFs because each human is different. Our personal HTRFs are specific to our individual ear shape and the size and shape of our heads. This means any HRTF we create for multiple users as a generic model is less accurate in the information an individual usually receives. This can be further complicated by the differences in playback devices such as headphones. A truly accurate HRTF would be modeled on our exact ear and head shape, but it would also take into account our hair and even our torso and shoulder shape and position. This kind of individualization is not feasible for most commercial applications of the new technologies.

Note: When referring to phase difference, humans can detect very small variations of phase, which is measured in degrees. Our rotational spatialization detection is not as accurate but rotational positioning is also measured in degrees. Although the term "degrees" may be used to discuss measurements for various aspects of audio, don't be confused when one paragraph describes poor sensitivity to changes in degrees and another paragraph describes excellent sensitivity to changes in degrees. The difference is in our ability to perceive these variations depending on the aspect of audio we are exploring.

Transcoding

"Transcoding" is a term that pops up quite regularly when discussing ambisonic and other surround formats. Essentially, transcoding is the act of converting a signal from one format to another—so, an analog to analog change or a digital to digital change of format. Converting a 5.1 mix to stereo is an example of transcoding. So while we may encode a file into 5.1 in the original production process, we may then need to transcode the 5.1 format to a stereo format to allow it to function effectively on certain platforms.

Transcoding is relevant for ambisonic content because the full spherical nature of the raw material will need to be transcoded into a suitable format for production and performance.

Flat Plane or Zero Plane

When I refer to the flat plane or zero plane in chapters of this book, I am referring to an invisible plane around the same height as our ears. This is relevant because most of the sound and music we have encountered so far exists on this flat plane. When we listen to a movie or our favorite band, we can hear sounds move back and forth, we can hear the drums on the left side and the guitar on the right, but all these sonic examples exist on a flat plane. They are like boats floating on a still sea.

Conventional media had not moved beyond the flat plane until Dolby Atmos introduced the idea of audio content coming from above. Atmos effectively added a lid to our surround sound box. There have certainly been projects and experiences that have utilized output

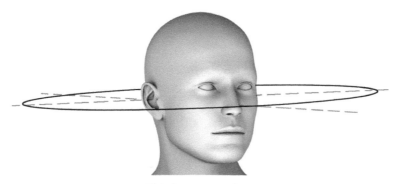

Flat plane or zero plane.

channels above and below the listener's position, but these have been for specific installations or performances. The standard media consumed by most people has been limited to this flat plane of audio. Moving outside this zero plane is essential to creating successful and convincing new reality experiences.

Diegetic

The term "diegetic" is derived from the Greek *diegesis*, meaning story is told or recounted instead of shown or enacted.

In the context of this book, I will use two related terms: "diegetic" and "nondiegetic."

A diegetic sound or piece of music is part of a narrative; it exists within the game world or experience as a part of that world. So a character switching on a radio will trigger diegetic music and we can consider that the character can hear and is aware of the music playing on the radio.

A nondiegetic piece of music is the music that underscores the gameplay. This music is for the sake of the player and it may herald events or provide the emotional undertones of the narrative, the soundtrack if you like. The characters in the story are unaware of the musical score.

In *Star Wars*, the main theme is nondiegetic and the cantina music is diegetic. Both of these terms relate to 3D audio for the new realities. This technology provides new and advanced methods for presenting music to the audience. Carefully consider the impacts on the design when selecting diegetic or nondiegetic music (or both) for your project.

Formats

"Format" is a tricky term as it can cover a wide range of different things: from describing the ways we encounter content (film vs. VR vs. monitor screen) to the kinds of files we are using to deliver content (sound files, sound banks, etc.) or even platform requirements, such as surround sound files for a console or other formats for mobile platform requirements.

Related to implementing audio for the new realities, there are a range of audio capture, production, and delivery formats that are essential to understanding the possible workflows for the new technologies.

Localization

I have included this term (localization) because it can have multiple meanings for media production. It can be used to refer to the process of translating written and spoken content from one language to another. So, a project developed in English may be localized into Japanese for release in Japan.

In this book, the term "localization" will usually refer to a human's ability to locate the position or origin of a sound they can hear—our ability to listen and triangulate where a sound is coming from.

Channel-Based Audio

As the name suggests, channel-based audio is any content where the primary delivery format routes an audio signal to an output channel. Technically, any audio produced through a speaker can be referred to as being routed through a channel, but the term has a specific definition that allows us to differentiate it from other formats.

Channel-based audio for our purposes refers to how the audio is spatialized. All traditional formats of sound production fall into the category of channel-based audio. From the original mono gramophones, through stereo, quadraphonic, and surround theater systems, these are all channel based. A number of speakers are defined before production starts and the content is produced designed to be routed out of those available speakers. Anything beyond mono lets us create a spatialized output. By balancing the content between the output channels, it is possible to create the illusion of a sound source being positioned between a set of speakers rather than wholly being produced from the actual speaker.

What defines this format as being channel based is that a decision is made for each signal as to its ultimate routing to an output channel. Regardless of how many channels exist and how a signal is panned through the various outputs, it is a linear and locked format. The number of channels and the position of the speakers define the shape that the audio will form in the performance space. A 5.1 system creates a box in which the audio is generated. A 22.2 system will create more of a spherical space in which the audio is generated. The performance space will influence what the audience hears, as sound is reflected off objects within the space and off the boundaries of that space (the walls). Even Dolby Atmos is essentially a box with a lid. The limitations of channel-based audio are practical and sensible.

A complete sphere of speakers would be expensive and impractical as only a single listener could really occupy the central sweet spot. Theaters and lounge rooms need to be able to accommodate people in a practical real world, everyday usage environment. So positioning speakers around the audience space in a square or cube has been the most suitable design so far.

Binaural

Binaural is a recording technique that utilizes two or more microphones in a specific way to capture a "3D soundscape." Binaural has been around as a technique since the late 1800s and has been used on and off in various ways since then. The output of a binaural recording can be effective but the process never gained serious uptake as a consumer format. Unfortunately, in the 1950s the record industry often used the term to refer to the more common stereo format and this created some confusion and misunderstanding of the format.

Mid-Side (MS) Recording Format

Before we jump into the ambisonic recording format, it is worth introducing or refreshing what MS format is all about. This is because MS utilizes the same general idea as Ambisonics, but it is a simpler setup and as such works well to introduce the concept in a simpler manner.

MS microphone recording is a technique that is used to capture a stereo field that is an alternative to the XY stereo format. XY is often adopted by both microphone producers and recordists because it is a natural approach to take. The matched pair of microphones arranged in a coincident pattern replicates how our ears work by recording sound with a time delay between the two mics that mimics the ITD of human ears. So it is easy for us to understand conceptually and also fairly easy to set up.

MS recording is somewhat more complex, but it has some significant advantages over XY format. First, it very easily collapses down to mono, but it also allows for adjustment and widening of the stereo image. The combination of the two microphone patterns is what gives the MS format its flexibility.

The mid mic can be either a cardioid or omnipattern microphone. This mic functions as a center channel; it essentially captures everything. The side mic as a figure-eight microphone is set up as close as possible to the mid mic, but at a 90-degree angle to the mid mic.

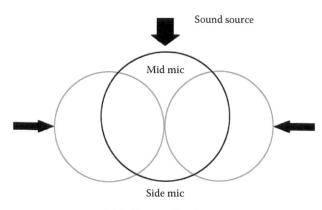

Mid-side recording format.

As a figure-eight microphone captures content from both sides, but with a 180-degree phase difference. All material is recorded onto two channels, one for each microphone.

The decoding is what lets us create a stereo field. The figure-eight side mic content can be copied into two tracks with one of them set to create a 180-degree phase-shifted version of the signal. Each of these tracks is then hard panned to the left and the right—the front of plus + side is most usually pointed to the left of your recording space, while the negative is pointed to the right.

The decoding of the three channels is applied as

Mid + (plus side) = your left channel and mid + (minus side) = your right channel

The mid channel on its own provides a mono signal and as you increase the levels of the two side channels you can hear the stereo image. The more side channel output in the mix the wider the stereo image becomes; therefore, you can vary the width of your stereo image quite easily.

The reason why MS format is relevant to understanding ambisonic recording is that ambisonic format is essentially an extension of the technique. While MS has mono central and then left and right, ambisonic has mono central, left/right, front/back, and up/down.

Ambisonics

The first thing you need to know about Ambisonics is that it is not a new format. Ambisonics was developed by Peter Fellget and

Michael Gerzon in the 1970s and is also a nonproprietary format. Despite the early start, it never really took off as a mainstream consumer format because there were no obvious applications for the technology. The advancements in VR and AR technology have seen renewed interest in ambisonic recording and production processes and technology.

The main reason for this is Ambisonics is not limited by channels. The more channels, the higher the directional resolution; so using four channels will give you full spherical directionality, including elevation and declination. In addition, using Ambisonics facilitates spherical panning. Let's take a look at how Ambisonics works.

At a basic level ambisonic recording consists of four signals W, X, Y, and Z—the horizontal plane is W, X, and Y; Z is for height information.

W is omnidirectional.

X, Y, and Z are figure-eight patterns.

Fortunately for us, Ambisonics has been around for a while and it is quite clearly defined. Stereo sound can be captured in many different ways, some of which may not be compatible with certain kinds of project content. Ambisonics has a single defined method of capture, and even when you add higher orders they are all based on the same methodology.

Ambisonics captures sound equally within the sphere, which means it is as suitable for four speakers as it would be for 40. The renewed interest in the ambisonic format has led to several significant developments in software. Previously, transcoding and formatting of ambisonic material required costly hardware components. Now there are

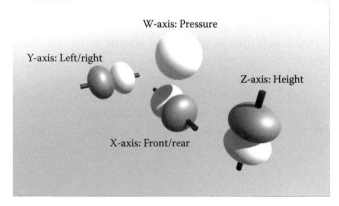

The ambisonic field axis.

multiple software solutions that provide the ability to format ambi-sonic content into a range of channel-based formats, and many of these solutions are inexpensive or even free.

Ambisonics can also be increased in resolution. The above dia-gram illustrates a first-order ambisonic format. This means there is a single figure-eight capture for each axis. It is possible to add more microphones on each axis (this must be done uniformly) to increase the capture resolution. So—second order, third, fourth, etc. The additional microphones function somewhat like increas-ing the pixel count for a photo. In a photo, you get more clarity and detail with increased pixel count. With Ambisonics, it means there are more microphones capturing each axis. So instead of the front/back axis being captured with a single figure-eight pattern, there could be multiple microphones so there are more points as you move between axes.

Ambisonic microphone with multiple capsules.

Ambisonics is a significant aspect of spatial audio and is likely to become central to many processes; therefore, it is worth investing some time to both define what it is and how we can use it.

Simon Goodwin has used Ambisonics in game development probably longer than anyone else and his understanding of the technology allows him to provide a detailed discussion on the topic.

Ambisonics explained for 21st century sound designers

by Simon N Goodwin

Ambisonics is a generalized way of representing a "soundfield"—the distribution of sounds from all directions around a listener. It can use any number of channels—the more you give it, the greater the spatial accuracy of sources in the soundfield.

Before Ambisonics, mixing was a one-step process. Individual recordings—stems, samples, synthesized audio, and location recordings—were combined into a mix, usually in stereo but sometimes in mono for radio, or 5.1 or 7.1 channel loudspeaker surround typically for cinema, which was then delivered as finished work to the listener. The accuracy of the result, in terms of relative levels, timbre, and source directions, depended upon the closeness of the correspondence between the system used to mix the master copy and the consumer's system used to replay it.

Ambisonics recognizes that there's no longer a standard mix configuration which can be created and then archived as part of the production process. Movies are more likely to be consumed at home via whatever speaker arrangement suits the furniture, or while on the move—in a plane or on a phone or tablet, via headphones or small battery-powered speakers—than they are in a THX-certified cinema. The same applies to new media, from 3D games on consoles and set-top boxes to VR, but much more so because:

- New media is interactive and consumed in more varied environments than old passive content like a film or LP.
- Interactivity implies flexibility and customization, and consumers have grown accustomed to this and expect it.
- Interactive media is optimized for a single consumer—whereas films have to be mixed to suit theaters large and small (hence optional features like low-frequency effects [LFE], and techniques like fold-down) and many listeners at once.

In interactive media like games, and VR most of all, the player controls the camera and there is no preferred direction where the content can be conveniently located. As the player moves, the sides become the center, the front the back, from moment to moment. We can't dedicate a row of speakers at the front for the "action" and reserve a few more for "immersion" so that the people in the cheap seats get some sense of being there—gamers and people seeking to explore a virtual environment need accurate spatialization, not just a vague sense of envelopment.

Immersion in passive media is nice to have, but not essential—it enhances the experience, but you can still follow the story even if the dialogue does not track the actors, or the things you can't see are not accurately placed in the listeners' ears—whereas knowing the location of things you can't see, whether to find them or run away, is typically a matter of (virtual) life and death to an interactive player!

Even before VR, there was pressure on ambitious sound designers to cater for a wide range of audio output configurations. Quadraphonic surround, then cinematic 5.1 surround (via DSP-enhanced consumer devices like Soundblaster Live and the first Xbox) were adopted by PCs and game consoles, to deliver legacy content and new experiences. Gamers use different panners to suit, assuming the user config is apparent.

The 7.1 surround system came in several flavors—the horizontal cinema version, plus early 3D variants like the Aureal layout, analog sound cards like Vortex3, Audigy, and XFi, and before long "standard" 7.1 channel analog output on PC motherboards, soon followed by one-wire solutions like HDMI which (from release 1.3 in 2006) supports 8-channel 192 KHz 24-bit digital audio by default, now implemented on consoles, computers, tablets, and even phones.

It was a mess. Even if you had a 7.1 channel mix to listen to, and all the amps and speakers or headphone virtualization tech to deliver it, you could not be sure that the channels delivered would correspond in positions or even order to your local rig—even working out how close you were was a challenge. Dolby and Creative Labs (among others) differed on the locations of the two extra speakers added in transition from 5.1 to 7.1.

Microsoft muddied the waters considerably by changing the assumed positions of those speakers between the rear and the sides, between two service pack releases of Windows XP! The advice for audio pedants was curt—if this matters to your customers, consider providing a switch to swap side and rear pairs over. Besides passing the buck to already-confused consumers, this introduced new ways of getting the mix wrong, irritating enough for passive consumers but potentially deadly for explorers, drivers, and shooters.

Combine that with the lack of any standard (there's no 7.1 equivalent of ITU 5.1 layout), several 3D variants like Aureal, 3D7.1, and Atmos which offer 5.1 compatibility but add height in diverse ways—consumer surround sound was broken at the start of the 21st century. For interactive audio designers and engineers looking to surpass the achievements of Hollywood in a market fast outgrowing cinema, it was no longer possible to pick a format and hope that consumers would follow suit.

They needed to have a way to hedge their bets, to pass some of the control to the players paying their wages—to avoid making decisions on behalf of listeners that would compromise their experience, whether they were on a basic TV, earbuds, home cinema rig, or early adopters of the latest Atmos, DTS-X, or similar package.

B-format *(this is a vital bit, not sure yet where this should be inserted—it will need good pics, e.g., input and output waves and spatial patterns, e.g., https://en.wikipedia. org/wiki/Ambisonics#/media/File:Spherical_Harmonics_deg3.png).*

You'll hear a lot about B-format when you first encounter Ambisonics. B-format is not all of Ambisonics but a single simple embodiment of it—a minimal representation to give full-sphere surround sound. It uses four channels, all the same format and bandwidth (typically LPCM), though codecs like ATRAC, AAC, and even the venerable MuLaw (the 2:1 codec which is faster than loading raw PCM) have been used. There's no concept of main and subsidiary channels, as in MP3 joint stereo or the low-bandwidth cinematic LFE .1 channel. Ambisonics prizes symmetry and orthogonality—all the channels match in capability, and to add or remove options you add or remove whole channels, rather than scrunch them up differentially.

B-format uses four channels, named W, X, Y, and Z. The assignment of the last three letters to directions follows mathematical rather than gaming conventions (and game systems still fight holy wars about whether positive Z is forward or backward); so if you remember that the X-axis goes from left to right, as it did in grade school, you're probably best off ditching the letters and just remembering the order. The four channels are ordered as follows:

1.	W	*Omnidirectional component*	*Parts of the sound heard equally in any direction*
2.	X	*Front/rear component*	*Front minus back (separated out in decoding)*
3.	Y	*Horizontal component*	*Left minus right (as in the extra FM radio channel)*
4.	Z	*Vertical component*	*Up minus down (sometimes empty, see later)*

What happens if you get them in the wrong order? It's vital to get the first one right—this typically carries the most power and is the channel against which all the 3D channels push or pull. Swapping the others over is equivalent to reorienting the listener, leaning forward or back or maybe rolling over—it changes the directions without adding or removing any content. There's no reason why front/

back comes second, for example, but we need to agree on it; it's convenient that height is the last B-format channel, as this means you can extract a horizontal-only soundfield (so-called pantophonic as opposed to periphonic; 360VR is pantophonic, not actually 3D—yet) by just ignoring the last channel, saving a third of the bandwidth at the expense of delivering sounds which respond to elevation and roll.

A sound source from any position on a sphere around the listener can be modeled by mixing the source wave into appropriate parts of the four components. If it's directly above or below the listener it will involve just the first and last channels, and so on. Instantaneous matrix math allows us to redistribute the directions smoothly, rotating the entire mix losslessly. Manipulation of the W component allows us to move sounds inward, to the point where an in-head experience plays on the W channel alone, and a well-aimed rocket sound can move smoothly up your spine and out of the top of your head just as hyperreality insists it should!

If this is B-format, what happened to A-format? A-format is an efficient way to capture B-format data—an alternate arrangement more practical for microphone designers. In theory, you could make a B-format microphone with one omnicapsule and three figure-eight mics (e.g., ribbon mics). However, for this to work you'd need to make all four microphones coincident, which defies current design expertise, and perhaps the laws of physics. You'd also need to match the different types of mic very carefully in acoustic as well as spatial properties.

An ambisonic or *soundfield* mic uses an alternate arrangement which is easier to make, with four matched directional microphone elements arranged in a tight tetrahedron, as close together as the designers can get them without compromising fidelity. This also generates four signals, but they're not separated out into mono-, omni-, and orthogonal directions. Electronics or software—or both, potentially customized for each instance of the mic, for best results—converts these four A-format signals into four B-format ones for ease of manipulation.

There are also some G-formats—output mix arrangements for a specific speaker rig which contain all the information needed to reconstitute B-format, and then derive signals for other speaker positions not explicitly provided. The four channels of a regular quad mix, with speakers at right angles, are a G-format, as is the regular hexagon implicit in cinema 7.1 once LFE and front center components are factored out. This can be decoded into pantophonic B-format plus some additional spatial information (which can inform second order ambisonic channels). Likewise the 3D 7.1 format, which some games output can be losslessly decoded back to B-format, with a full periphonic height channel. You can then re-encode it for any number of speakers, anywhere around you! Get up on that wire-mesh floor and experiment!

G-formats are interesting for recovering data from old recordings and titles, or customizing those to play better in your own listening environment, including HRTF-based 3D headphone systems, and A-format is worth understanding if you're using live captures in your mix, but for most purposes B-format is the key concept. There are many advances over B-format, which come from adding extra channels, corresponding to intermediate directions or internal positions, but they all build on B-format channels as a base, and refer to a common W channel; however, many extra spatial channels are added. These extensions are referred to as higher-order Ambisonics and will be explained in more detail later.

So Ambisonics is primarily an intermediate format—between the location recordings, spot FX foley and "object audio" compiled by the sound designer, and the final mix customized for the players' ears and environment. Rather than making a custom mix for each listener, or some one-size-fits-none populist compromise, the designer populates an ideal soundfield with no preferential layout or even direction, monitors and demonstrates it on speakers and headphones as usual, and ships the raw material in the form of objects and soundfields, with the manual and smart automatic options (like endpoint detection) needed for the consumer to decode it optimally. If a new custom HRTF or spatial decoder like Harpex comes along, the consumer may get a better mix than the original designer. That's fine—that's progress! The packaged soundfield is essentially an ideal mix for a perfect replay environment (subject only to your channel and disk budget). It's future-proof, in a way that an ITU 5.1 mix cannot be.

No wonder that the BBC, when faced with the challenge of evergreening thousands of archive shows with stereo masters and raw multichannel sources, has opted to create soundfields rather than custom 5.1, 7.1, Atmos, binaural, and 360VR mixes. That way it captures all the possible source directions, and can pick the one or ones a given TV customer needs from it. Even a decade ago, it was a no-brainer for designers at Codemasters to author horizontal B-format mixes rather than the four main mixes needed for contemporary game platforms. One B-format ambience, with three or four channels, can be decoded at negligible cost to 5.1 (regular square or irregular pentagon), 7.1, binaural headphones, or stereo speakers.

You save loads of disk space, as well as design and QA time—prerendered speaker and headphone stereo, and 5.1 and 7.1 channel mixes need 18 channels, versus three or four for the soundfield, or maybe six for a hybrid horizontal mix that gives greater precision for irregular 7.1 and ITU rigs. Even allowing for separate localization tracks (or soundfields, if you want those spatialized too) the result is a lot more future-proof than a set of custom mixes. Add crosstalk cancelation and you can even do front/back and side surround from a soundfield via just a front stereo pair, as long as you know the listener is going to keep still.

The most common config of Sega's Showdown arcade racer does just this—it helps to design the seat and speaker layout at the same time as the game. But if you can make appropriate measurements on the fly, Ambisonics allows even this to be achieved on hardware that might not exist when the assets are authored.

One ambisonic soundfield can support any number of sources—just as one mono, stereo, or 5.1 mix can—but unlike a conventional multichannel mix, the soundfield can be smoothly rotated in 3D to any orientation, varying yaw, pitch, and roll, without loss of spatial information. It's this feature that has made Ambisonics especially useful for AR and VR sound design. In VR, the player controls the orientation of the camera and the corresponding audio mix, typically through fast head-tracking, and it's vital that the mix remains consistent throughout.

To understand the significance of this, consider what happens when a four-speaker surround mix is rotated, using conventional pairwise panning between speakers. When all four channels of the mix correspond to speaker positions, the mix sounds as the designer intended. When the listener turns, all the sources are panned to positions between speakers. This works fairly well for a narrow angle between the front speakers—it's the basis of stereo—but much worse to the sides and rear, due to artifacts like head masking, where part but not all of each pair of signals is blocked by the listener's head.

The result is a sound that goes in and out of focus as the channels move into and out of particular speakers—spatialization of sources between the side and rear speakers is much poorer, breaking the sense of immersion. For sport games using pairwise mixing (such as Brian Lara Cricket, and sundry soccer titles), it was soon found better to leave crowd ambience pegged to speakers than to try to rotate it with the listener.

The smooth fading of Ambisonics, which involves all the speakers regardless of the source orientation, makes it practical to rotate the soundfield and decode it appropriately on the fly, rather than taking a prefabricated speaker-specific mix and crossfading it between the nearest speakers, which doesn't work anywhere near as well. The ambisonic approach keeps the spatial components of the mix distinct, whereas speaker mixes cannot—and unmixing and remixing is a lot harder and more error-prone than making a custom mix from data which keeps the spatial content as separate as possible, for a given channel count.

A particular problem, demonstrated at the 2016 AES International Audio for Games Conference in London, relates to fold-down and source positions in-between speaker positions presumed by the original mix—repanning boosts the level of sounds in such positions, interfering with the distance cues, which are so important in games and AR. It sounds as if sources in-between speakers are closer than those which happen to fall on a speaker location. This undermines the player's ability to work out the locations of threats that they can hear but not see—most of the scene, inevitably, in a busy world and even whether they are approaching or going away from the player. All this potential confusion goes away when you avoid making final mix decisions till you know the player's listening setup.

Ambisonic standards, as used in console and PC games like the *RaceDriver Grid*, *Dirt*, and the *F1* series from Codemasters, also allowed one mix to be made and rendered for 5.1 and 7.1 mixes with comparable quality, even if the layout and exact speaker angles for the final replay is not known at the time of encoding and unlikely to match that used by the original sound designer. More will be said about this later, in the section about practical uses of Ambisonics in modern games. The separation of ambisonic processing into two stages, encoding and decoding, allows flexible delivery.

This matters because even if you don't know the exact details of the listener's setup when you design a game, a good audio programmer or middleware package like Wwise should be able to customize your design to suit each particular listener—including other designers, testers, producers, and fellow team members, in the course of development—without the need or false confidence of standardizing listener setup across the development team. Their experience will vary, but it'll be closer than if you made a one-size-fits-all mix, with upmixing or fold-down to plug the gaps, and easier to build, test, and balance than one made with group volume tweaks and asset-swaps to adjust between headphones and all the possible speaker mixes.

Even in a VR experience optimized for a single listener, there's often a requirement to make a simultaneous conventional speaker mix for players waiting their turn, or a stereo or 360 surround (horizontal only) version to upload to YouTube. Since Ambisonics separates encoding and decoding, it's relatively easy to derive these multiple endpoints from the full set of data used to make the full 3D mix delivered to the main player. For instance, a stereo mix of arbitrary width can be derived from two of the four B-format signals—mono and left/right difference—or 360 surround, by discarding only the height channels.

Encoding

Encoding involves combining recordings or positioned sources into a layout-agnostic set of related channels, according to mathematical rules which are optimized to economically preserve spatial information for later use. Decoding takes those and distributes them appropriately for the known properties of the listening environment. The more we know about that environment, the more accurately the mix is delivered, from a given set of encoded channels.

Encoding is also a fast process, at least on modern computers. Comparisons between the pairwise 5.1 mixer built into Sony's Multistream console audio middleware, which uses standard pairwise mixing techniques similar to those in Apple and Microsoft firmware, show that games could encode a source to hybrid third-order Ambisonics (eight directional channels) and decode it back for a 7.1 speaker layout in 2D or 3D and regardless of exact layout, faster than the default 5.1 panner could work out which pair of speakers to address and mute the others.

This is partly because ambisonic encoding and decoding treats each output and input channel equivalently. The code performs the same operations on each audio stream, varying only the intensity and polarity of the signals in each channel of the soundfield. The values of the coefficients computed by the encoding panner, and the decoding renderer, vary the proportions of input signals used and how they reach the player's ears, but the system workload is identical, since it takes the same amount of time for a CPU to multiply by 0.707 as it does −0.001.

The coefficients encode the source and output positions, the math does the rest. As a designer, you just provide 3D positions, sizes, velocities for sources and the orientation, and speed and position of your listeners, just as you would in any game made in the last 20 years. The encoder uses those, and the decoder uses additional information about the replay environment—or environments—to get as much of that information into the player's ears as the input data, intermediate format, and output gear can handle.

Efficiency

It's reasonable to expect that this is an expensive process, but actually Ambisonics itself is fast—almost instantaneous, though delivery codecs and HRTF processing may add output lag, as they would for any panning system— and well suited to the way DSPs work. Since modern processors, especially the power-constrained cost-reduced ones in consoles and mobile devices, are fast at sequential operations but soon get bogged down handling interacting conditions (a consequence of hardware pipelining), this makes Ambisonics a particularly good fit for VR and AR.

It also means that there are no performance spikes which could cause unsteady frame rate, breaking the illusion of "being there" by introducing erratic lag. In game performance, only the worst case matters, and in ambisonic games the worst case is both predictable and relatively quick. This allows you to mix more sources for a given CPU load, or combine premixed soundfields and foreground object audio sweeteners for a more varied and immersive mix than would otherwise be practical.

Ambisonics also scales well, up or down, which matters on mobile or PC gaming where the difference in capability between a mass-market, low-end device and the latest hardware may be a factor of 30 or more. Your producer may be pressuring you to maximize sales potential and support millions of low-end devices, without sacrificing quality on the best kit which reviewers will have and use to judge you against the top-flight competition. So it helps to have a quick way to trade performance and fidelity which does not sacrifice content, but only spatial detail, in the quest to keep the frame rate up on older devices.

Decoding

The main area of differences between ambisonic systems involves the decoding and playback stages. Filtering, crosstalk processing, and other DSP tricks are used in proprietary ways. Since the input—the soundfield representation—is the same for all ambisonic decoders, this means content producers don't have to worry about the differences in rendering, except to note that their work will take advantage of the various proprietary techniques on offer. This may be advanced and customized HRTFs, feature extraction—like the Harpex library which uses DSP analysis to derive higher-order data from a B-format mix—or custom adaptation for the listening environment, headphone characteristics, etc. Since you're using standard ambisonic intermediate channels, you or your customers benefit automatically from standardized encoding now, and future advances in decoding yet to come.

Ambisonics is well-established nonproprietary technology, mathematically rigorous yet simple to apply, and scales progressively up and down from mono to any number of channels. As you add channels it becomes mathematically equivalent to wave field synthesis, an alternate approach to surround sound which typically relies on a very large number of speakers. One key practical difference is that you can add channels progressively to an ambisonic representation.

Ambisonics was first used in the era of quadraphonic sound, where it offered forward and backward compatibility. Forward—to larger horizontal speaker arrays, like the hexagon central to modern 7.1 cinema, and beyond to true 3D sound with speakers (or sound sources) above and below the listener. Backward—to mono and stereo, without the positioning discrepancies associated with fold-down, where the correlation between channels affects balance of mixed sounds (fold-down makes conventionally panned sounds louder if they're between speaker positions).

Unlike mono, stereo, quad, or transitional arrangements like cinema 5.1 or 7.1, the number of channels in an ambisonic mix does not correspond to the number of speakers. As soon as you get past stereo, Ambisonics requires fewer channels for a given number of speakers than would be needed for a direct per-speaker mix, and the more channels you have the more speakers—or virtual source positions, in an HRTF-based headphone system—it can accurately drive.

History and Fundamental Concepts

Ambisonics stems directly from stereo and the work done by the inventor of stereo, Alan Blumlein—who considered height and depth, as well as left/right panning, from the start. We tend to take stereo for granted, but an understanding of its subtleties makes Ambisonics easier to grasp—in fact almost inevitable, with stereo just an obvious first step. Indeed, Blumlein used the term binaural to describe stereo, anticipating HRTFs, ERTFs, and custom headphone mixes as well as twin-speaker rendering.

Almost all his 100+ patents use sum and difference techniques, as do stereo vinyl records, stereo FM radio broadcasts, and even the high-compression "joint stereo" MP3 formats. In Blumlein's days, this separation, combination, and mixing was mostly achieved with transformers; in the 1970s, heyday of analog synths and the birth of surround systems, they were done with op-amps. Nowadays we get the same results effectively for free—more accurately and with less noise and conversion artifacts—with DSP instructions, especially the parallel multiply-add operations which modern CPUs eat for lunch. It's still possible to decode an ambisonic mix for any arrangement of output channels with nothing more than transformers, but nowadays the DSP approach is easier!

You don't need to understand the math and physics as well as Blumlein or Gerzon, but they were both practical engineers with extraordinary talent for lucid explanation. A well-trained sound designer will know far more about psychoacoustics than Blumlein, and some things discovered since even Gerzon's death—but it's worth looking at the original papers if you want to really understand the full picture, and anticipate what's yet not done, but still worth trying.

further reading

Andersen, Asbjoern. "Creative audio for virtual technology." A sound effect. May 20, 2016. Accessed October 10, 2017. https://www.asoundeffect.com/creative-audio-for-virtual-reality/.

Bridgham, David. "Hearing a Universe: Why 3D Sound is Key to the VR Game Experience." Maximum Games. May 4, 2016. Accessed October 10, 2017. https://www.loading-human.com/hearing-universe-3d-sound-vr-game-experience/.

David Bridgham. 2016. Maximum Games. [ONLINE] Available at: https://www.loading-human.com/?s=hearing+universe. [Accessed 1 August 2017].

Nguyen, Tuan. "3D audio is back, and VR needs it." PC Gamer. April 1, 2016. Accessed October 10, 2017. http://www.pcgamer.com/3d-audio-is-back-and-vr-needs-it.

Lalwani, Mona. "VR needs 3d Audio." End Gadget. January 22, 2016. Accessed October 10, 2017. https://www.engadget.com/2016/01/22/vr-needs-3d-audio.

why isn't this easy? The many challenges of the new realities

the challenge of 3D audio

Audio production is hard. Audio production in 3D is very hard. There is a level of accuracy and realism that needs to be achieved to help sell a convincing experience for the new reality formats. But what is so hard about this format when compared to regular audio production?

I am going to start this chapter with a contribution from Garry Taylor, audio director for Sony Europe. Garry has been heavily involved with the development of virtual reality (VR) content and so has a clear perspective on where we are now and where we may end up.

VR Audio

Garry Taylor

How VR has changed (or will change) audio development?

Long ago, when one of the most debated questions was "which speaker should the dialogue be coming out of?" the sum of our work was presented to the player on a flat plane, on speakers in front of them, usually either side of the screen. If, as a consumer, you were lucky enough to have more than two speakers, the chances of them being in the same place as the speakers the engineers mixed the game on were virtually nil. Let's face it, next to no-one has a 7.1 speaker setup at home. That doesn't mean that we shouldn't be supporting these large surround formats; after all, people that have invested in such systems should definitely be rewarded, but we do need to remember that the average person probably wasn't listening in surround.

These days, in VR, we tend to put our trust in 3D audio rendering systems that don't care where your physical speakers are. This is a good thing. If you want to put a single surround speaker on the bookshelf next to the door, your system should be able to accommodate that. But it also needs to know where that speaker is in space in order to render audio to it accurately. That's tricky.

However, if you're playing in VR, the chances are you're wearing headphones. This is also a good thing. If we know the orientation of your head, relative to a fixed point, we know what direction you're facing, and by extension where your ears are likely to be. This means we have the chance to simulate the acoustic properties of any virtual environment and the sounds in it, and reproduce them correctly at your ears.

Since before you were born (my daughter used to kick her way through Groove Armada albums in the womb) we've learned to localize sounds in space by the way the sounds bounce off our ears and around our head. If you're trying to locate the source of a sound in the real world, many small unconscious head movements subtly change how the wavefronts arrive at the ears and allow us to pinpoint the direction of a sound source. This is especially true of sounds above or below you, which rely on the shape of your pinna, the flappy bits on the side of your head.

Three-dimensional audio rendering systems have taken advantage of this by creating models of people's ears and deriving head-related transfer function (HRTF) models, which simulate the acoustic effects of the head and ears. It works very well. There is a drawback though; when these systems are built, a measurement of a person's head is made by placing a microphone in each of their ears and recording a sound from many positions around the listener (usually a sine sweep that contains all audible frequencies). From these head-related impulse response (HRIR) recordings, a set of filters and delay lines is generated for each ear for each position in a sphere around you, and if you put a sound through it, it really does sound like it's coming from the direction you want it to come from.

However, because everyone's ears are different, you're effectively listening through someone else's ears, which are going to be different from yours. The directionality they produce doesn't work for everyone, especially when it comes to sounds coming from above or below you, but for the most part, it works fairly well for the majority of people.

So, now we have the ability to track the player's head, and we have enough processing power to run multiple filters and delays in real time, and we can do this in VR. That's great!

You'd think that this was a straightforward evolution of playback technology, and it is—but it has had the added effect of bringing into sharp focus how much we've essentially faked things in the past. It also means that we've unwittingly entered the uncanny valley of audio, similar to the problems our brothers and sisters in the business who animate and render models of human characters have.

Now, we're actually in the world, as opposed to watching a moving picture of the world on a screen, and the sum of our life experience has taught us how sound behaves in the real world. We instinctively know it, even if we can't explain it to someone. Or more accurately, we notice when something is wrong, even if we lack the vocabulary to explain why it is wrong. It doesn't "feel" right. Our brains are extremely adept at recognizing patterns, whether it be visual or auditory, and when something "isn't quite right" we briefly stop thinking about the content we're experiencing or the game we're playing, and our brains go into "trying to work out what's wrong" mode.

Everyday objects, for example, usually don't have a single sound when you examine them up close. The sound of any object is usually made up of multiple moving parts, and the closer you examine it, the more those separate sounds diverge from a single point. The real world has a lot more detail than we have ever created in a virtual world, and when you're examining a single object in VR, bearing in mind that with motion controllers you can rotate any object and bring it closer to your virtual ears, the illusion falls down. That's not to say it's a bad approximation, because it's not. It has served us well in the past, but now, we're beginning to see that it was always an approximation. And as time goes by, it'll annoy people, mainly those who create audible illusions for a living like us, audio designers.

Our audio creations lack detail, and their behaviors lack nuance. And VR has brought these facts to the fore.

There are a number of acoustic effects that happen in the real world which we don't usually have the processing power to compute in real time.

Things like atmospheric absorption, as sounds travel through the air we breathe, and the reflection of spherical sound waves off a multitude of different surfaces and materials, at different distances, each of which imparts its own fingerprint onto the sound bouncing back. We approximate them, or attempt to at least, but doing so in great detail takes significant computing resources.

The way we simulate distance is absolutely crucial in giving the player the positional cues they need in order to accurately place sound sources such as objects and people in the world. Psychoacoustic theory tells us that in order to accurately judge the distance of a sound source there are multiple cues we need in order to do it accurately.

First, we know how loud certain things are intrinsically. For example, we know how loud the human voice is generally. We know how the sound and intensity of the voice changes when we shout. So, if we know how loud something is in reality, we can judge with a fair amount of accuracy how distant it is by the sound pressure level we hear at our listening position.

Second, the ratio between the dry sound, the one that travels directly from the source to our ears, and the early reflections that bounce of the surfaces around us is the main signifier for distance, as well as giving us valuable clues as to the type of environment we're in. For example, if you shout in an enclosed space, the amount of reverberation bouncing around the room is always constant, regardless of how close the sound source is to you. Therefore, if the dry signal is prominent in relation to the reverberation, your brain will tell you it's close. As the sound source moves away, the dry signal will decrease, but the level of the reverberant field will stay the same.

Third, there's air absorption, which very gently filters the sound as it travels through the air. The effect of air absorption on distance perception is slight, but it is a factor, especially when the source is at greater distances.

The behavior of acoustic modeling systems currently used in game development is very coarse, it's an approximation. A lot of the time, it's a bad approximation that only gives us information about the state of the game (e.g., a sound effect), but not necessarily accurate information about the acoustic environment.

The buzzword for VR at the moment is "presence." That is the sense that you're actually there, "in the world," and can affect the world in some way. Good audio design is absolutely essential for that feeling of presence, but the way we model acoustic environments needs to improve, if we're going to blur the lines further between the real and the virtual.

Where will VR audio be in 10 years' time?

I wouldn't be foolish enough to say with any certainty what might happen in the next 10 years. Who would have seen VR coming 10 years ago? Most of us can't even predict what might happen in the next 10 hours.

Who'd have thought that ambisonics, a spherical sound encoding technique from the 1970s, would see a resurgence in use, specifically for a very 21st century entertainment platform like virtual reality?

However, given the history of computing up to now, as well as the knowledge of the evolution of interactive audio systems, we can make an educated guess about some of the technological advances that are likely to occur. We'll probably miss out some ground-breaking "thing" that no-one saw coming, but that's true innovation for you. Most people never see it coming.

Accurate acoustic modeling takes a lot of computing power. But as we know, computing power is increasing, and will continue to increase, even if Moore's Law is showing signs of stumbling. This will give us increased processing power that can be put to good use simulating the behavior of acoustic energy bouncing around an environment. That's not to say that we'll be modeling acoustics with perfect accuracy; it only has to be "good enough." But at the moment it isn't good enough.

Personalized HRTF sets would increase the perceived quality of audio rendering significantly, but it's a tough nut to crack. Not generating them—that's relatively easy—but giving the general public a way of generating them that's very easy and quick to do. That's the hard part. Most nonaudio people wouldn't have the patience to go through a process that might last 10–15 minutes in order to accurately build up a model of their head and pinna, especially if they don't actually understand how it works or what the tangible benefits to them are. This is more of a user experience (UX) and user interface (UI) problem, and it's a process that's in dire need of innovation.

With the rapid rise in complexity—not only of games generally, but also in the tools we use—new ways of developing audio for games, as well as the games themselves and other interactive systems, are required. The tools we need to build more complex systems need to get smarter and quicker. Managing that complexity is key. To be honest, given the current complexity of game systems, I'm kind of surprised that we manage to build anything at all these days.

We need audio tools to know what we want to do, and for them to assume much more than they do now. With the rise of machine learning, voice recognition systems, and natural language understanding, a new generation of tools could cut the cost of developing games significantly. I know I'd much prefer to tell a machine what I want it to do, as opposed to sitting in front of a crude input device like a keyboard and a mouse, and manually typing in commands.

The truth is that I don't know how we'll be making games for VR in 10 years, or what those games might be like, both technologically and artistically. But I'm looking forward to it.

adapting to new formats

Our approach to audio production for the new realities may need to be adapted in several ways from how we created content for previous forms of media. Because of the level of interaction that is possible and encouraged with the new formats, it can mean that the old techniques of asset capture, creation, and implementation do not always provide the required level of flexibility needed for immersive reality experiences.

A similar evolution in asset creation was required for interactive media production. In a movie, a car may pass on screen from left to right. All we need as a suitable asset for this would likely be a single recording panned to track the screen movement. Interactive media made it possible for the audience to move along with the car, move around the car, or even stop the car from moving. All of these actions required very different assets to support them. So the car needed sound modeling to allow for the interactive nature of the experience. The more agency we gave the audience, the more the car evolved from a single sound panned to suit screen time, to an interactive sound model.

The new realities will often require this process to evolve further. VR/360 video and alternate reality (AR) will often deal with real-world scale of 1:1 and as such the audience will be interacting with virtual objects in a manner never previously experienced. Our virtual car might now be an object that the audience can walk around, lean close to, and kneel in front of. This more intimate proximity to virtual objects means that the car will require many different sound sources all accurately positioned to simulate a real car and how it generates sound. The level of detail we put into virtual experiences may need to be considerably more than that previously required for linear or interactive media.

how and why we hear

I suspect that anyone who is reading this book already has an understanding of the basics of sound production and how the human ear captures sound. As a quick refresher, vibrations generate sound waves that travel through a medium (usually air) and are picked up by the ear to be translated into electrical signals that are interpreted by the brain. A microphone and loudspeaker system work in a similar manner.

All the other factors that influence how sound behaves are important in media production and critical for the new realities. We cannot afford to ignore why we hear certain things in certain ways and why our brains interpret sounds in the ways they do. Psychoacoustics plays an important part in how we communicate with our audience. As we explore new technologies, we will encounter not only new functionality but also real limitations that we must understand and either work with or around. To start with I think it is important to explore the concept of the uncanny valley.

The Uncanny Valley

The uncanny valley refers to how humans react to representations of real things, often living things such as creatures or people, but the uncanny valley effect can be applied to anything. Think about cartoons—when we create a stylized cartoon character we tend to create exaggerated caricatures of people. Big round noses to emphasize comedy, large doe eyes for innocent characters or children, long thin limbs and torsos, gravity-defying features. We stylize people or create anthropomorphic animals that we and our children love to watch and have no trouble relating to. We can do this because the simple bold lines and saturated color of a cartoon are so very distant from our reality that we simplify these images in our mind and tell ourselves they are "real."

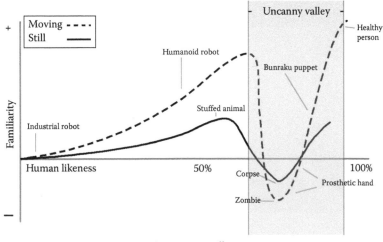

The uncanny valley.

If we encountered a typical animated character in the real world, it would most likely be utterly terrifying. Eyes that take up half the face, arms, and legs impossibly thin and twice the length of a normal human, a torso so thin it could not even support its own weight.

The uncanny valley refers to the trouble we run into when trying to make things more and more realistic. The closer we get to reality, the more the inconsistencies will out. Some big budget movies have been criticized in recent years because as they get better at creating realistic CG characters, things like eyes not blinking and tongues not moving accurately inside a character's mouth have a huge impact on how we perceive these characters. The more "human" they look, the more we notice the little things, which makes us uncomfortable and the characters seem more like monstrous mockeries of human beings than the real thing.

Star Wars: Rogue One (2016) used technology to bring back Admiral Tarkin and a young Princess Leia, to not so great a reception. Do a quick Google and see how well (or not) that was received. The uncanny valley really came home on this one.

Why the uncanny valley matters to the new realities

Virtual *reality*, mixed *reality* (MR), augmented *reality*. *Reality* is the key here. Up till now most of our gaming experiences and linear stories in film and television have been all about escapism, looking through a window into a fantasy world. We rarely try to convince the audience that we are transplanting them to a new location.

The CG characters in *Yonder: The Cloud Catcher Chronicles* are vastly different from how a real person looks, and yet we accept them easily as a representation of a human. (Copyright Prideful Sloth 2017: Used with permission.)

Even deeply interactive games and super-high-quality cinema experiences such as IMAX or 3D film still have to deal with the fact that the audience is sitting in a lounge room with a controller or an auditorium where the guy behind you might be texting his friend and eating popcorn. So while these experiences can be really entertaining and engaging, we are not suggesting to the audience that we have transported them to a new reality.

One interesting exception here is the theme park rides or simulation games where you're in a pod that resembles a cockpit or racing car. These are coming much closer to what we're looking for in simulating reality, but are completely impractical for the average household user. The use of real-world props and settings is what sets these examples apart.

When you place a VR headset on, things change. We are replacing our audience's entire visual range and responding to their movements. In addition, we are replacing real-world sound sources that connect them to their own environment with sound cues that represent their new virtual environment. Our goal is to make our audience feel like they are truly inside the new environment and become deeply immersed in the experience we have created for them. From an audio point of view, this is incredibly difficult to get right.

Sound in the real world is complex, really complex. There is not a technology available today that can accurately simulate all the elements of how audio works in the real world, at least, nothing that is feasible for use in new reality experiences. The cost in resources would simply be too high to run on our current devices. Since we can't emulate real-world audio completely, we have to get as close as possible. This tiny gap between what we can do and what the real world does is our uncanny valley.

The following is just one example of the many areas we encounter in audio's uncanny valley.

Placing an object into a world space for audio is complex. Even if we start with a small empty room, there are many factors we need to consider. If the listener is in the center of a 10 m x 10 m room and a sound source is directly to their left 5 m away, then we would need to consider the following if the sound source emitted a single beep:

- The materials used to create the room will affect sound reflection and absorption.
- The exact distance the object is between the listener and the outer wall will affect the time that sound waves take to move

directly to the listener as well as indirectly move toward the left-hand wall and bounce back to the listener.

- If the walls reflect sound, any reflections will bounce around the room creating echoes and each of these must travel to the listener's position to be heard.

- The listener's clothing will affect reflection and absorption of sound.

- The distance from the sound source between the floor and ceiling will also affect the timing of certain reflections and how they contribute to the overall propagation of the sound.

- The nature of the environment will determine how long it takes for the energy from the single beep to dissipate from bouncing around the room.

All of these factors, and various others, need to be calculated just for a single beep in an empty space detected by a stationary listener. If we add just a single factor to the original scenario, the entire process becomes significantly more complex. If either the sound source or the listener is moving, it will affect the reflections; if other objects exist in the room, they will also affect the sound behavior.

How we deal with these challenges defines the effectiveness of the final experience. Many of them require efficient solutions to manage limited resources, so we rarely have the luxury of applying the most effective solution. There is always a trade-off between effectiveness and efficiency.

Why What We Hear Matters

Of all our senses hearing is our most critical warning system. When we sleep, we close our eyes and our sense of smell shuts down. This is why we use audible smoke alarms to warn us of fire. If there is an emergency situation when driving, a car horn alerts everyone around to be careful. This is because our hearing is a 360-degree sphere around us, so we can be aware of what is happening in any direction as long as the sound is loud enough to hear. Our hearing functions as well, if not better, at night when our eyes can struggle for definition. When it comes to music, our hearing is the primary sense for conveying emotional information. A picture may speak a thousand words, but a single spoken sentence or phrase of music can convey more emotional content than a book full of images. We have a rich range of emotional shorthand that

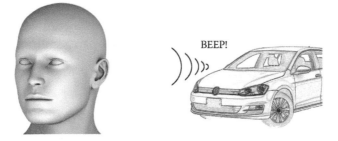

3D spherical hearing alerts us to danger all around us.

we can access through sound and music, which provides a critical means of connecting with our audiences and engaging them.

We underestimate how much we rely on and accept information from our ears. Humans will often call into doubt what they are looking at and wonder if a news report has been touched up with graphic effects. We wonder if the wood grain surface is, in fact, plastic so we reach out and touch it. Our eyes can deceive us and so we have learned to question what we see. With hearing we can also be tricked, but we are far more likely to accept what we hear as real. We are all very familiar with optical illusions; they can be fun and a challenge to understand why our brain interprets certain visual images in a specific way. Auditory illusions also exist, but are less commonly shared or explained, so people are less aware of how their hearing can be tricked.

If we stand in the middle of a built-up city and we hear a helicopter, we assume a helicopter is flying somewhere close by. If we turn around, look up, search, and find that we can see no helicopter, then we do not assume there is no helicopter; we just assume that something is obscuring our sight. It must be behind a building or too far away to see and the environment is bouncing the sound around. We never think that there is a giant speaker somewhere playing the sound of a helicopter just to trick us.

If the sound of the helicopter is very faint, we tell ourselves it must be far away. We do not assume it is just a quiet helicopter. We have established a certain baseline for what we know about the way a helicopter should sound. We have probably seen them in real life, we have certainly seen them in movies and on TV, and we know they are a large, noisy piece of machinery. So even a young child or someone with limited experience with aircraft will still, without even thinking, identify that sound as being from a helicopter that is further away.

It is the effective act of hearing and processing that humans do so naturally that provides such a great challenge for audio production. Most people are not aware of how effective their listening process is. They may not be very good at listening to their friends or remembering what their teachers have said, but they do have a very good instinctual hearing ability tuned as a danger sense and a navigation tool. So when we create a virtual experience, the audience may not be able to identify exactly what is wrong, but they WILL notice if the audio behaves in a manner different from what they hear in the real world.

If we want to avoid the uncanny valley of audio, we need to understand various aspects of how we hear and why we hear. This will let us focus on the right things when we create audio for the new formats. This understanding will also help us to fool our audience with various techniques and take advantage of the weaknesses within human hearing. Since we most likely cannot 100% accurately recreate a true simulation of audio behavior, we need to take advantage of certain aspects of psychoacoustics and utilize "smoke and mirrors" techniques to create the right experience. This is key, since in most cases what we are creating is entertainment or utility in our products to benefit our audience. If we can create an enjoyable, believable entertainment experience, then the exact way we do that is not important. Equally, if we can create an effective reliable utility application, then, again, the ends can justify the means.

If our project is designed to be mission-critical and lives and audience well-being rely on the outcome, then the need for accuracy becomes more important. If all we are doing is providing a certain sound that functions in a certain way, we can work with a less than completely scientific approach to achieve the desired outcome.

I would like to clarify here that I am not understating the importance of scientific data and the correct application of our knowledge of physics, math, and the other factors that affect audio. These all help to calculate accurately how sound behaves in the real world and how humans receive and process sound information. Everything we design should be based on solid physics and scientific practice. We also must acknowledge how the human body and brain works.

An excellent example of this principle comes from a documentary I viewed some years ago. This program was talking about the process of constructing the Parthenon in Athens, Greece. Considered one of the ancient wonders of the world, the accuracy, and quality of the construction, is incredible considering when it was built.

The Parthenon in Athens.

The building has several elements to its construction that are very good examples of mathematical precision. It has the reputation of being the most perfect Doric temple ever built.

However, the "perfect" nature of the Parthenon is a result of its deliberately imperfect construction. When looked at from the front-side corner, a viewer can see both the front face and the side of the Parthenon and all its columns. This angle presents the entire building and all its perfectly aligned elements. But because of the way in which the human eye works, the only way to create the illusion of perfect perspective was to create the long sides of the Parthenon so the columns form a slight dip in the level of the top edge. Our senses and the way our brain processes information are far from exact and do not align with the perfect mathematical nature of things like physics. The architects of the Parthenon made a deliberate decision to skew the values during construction so that humans would perceive the building in a certain way.

In the same way, although environmental audio should be based on math and physics, the practical production of an experience for a human audience may require some "trickery" to enhance how it is perceived by the audience.

Keep in mind, very few humans are completely symmetrical; in fact, if you did see a perfectly symmetrical human face, it would look creepy. This applies to the position of our ears and the shape of our head. The math and science we apply to our current technology cannot account for each little deviation of ear placement and head shape for every user. So we apply a general "best fit" that hopefully works for most people most of the time.

Hearing versus listening

People often do not pay much attention to audio, they hear but they do not really listen. So that means we can get away with anything right? Wrong! Exactly BECAUSE people don't listen is the problem. Our hearing works instinctively and as such, it's quite hard to pull the wool over the eyes of the listener and fool them into thinking things are okay. There are tricks we can use, but even these tricks need to be used carefully. Otherwise the audience's instincts kick in and they will feel like something is not right. They probably can't explain what is wrong, but they know something does not fit as it should.

The other issue has to do with modeling sound for each listener. We all hear differently; we are different heights, have different heads, and different ear shapes and sizes. Then we have variable hearing sensitivity; some of us have lost some range of hearing, or have certain aspects to our hearing that are unique. So when we present a 3D sound experience, to get it absolutely perfect for each listener we would need to model the data on their personal hearing capabilities. In the same way that we should tune a VR headset and make it fit the user exactly, compensating for any vision issues and setting it for their interaural phase difference (IPD), we should be adjusting for their hearing. Unfortunately, at this stage we cannot actually do all this, so we look for the middle ground—a best fit approach that will suit most audience members.

If you want to test this in practice, buy some dummy ears from a costume shop and put them on. Now try triangulating sounds you hear, how hard is it to localize sounds? Most people find they are much less accurate when the shape of their ears is changed.

There will likely never be a single solution for audio capture and creation for the new realities. But don't panic. Keep in mind how movie, TV musical recordings, and games all use many sources captured and used in many ways. Even the isolated dialogue from a film has probably been captured with several microphones simultaneously and blended to create the most effective end product. Audio production is complex, and the new realities will do nothing to reduce this complexity.

random or designed: the battle between order and chaos

It reads like the script for a Hollywood movie, but often when creating audio for interactive experiences we need to find a balance between order and chaos. On the side of order, we have the desire to accurately map the scientific behavior of sound in the real world. Spatial reflection, distance attenuation, environmental filtering, and localization within the world space are all examples of where audio teams want, as much as possible, to simulate exactly how science defines sound behavior in the real world and apply that to a virtual experience. The math behind real-world behavior is the foundation of a solid simulation.

The flip side of this is the chaotic nature of the world we live in. The nearly unlimited variables affecting how sound is produced and propagated mean we need to introduce many aspects of seemingly random behavior to our sound design. An accurate application of physics in the real world will often look chaotic and random to the average audience. Footsteps that vary significantly to avoid repetition, a large selection of different bird calls to create a realistic environment and constantly varying tempo of musical tracks to account for humans not being able to keep absolutely perfect time when performing. While we are trying to adopt a rigorous scientific approach to our audio behavior, we have a need to add unpredictable randomness to avoid our audio sounding fake, since the real world has so many factors that influence sound behavior.

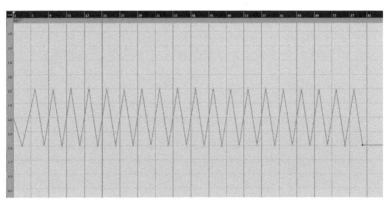

Midi tempo track: The constant variation simulates
the tiny variations in tempo of a live performer.

The above diagram illustrates a very simple technique in music production to break the "perfect" nature of sequenced music. Humans are mostly unable to keep perfect timing when performing. An ensemble that consists of multiple performers would struggle even more to maintain clock-perfect timing without a reference guide. This image displays the tempo track from an audio workstation for a piece of music with a constant tempo. The "constant" tempo of this piece of music is 120 bpm. But a computer can keep absolutely correct and accurate timing, so when played normally, the piece of music is played at exactly 120 bpm at all times. Considering that one of the main goals of working with sampled instruments and sequencers is to attempt to create realistic sounding music, this perfect timing is not really what we want.

Varying the tempo constantly over a very narrow range can break the computer-perfect playback. In the image, the tempo automation constantly shifts between 118 and 122 bpm. This means that the tempo is never static. The shift is only very minor and most listeners, even experienced ones, are unlikely to notice a shift of only 2–4 bpm, but it significantly breaks the feel of perfect timing. When I listen back to this technique, I cannot hear exactly what has changed, but I can clearly hear that the music sounds "better"—more organic, more lifelike. A real-world performance has almost limitless factors that will affect the ultimate tempo we hear as an audience. The exact nature and cause of these factors is not as important as the end result itself, the fact that we will not hear perfect timing in live performance. So in the case of producing computer-based music, this aspect of "randomized chaos" helps to produce a result that we find more closely matches a real-world performance.

Some of the variation we hear in the natural world could be simulated with precise scientific data, but in general the cost of doing so would not provide us with enough of a benefit for it to be worth the effort. The sound of footsteps in the real world may seem to vary randomly to the untrained ear, but each step is the result of a range of variables, including:

- Surface material (dirt, sand, snow)
- Additional surface elements (leaves, gravel, twigs)
- Shoe material and type (rubber, leather)
- Foot impact strength (walk, run, heavy person, light person)
- Foot impact angle (tall, short)
- Surface angle (flat, slope, uneven)

If each of these factors and others were tracked with absolute accuracy, then a simulation could calculate the seemingly random footsteps that we hear, but this would be incredibly costly to track and calculate for very little benefit. The variation we hear in the sound of footsteps can be effectively simulated using randomization of some basic variables, such as surface types, impact force, and movement speed.

Randomization of sound events like this is an efficient way to simulate sound behavior that would be very complex to track and predict accurately. This works well for sounds that most people will accept as being random in nature. Taking a smoke and mirrors approach in this case gives us the same result as applying rigorous mathematical accuracy, but without the negative impact on our resources.

Using sound design techniques to provide adequate solutions that the audience will accept and enjoy lets us free up computing resources for things that we cannot create convincingly with smoke and mirrors, such as positional data and accurate room reflections. In the fight between order and chaos, we pick our battles carefully.

Sometimes you need to deal with a little chaos.

choose your reality

As we have discussed so far, there are a variety of differences between VR, AR, and MR. Many of these differences are defined by how the technology works. Another key difference is the way the technology is utilized. Although there are distinguishing factors, I think we are still quite a way from defining clearly where VR stops and AR starts. Perhaps that line will never be entirely clear.

How Far Down the Rabbit Hole Do We Go?

One common issue that affects all aspects of surround audio production is the sheer complexity of the whole thing. There are so many interlocking factors that affect how sound is transmitted, influenced, received, and perceived that there is no one solution that can model the behavior with 100% accuracy. Essentially, it is too difficult with current technology to account for all the factors involved. I would even go so far as to suggest that we may not even fully understand all the factors that influence how humans hear and how we localize sound sources.

There are a great many characteristics that impact how sound is transmitted and received. To complicate matters further, many of these characteristics influence each other. This makes exact examination of specific behaviors difficult. To fully understand a single behavioral characteristic you might ideally want to isolate that characteristic so you can more thoroughly and accurately measure its variables to define it correctly. When there are so many elements interacting with each other's behavior, it becomes very difficult to isolate them accurately. The act of isolating itself changes the behavior of the characteristic you want to observe, which reduces the accuracy of any tests.

This means we often have situations where certain areas of understanding about sound behavior can be very interesting and engaging at an academic level, but may not be useful in a practical application for commercial products. Excessive cost, lack of processing resources, or practical understanding can result in certain characteristics being left out of technology development. In some cases, we know there are many different important characteristics to sound behavior, but we may not have a strong enough understanding of just exactly how all these elements come together to put it to use in our audio designs.

Example: wavefront curvature

Wavefront curvature is a term I first heard in 2016. When I heard the words assembled in that order, I stopped and processed what they could mean. A colleague from AES gave me a simple hint: "How the curve of a sound wave alters as the wave expands outward." This was all I needed to realize the impact and importance of this one aspect of sound behavior and the huge ramifications it had for spatial audio. But after I did some searching, it seemed that this aspect was not being discussed or included in information about spatial audio processes. I suspect there may be several technology companies who are dealing with wavefront curvature in some form or other, but the current secrecy around many of these solutions makes it hard to find out exactly what might exist.

This was a good example of a characteristic of sound that was important, but either too complex or too costly to be effectively utilized by the tools being developed.

Both curves represent a 90-degree slice of their original circle, but the largest diameter has a far gentler curve than the smaller one. This flattening of the curve can be an indication that that portion of the emanation is much further out from the origin point than the original point source that created the wave.

Wavefront curvature has significant implications for spatial audio accuracy. The "splash in a pond" analogy representing sound propagation gives us a convenient way to illustrate why wavefront curvature is important. Humans often determine the proximity of a

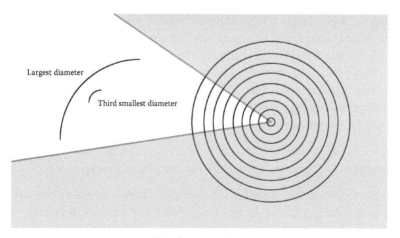

Wavefront curvature.

sound based on how loud it is. Using this analogy, the size of the ripples in the pond indicates how close we are to the initial splash. As we travel away from the initial impact, the waves get smaller and smaller, so the volume decreases. The problem here is that this only works if we know how big the initial splash was. If we encounter a wave that is one inch high, does that mean it came from a small splash a foot away or a massive splash that occurred a mile away but that has diminished so much that we are left with only an inch of amplitude?

When the initial splash in water or creation of a sound occurs, the waves expand outward from the point of origin. If we are close to the source, the curvature of the waves will be quite small. If we are miles away the curve will be extreme as the waves have expanded as they travel. So regardless of the amplitude of the wave when we interact with it, the curvature provides us with information as to how far it may have traveled. Using this, we can evaluate both the current amplitude and the wavefront curvature and surmise that a massive curvature and a one-inch amplitude was most likely caused by a very big initial splash.

So wavefront curvature is one of the many ways we localize sounds. How important it is or to what extent we utilize it I am not sure because, as I said, finding research on it is quite difficult. It may be that other species of mammals utilize it more effectively than humans do. It might even be the case that exaggerating wavefront curvature information in spatial audio could enhance a human's ability to detect sound source localization in virtual experiences beyond our real-world abilities. This opens a very interesting topic of conversation that is perhaps better left for another book. Is it possible for our technology to make us better able to listen and localize in virtual spaces than we can in the real world? And what is the implication of that for both entertainment and practical experiences?

This is only one example of a sound characteristic that has real value to spatial audio that may or may not be utilized in all processes because of the complexity involved in simulating it.

Challenges Common to All New Reality Formats

Before we explore the individual formats, there are a range of challenges that are common across all the new reality formats. These will not all apply all the time, but they are worth considering for all formats.

Generally, the new reality formats present sound and visuals for either entertainment or practical application. By necessity, we need to provide the audience with visual information that has some meaning. Swirling lights and patterns may be interesting for a short period of time, but they also risk disorientating the audience and even causing nausea. In fact, nausea is still a very real risk in many VR experiences as we continue to test the boundaries of what is comfortable for the average audience. Sound has its part to play in this process, with some basic functions that it needs to provide in order to support a VR/AR or MR experience.

So before we even think of how to make amazing sounds or immersive environments, we need to consider some of the baseline challenges of working with audio for the new realities.

Balancing Information and Entertainment

I love fun action movies; I also love the escapism of a good movie, television program, or game. I understand that much of what we do when we create media is to exaggerate the real world to make the story more appealing. For example, I love that, in *Raiders of the Lost Ark*, Indiana Jones' handgun sounds more like a howitzer. Every time he pulls the trigger it explodes like a weapon four times its size. For the audience this helps reinforce that Indiana is our hero. Sonically, the action of him firing his gun is important, so it is loud and powerful and we are left with no doubt of that fact.

If we are trying to create a convincing illusion that the audience is inside a virtual environment, we need to utilize many aspects of how audio works to support that illusion and convince the audience that what they see and hear is as "real" as possible. This is where we may encounter a conflict between the need to support the narrative design and the technical requirements of immersion.

In the bar fight scene set in Tibet, Indiana fires his handgun for the first time. It is a huge bang of a sound with considerable low-frequency content and it reverberates around the space. But if this was a virtual experience would that same effect work as effectively?

The bar is reasonably large, but it is unlikely to result in quite so much reverberation in real life. So if we model the bar space virtually and allow the audience to explore it prior to the fight scene, they audience need to experience a convincing environment. We want the audience to believe they are really in that bar. The average audience may not understand exactly what reverb is, or how it works, but people have very good senses when something feels wrong. So exaggerating the reverberation in a space such as the bar is likely to trigger people's sense of "something is not right." Similarly, if the reverb for the bar is modeled correctly but the gun shot was created with significantly more reverb added to it, it may also sound out of place.

When producing content for the new realities, effects such as reverb are much more than "adding some echo" to a sound to make it sound fat. Reverb reflections are a critical aspect in localizing a sound source. We also utilize much of the frequency range of a sound to help us localize it. The level of importance of these characteristics depends on exactly how accurate you need the sound to be. If you only need to know that Indy is off to your left somewhere, then it might matter less if you utilize an exaggerated reverb on a sound with lots of boosted low frequencies. But if accurate localization of the sound is needed to the point of knowing if the sound is 2 m from the audience or 10 m then the technical considerations of the sound design may be more important than the aesthetic considerations.

Here is where science and art may clash. If we wish to spatialize a sound accurately and create a realistic simulation of a real-world space, there is a range of physics rules that guide how we would create this scene. The room is of X dimensions and is made out of materials that absorb sound in various ways. To position a sound accurately within that space so that our audience can accurately localize it, we need to calculate many aspects of the sounds' behavior, its frequency content, and the room reflections.

Or ...

We can just add some reverb.

While this alternative may sound flippant, we need to keep in mind the purpose of our project. If the narrative for our audience is that there is an action gun fight occurring in a bar in an exotic location and our hero is busy defeating some villains, then as creative producers we need to ask in all seriousness, what is more important; narrative effect or mathematical accuracy? Sometimes it may be an element of both, but often for the sake of the audience we simply need to convey that we are in a large space, and that there is a lot of loud action taking place. It may seem like I am contradicting what I've said earlier, and in fact my viewpoint on this changes in particular ways as our discussion progresses.

A friend and mentor George Sanger once told me that recreating reality is only the first step; after that we need to ensure that we also include FUN. In the case of narrative media, fun can mean many things, but I like to think of it as the embodiment of entertainment. Whether we are scared during a horror movie, inspired by our heroes or engaged in a complex drama, we seek entertainment for the fun of it and it is critical that as creative producers we avoid killing the fun in our effort to create more accurate simulations. I find this contradiction and ongoing challenge in the production of creative media and will continue to explore it throughout this book.

the triangulation challenge

Humans are not very effective at triangulating or localizing sound sources that are directly in front of them. Our hearing allows us to detect the position of a sound to the left or to the right because of the delay in the sound reaching the opposite ear. When outdoors we may still find it tricky to pinpoint exactly where a sound is coming from. Factors like being surrounded by tress that obscure the direct sound or surfaces that create reflections can confuse our sense of direction. When we encounter this we often turn our head slightly from side to side to more actively triangulate the sound source (cats and dogs do the same thing by moving their ears). The continuous update of information to our left and right ears allows our brain to more accurately detect where the sound is coming from.

When a sound is directly in front of us, it reaches our ears at the exact time and the lack of difference in the received information makes it difficult for the brain to process. We can turn our head back and forth to pinpoint the sound, but without head turning the brain relies on another important piece of information—our sight. As a general rule if we can hear an audio signal evenly between both ears, our brain will then try to confirm the position of the sound by looking for an appropriate sound source that we can see, such as a person in front of us talking.

If there is no visual reference for the sound we are hearing, the brain will generally tell us "the sound is behind you!" This is quite useful if you are out in the forest and need to know about the tiger creeping up behind you. This is why a binaural recording of something behind you can be so convincing. The lack of a visual reference has already convinced the brain that there is something to the rear. This is a most useful "trick" that we can apply to other spatial sound positioning.

Localization and Spatialization: Defining the Issues

So why is accurate localization and spatialization of audio in spherical 360-degrees difficult? The answer to this question forms a long but important list. Some of the challenges are due to the complexity of replicating real-world physics and the expense in resources to recreate. But there are also issues with how we function as humans.

The Human Problem

If you look at a cat, dog, or many other mammals, you will see their ears are positioned on top of their head. If you observe them in action, you will notice most can rotate their ears individually to help them track the source of a sound. These animals have excellent triangulation abilities and rotating the ear cone goes a long way to helping with it. This is why humans will often turn their head to help in locating the source of a sound. Rotating our head slowly back and forth provides us with additional information that helps us pinpoint the sound source. Think about if you've ever tried to find an insect, like a cricket, you hear buzzing in the grass. What process do you follow to locate the insect when you cannot see it?

Many mammals can rotate their ears.

I performed a very basic test in 2016 when I was doing research into sound localization. This is a very easy test for anyone to perform with the help of a friend.

Stand outside in a park or in your garden, or even on the beach. Close your eyes and ask a friend to quietly walk around you at a distance of a few meters. Your friend should stop sporadically and either make a noise with an object or ask, "Where am I?" Keep the phrase or noise fairly short, only a second or two. Your task is to stand there with your eyes closed and whenever you hear your friend you point to where you think the noise has come from. Get your friend to record your performance with their phone or camera and then review how you did.

Both I and a colleague performed this test in completely different environments with similar results. Most of the time we would be reasonably close; maybe out by 10 degrees or so. But occasionally we would be out by as much as 180 degrees. When we got it wrong, we got it VERY wrong. Also, if our assistant crouched down or climbed up higher so they were not on a flat plane relative to our listening position, we often could not tell. This test very clearly and easily indicates one of the primary issues with accurate localization for the new technologies. Humans are not great at pinpointing sounds, especially with eyes closed. An outside environment further complicates this as we have no spatial reflections to assist our attempts to locate the sound source.

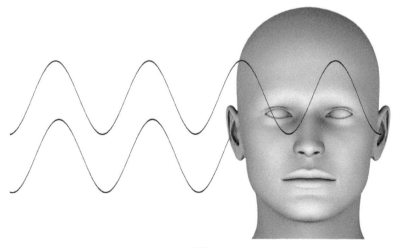

ITD.

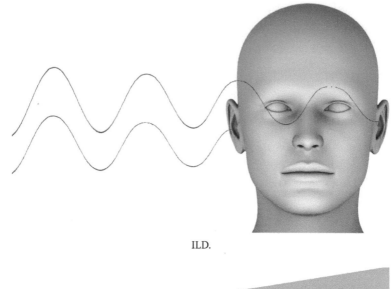

ILD.

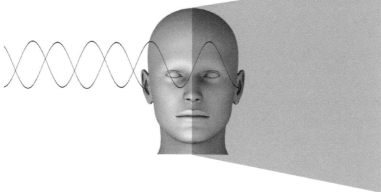

IPD in a row.

Much of how a human localizes a sound is due to context. If I hear a sound and there is an object in front of me, I will often link that sound to the object and decide it emanated from that location. This is especially true of sounds directly in front of us. Interaural time difference (ITD), Interaural intensity difference (IID), and IPD all combine to assist humans in localizing sound sources, but even those aspects struggle to allow us to accurately map elevation and declination. So when we close our eyes and lose the visual context of our world, we lose a significant part of our ability to pinpoint sound sources. Like many other skills you could probably train yourself to be more sensitive to your environment and improve your ability to localize, but for the average human it is not an ability we refine.

The human problem becomes even more apparent when attempting to design an effective HRTF system. Since HRTF is based on the characteristics of each person's ITD, IID, and IPD, and these factors are unique to each person based on their head shape, bone density, ear shape, ear positioning, and many other factors, creating an HRTF system with broad application is challenging. People do not have symmetrical heads and most will have one ear placed lower than the other. No matter how we create an HRTF system for consumer use, using one set of equations to calculate all the data is going to have significant accuracy issues as the data will vary significantly for individual HRTF values. It is kind of like trying to make one set of reading glasses that will suit everyone's eyesight variations. That is essentially what a magnifying lens is; it will make everything you view bigger for everyone, but it will not overcome the individual issues we may have with blurry vision or other challenges.

An interesting observation I made when researching this book is how a cat can react to reflected sounds. Our cat often sits in the front room as she enjoys the sun coming through the window. This means I can see her as I walk down the stairs to our front door. However, if I call out to our cat as I approach the front door, she will always turn her head away from me by 90 degrees. She is turning her head to face the direction of where she is hearing the sound the loudest and that is through the open door to the room she is in. So my voice travels through the front screen door and then around the 90-degree bend to the doorway of the room she is in. I know for a fact that you can also hear sound through the window if you are in that front room, so she must get some of my voice traveling through the glass, but it is relatively much quieter than the reflected sound that comes through the doorway.

Maybe because a cat can rotate her ears to lock onto the strongest audio source they are far less likely to rely on reflected sound in the way humans do to localize a sound. So she is much more accurate at localizing a sound in an outdoor environment than a human would be, but once reflected sounds need to be processed to accurately localize the source of the sound, this confuses her. She locks onto the stronger reflected signal and turns her head toward it, even though she was almost facing me and only needed to look through the window. Most of this is guesswork based on a handful of observations so it is not very scientific, but it was interesting to note at the time of writing this book.

Delivery

Moving on from human nature, we also have the inconsistencies of delivery platforms. Even if we agree that all content should be presented on headphones instead of speakers, there are a huge number of different headphone manufacturers. Professional headphones often have a good flattish frequency response, but it is almost impossible to get a completely flat response. Consumer headphones can vary wildly up to extreme cases with terrible bass boost and built-in effects to attempt to impress the uneducated consumer. These processes can significantly impact how spatial content comes across to the audience.

A discussion of headphones brings us back to human nature and the fact that different individuals can be sensitive to certain frequencies or even deaf to some frequency ranges. For years, I thought I was sensitive to low frequencies as I always loved bass content, until I realized I was actually more sensitive to high-frequency content, which is why I always turned the bass up. So even if we wear the same headphones, I will hear content differently to other listeners. I am aware of at least one studio producer who keeps a cupboard full of the same brand of headphones that he works with and ships a pair with all his work so the client at least has the same delivery platform that he worked on.

Spatialization

Spatialized plugins is an area where our first "Wild West" snake-oil warning comes in. Over the past few years I have been involved with, and spoken to other people who have been involved with, evaluating the rapidly growing field of spatial plugin technology. At one stage, new technology companies seemed to be popping up every week, all making grand claims about how effective their solutions were. There are some really excellent solutions available, but beware, there are also some plugins and tools that are borderline fraudulent.

During one series of tests I discussed with some industry colleagues it was discovered that the spatialization plugin was literally just playing basic stereo sound files. I have seen crowd funding campaigns for devices that claim to spatialize any audio content and other similarly wild claims. The message here is that there are some very dubious claims being made by certain companies and individuals and it is really worth investing some time to check out how effective and reliable any specific tool really is.

Talk to your industry friends, ask questions on social media and really put these claims to the test. This is for the benefit of all of us. For this new technology to succeed, we need to isolate and remove those who would damage the industry for all of us simply to make a quick buck.

Do not be afraid to question and confront product makers when we speak with them at conferences. Always be polite and always check your facts. But if you listen to a demo that claims to be 360 audio and you cannot hear any elevation content, then ask the demonstrator why that might be, investigate what it is they are showing off and also provide feedback. This will help them develop their products if they are serious about building something useful and show them up if they are trying to mislead people.

Physics Is Expensive

A good understanding of physics is what allows us to attempt to simulate how the real world works. We utilize many areas of physics to assist with calculations, the behavior of sound and light waves, simulated gravity, and understanding how our universe actually works. The problem is that physics can be really expensive. Well, it's not that physics itself is expensive, it's just that there is so gosh darn much of it!

As we explored in the introduction, calculating the reverb of even just one sound in an average room requires a lot of work. The more factors influencing reflections there are in a space, the more calculations you need to include. Multiply that by every sound you may want to include in your project and the cost of your physics simulations can get prohibitive.

Most interactive projects have utilized a fairly simple set of equations to simulate audio behavior. We attach a sound to an object in a 3D space, so we know where that sound is located. Information about attenuation is usually the first factor to be included. So as we move away from the sound source, what we hear drops in amplitude. Most software tools let us define the shape of the attenuation curve. So you can choose from a linear drop-off or a section of curve shapes to best suit your specific needs. Frequency behavior over distance is also often included. So as you move away from a sound source, the high-frequency content tends to attenuate faster than the low-frequency content.

This basic set of functions has been available for developing 3D game environments for quite a few years, but this functionality is limited and already has shortcoming before we even consider environmental reflections. Obstruction and occlusion, while possible, have not been utilized much in game projects because of the resource cost involved. These are the most basic elements needed before you can start to include sound wave reflection behavior.

Obstruction and occlusion deal with objects existing in the world space. These objects will either fully block sound from passing through them or filter sound when it can pass through them. This is the "closed door" scenario. If I speak to you from the other side of a closed door, then my voice is muffled. If the door is then opened, my voice has a direct path to your ears and becomes far clearer. If the door is very thick and sealed like an airlock, the door may completely occlude my voice and you will hear nothing.

So why are obstruction and occlusion expensive? This question extends to all aspects of calculating reflections. If we place our clock on a table in a virtual space, we can hear that clock at the position of the virtual object. For occlusion to work we need to be aware of the position of the clock and also the position of the listener, but more importantly we need to be aware of anything and EVERYTHING that may influence the direct path of the sound from the clock to the listener. So instead of just being aware of the clock and the listener, we need to constantly be tracking the path between the two and checking to see if there is anything in the way. This process is called ray tracing. We track a virtual path between the sound source and the listener so that we can be aware if this path ever becomes blocked.

Doing this with a single clock and an empty room with only one doorway might be feasible. We can track the line of sight between clock and listener and if the door is closed use that information to filter the sound as it travels through the door. But a game or virtual experience is never going to be just one sound source in an empty room. Even if we stick to only the single sound of the clock, the room will have furniture and ornaments, and carpet or floorboards, window coverings, and all of these things may affect the direct path of the sound from source to listener. So the ray trace must be performed constantly and updated every frame to account for the listener moving and objects intersecting the direct path of the sound. Once we add in all the other potential sound producing objects into the world, we have a great many paths that have to be monitored to account for obstructions.

When we consider 360-degree spherical audio, where we want to add realistic reverberation reflections, we have just multiplied the potential number of paths by tens of thousands. Each sound source can bounce and then bounce again and again as the sound waves reflect off every surface and object in the space. Beyond this, we would also need to calculate exactly how the sound changes depending on the type of surface it interacts with. Hard shiny surfaces will reflect back more sound energy than a soft porous surface material. So now we are tracking a huge amount of ray trace data as well as calculating lots of different reflection coefficient values, all in real time, and all constantly. This type of mathematics tends to melt processors.

Fortunately, tools for calculating occlusion and obstruction do exist. Game audio tools such as Wwise and FMOD have built-in functions for amplitude and frequency modulation. These are all you really need to simulate how materials affect sound behavior. But accurate modeling is CPU-intensive; so many games choose simplified approaches to the challenge. Instead of accurately modeling the sound between two closed rooms for every possible combination of objects and materials, a simple template can be applied that is triggered as you enter or leave a room.

mixing for the new realities

One thing I discovered very quickly when I started working on new reality content was that mixing was going to be a significant challenge if there was only one person available to do it. Fortunately, over my years of working on interactive projects there have been new tools that have become valuable to the mix process of game development.

The ability to be able to link up a game engine to a sound engine tool in real time and alter your content while playing the game has been a huge advance for the quality of game audio. Prior to this technology an audio team needed to play a game, take notes on audio that needed to be changed and then go back to the software and make the changes, and then repeat the process until it was correct. Being able to play a game and instantly adjust the volume level or attenuation behavior of a sound in real time and immediately test the results makes the entire process of implementation more efficient and the final audio mix far more effective.

When we work on new reality projects, there is a new challenge that arises. For the new technologies, you usually need to wear a headset to be able to experience what the audience will ultimately hear. Head tracking and localization is a critical aspect of the mix

A new approach does not mean we discard old techniques;
it means we adapt them.

process, so you need to be inside the experience to evaluate it accurately. The issue with this is it is now very difficult to adjust those values in your sound engine tool while you are wearing a headset that is likely obscuring some or all of your vision.

A team I was working with discovered that the mix process worked better as a two-person task. One would wear the headset and run through the experience while the other made changes in real time in the toolset. So the team member that represented the audience would critically analyze the audio within the experience and provide immediate feedback and requests to their colleague controlling the tool, who could make adjustments that could then be immediately checked by the person inside the experience. This is a simple and obvious solution to an issue that is not a huge challenge, but still a workflow problem to be addressed, especially if you usually work as a one-person team.

unique format challenges

Beyond the challenges that are common to all of the new reality formats, there are some that are unique to each. In this next section, I will address many of the unique challenges that we have discovered so far. As the technology evolves, these challenges will also evolve and change.

Virtual Reality Challenges

Virtual reality usually replaces the audience's entire access to the real world, which means it has a unique set of challenges to overcome. Worn correctly, a VR headset should cover the eyes and prevent light from the real world from entering. Eliminating light serves two purposes: first, external light can reduce the clarity of the headset screens, but more importantly I think it can detract from the feeling of total immersion. I also think the same is true for VR audio.

Using closed-back headphones that completely cover the ears is the best way to isolate the audience from the real world and help replace their sensory input with virtual input only. Early VR rigs either did not include headphones at all or packed small earbuds in with the headsets. This would have been both for cost and size as a good set of headphones can be bulky and expensive. But I think this was a poor decision in some ways. Strapping yourself into a VR rig that simulates a giant mecha cockpit only to be able to hear your refrigerator humming in the kitchen and your family walking around the house instantly breaks any sense of immersion no matter how good the graphics are. In the same way, you do not want to be able to see the real world when experiencing VR, you also do not want to be able to hear the real world.

Audio is a key sense we use to position ourselves in the real world. Ask someone to close their eyes and then move them to any room in their house and they can likely tell you where they are just by listening to their own voice in that space. In this regard, one early VR experience did an excellent job of utilizing a very basic, but clever function to further immerse the audience.

The *Star Wars Battlefront* VR experience created by DICE and Criterion started with a simple empty virtual space in which your X-Wing Starfighter is parked. You can move around the space by selecting certain waypoints to get a number of different perspectives of the space and view the X-Wing model. It feels like you are in a large white room and the X-Wing is parked in front of you. There are various sound sources located around the room buzzing and humming. But if you speak while you are in this room the Playstation VR headset picks up your voice via its microphone and the experience plays it back to you through your headphones with the addition of appropriate reverb for the virtual space you are in. So if you speak to someone in the real world, you hear yourself as though you were actually in the virtual space. This is such a simple concept, but it works so well I think it should be adopted for all VR experiences; it did so much for placing me inside the experience.

This experience would have had much less impact if I had been wearing small earbuds or open-backed headphones. I would have heard myself in my real-world space as well as the virtual space, lessening the sense of immersion. The key concept to keep in mind at all times with VR is that we are trying to replace the audience's real-world location with a virtual one. So anything and everything that we can do to convince them that they are no longer in the real world is beneficial to the experience.

Because the listener is wearing headphones we also need to be aware of ear fatigue. Currently, many VR experiences are fairly short and so we have been able to avoid this issue so far, and experiences may remain short until the issues around player nausea are resolved. But as the format becomes more widely accepted and some of the technical issues are resolved, people may start playing games for extended periods of time in the same way they do PC and console games.

Ear fatigue has been an issue for headphone users for a long time. Long periods of listening to high-level content can strain the hearing, but with 360 surround audio we have not had enough time to test the impact of extended use. By simulating surround positional audio sources is HRTF at risk of causing ear fatigue sooner? It certainly may cause concentration fatigue as we are presenting the audience with far more stimuli than basic stereo content.

We may find the 360-degree format that might offer ways to reduce ear fatigue depending on how the content is mixed. The expanded panning area means we can spread out sound content, so a mix can not only include a range of frequencies and amplitudes to differentiate content, but it also has a wider space in which to position the content. Environments with more separation of content may be less taxing on the listener.

Head Tracking

I have been surprised by the number of people I have seen speaking about their experiences working on early VR projects who have said the clients have specifically requested no spatial or head tracked audio content. VR production companies sometimes specifically ask for audio that is fixed stereo. This is really worth discussing.

I do think, that for a specific type of video there is a very limited scope for locked audio content. If your project is a linear 360 video of an action sequence such as a car race, aircraft flying, or many of the extreme sport type of experiences, then playback of a traditional stereo music track could work quite well. The audience is there to participate in the experience of the individual performing the actions caught on film and the 360 view provides a unique perspective for the audience to see how it feels to be the driver in a racing car or a parachute jumper. Typically, these are presented a little like music videos. The link between the visuals and the audio is somewhat loose. We watch the visuals and there is an associated audio track that does not need to sync exactly to what we are seeing. In these examples, locked stereo music works well; we do not want the music perspective to rotate as we turn our head back and forth when experiencing the visuals as this will draw us out of the visual experience. The music is nondiegetic and accompanies the visuals as a background element. 360 video is the perfect platform for this format—linear video content that can be viewed immersive through VR headsets, but that can work well with traditional stereo music or narration.

If, however, we move to any audio content that is synced to the visuals or captured with the visuals, not including head tracking is going to cause a disconnection between the sound and visuals and almost instantly push the audience out of the experience. If I watch a video that places me inside an aircraft or motor vehicle and the engine is positioned to the front of my position, it must stay there when I turn my head. If I turn 90 degrees to the right and the position of the engine swings around as well, any sense of "being there" is instantly lost.

My concern with the content we are seeing in these early stages of the new realities is that there is a lot of misunderstanding and a general lack of knowledge about how significant this is to our audience.

why bother getting audio right?

Audio has often been an afterthought in interactive media production. For VR, this is a luxury we cannot afford. Underestimating how the audio needs to work can undermine the entire project.

What may be more important is the missed opportunity for 360 linear video productions. Surround sound added a huge new dimension to cinema experiences. Low-frequency channel content and rear and side channels, when utilize well, added a new level of impact for Hollywood-style movies. For VR experiences, I would suggest that the potential "value added" of well-produced audio content is even more significant. I suggested at the start of this book that good audio was critical for immersive experiences, but at a production level there is a simpler motivation that can be presented to media teams working in VR. Greater engagement results in greater financial returns. Essentially, good audio in your VR experience will result in better sales.

A simpler way of understanding this is by thinking about how a standard video feels if the audio is slightly out of sync. The words people are speaking don't quite match up to their mouth movements. The footsteps are played just a few milliseconds after you see the feet touch the floor. Even slight offsets to audio visual syncing can be noticed by most audiences. It becomes a distraction; it breaks the illusion that we are actually viewing the events and reminds us that there is technology involved and that, specifically, the technology in this case is not functioning quite as intended.

Neglecting head tracking or spatialized audio content for 360 video is similar to this. Because VR is a new format the audience may not be able to exactly pinpoint what is wrong, but they will instantly feel that something does not feel right. This will result in the distraction and breaking of the illusion. Even more, those projects that are getting it right will teach our audiences what to expect, and if your project misses the mark, it will come at a cost.

Aiding the Visual Experience

I have already mentioned how VR can have serious issues with the comfort of the audience. The very first time I tried the Oculus development kit I thought the experience was incredible, but within 20 seconds I had to take it off as I was suffering seriously from motion sickness. The technology has advanced significantly in the last few years and improvements in resolution and frame rate have helped reduce the chances of people feeling sick when viewing VR. But there are still certain content types that can make people feel nauseous.

Rapid movement, specifically turning, can be an issue on VR; this is because our inner ear does not sense any change in the real world. This is a key cause of motion sickness. The inner ear senses turning and leaning of the vehicle, but we cannot see where we are going so this disconnect makes us feel ill. I spent much of my childhood experiencing this and I can tell you it is very unpleasant. VR can cause the same issue but in reverse. Audio can actually help with this in a surprising way.

If the audience is about to experience being on an elevator or a rising platform, the sudden visual change without an accompanying change to their real body movement can cause this uncomfortable experience. We have found preparing the audience with sound cues can significantly reduce these effects. In the same scenario, if the audience is warned of the pending elevator movement with an appropriate sound cue it can reduce the feeling of unease. So if the elevator clunks into life and starts to wind up the motor, the audience then expects the imminent upward movement and the audio cues to the brain may override the lack of any physical sensation. So we trick the brain into believing that the body is about to ride an elevator and as a result the audience is less likely to feel sick. The same might be possible with audio cues for movement of vehicles and first-person perspective movement experiences. This is another aspect where well-designed audio is far more than simple sounds to accompany visuals.

360 Video

I have included 360 video here as a kind of subset of VR. I do this because 360 video often utilizes the standard VR headsets; however, content delivery wise 360 video could be more closely associated with AR depending on how it is presented. As with everything here, the blurry lines are blurry!

I think 360 video deserves its own category outside of VR because it has some significant differences to VR interactive content and it will likely grow much faster as a format. I say this because 360 is more easily consumable currently and also arguably easier to produce than interactive content. There are already millions of 360 videos shared across the various social media networks and 360 cameras are readily available and relatively inexpensive. So I suspect it is this format that will get everyday consumers used to wearing headsets and viewing immersive experiences.

There are already many questions being asked online about the best approach for producing audio for 360 videos:

- What microphones should I use?
- What format does the audio need to be in?
- What is the best encoding method?
- What is the best delivery method?
- How do I do this thing?

Like all new technologies, the issue is that there are dozens of answers to some of these questions and not enough answers to some of them. All the technology developers are approaching the different challenges in their own way, hoping their method will be adopted and will help their company grow. This is a natural approach from a business point of view, but it is often the worst point of view for the consumer. As the companies thrash out their various approaches and compete with each other for consumer attention, the consumer is left with a range of options that are incompatible with each other and often do more to block productive creation than to facilitate it. Codec A does not function with delivery platform B, spatial audio format X works well with platform B but not with codec A. While researching for both this book and my own work, I have dealt with this issue almost every day. Often the sequence of steps you need to go through just to combine the best visual format with the best spatial audio format feels more like you are trying to send a rocket into space rather than render a 30-second video.

This is the consequence of standing on the bleeding edge of technology. Those of us who brave this environment have to risk a bit of confusion and frustration. Hopefully doing so places us in a good position when the dust settles and the new formats become a little more standardized. This was no different for the first producers of movies, or for Disney and his team of animators, or for the pioneers of video game development. We certainly have more choices of technology to work with these days and that comes with both good and bad consequences.

In Chapter Five, we will go through the specific list of questions for 360 video production, and discuss how we can approach this format, and how it differs from the other new reality content.

alternate reality challenges

Alternate reality presents some interesting challenges that will make the presentation of more traditional audio content difficult at best. AR offers an interesting format for entertainment, but I suspect it is going to be utilized more for practical applications and tools. Regardless of the content being experienced, it does need to be approached in a different manner to VR content.

Unlike VR, AR is designed to not replace the audience's environment but rather to enhance it by adding virtual content. The primary wearable platforms for AR are currently the Microsoft HoloLens and the as-yet unreleased Magic Leap Sensoryware devices. Both of these are similar in that they utilize a "reading glasses" type of form factor. So the user wears an enhanced pair of glasses that provide them with visual and audio content. Nonwearable forms of AR include mobile devices, such as smartphones used to play games like *Pokemon Go.*

Because AR adds to the real world instead of replacing it the user can still see and hear the environment around them. Wearable technology allows the user to see the world normally and then superimpose virtual objects into the user's sight. The same applies for the audio content. The speakers do not fully enclose the user's ears, allowing the user to hear a mix of both the real world and the virtual content. This is the first and biggest challenge for AR content production.

Imagine if all the music and sound content you created for a project was going to be heard by an audience who had to share their space with the rest of the world. They are not wearing headphones that allow them to hear the audio material privately; they are wearing speakers near their ears as if they were holding a phone to their head. If the volume on the phone is too loud anyone sitting near them can also hear the sound from that phone.

AR devices are far more sophisticated than just holding a phone near your head, but some of the issues are very similar. The very nature of AR is designed so the user can hear the real world as well as the AR content, so in noisy environments the user may struggle to clearly hear the AR content. This means the design of AR content has to be considered very carefully before going into production as traditional media and media production methods are at a real risk of not producing appropriate material for AR experiences.

"Pardon?" AR Audibility

I think that if we are going to make entertainment content that is narrative driven for the AR platform we need to consider how we function in the real world. If you and I are walking through any busy city in the world, then we are constantly focusing and refocusing on each other's dialogue. We must actively block out the various sound elements of the environment that interfere with hearing the things that are important to us. If you are speaking to me, I will be looking at your mouth to help my brain interpret what you are saying, I will likely be constantly making minor rotations of my head to align the sound of your speech with my ears better and to block out unwanted sounds. And there is another function we constantly use that we may need to adopt for AR content—I have the option to interrupt the conversation at any time and ask you to repeat something that you have just said.

Even with our ability to focus on a single sound source and filter incoming content, sometimes our environment will just overwhelm our ability to hear. A truck drives past, or someone nearby yells, and some industrial machinery starts up. The number of things that could interrupt our conversation is unlimited. The simple ability to ask the speaker to repeat themselves is a basic function that we learn very soon after we learn to speak. If our AR experience is presenting the audience with content that is a vital aspect of the experience, such as any narrative dialogue or any functional explanations or warnings, then AR is going to need to provide the option for the user to ask for the information to be repeated. The simple act of saying "can you please repeat that?" should probably be as core to AR functionality as the UNDO function has become for computer software. This simple function aligns itself perfectly with the concept of AR working in concert with the real-world environment.

Turn that Racket Down!

Related to the issue of missing content is the very nature of how the audio is presented. Because the audio is presented through nonoccluding speakers it is possible for external sounds to interfere with what the listener hears. But the opposite of that is that the AR content may also invade the real-world space of others in the listener's immediate location. This is the principle reason why just increasing the volume of the AR content is not always going to be the best option to improve clarity to the listener. If the user of an AR device is sitting on a crowded train, then high-level output is going to be like someone having a phone conversation on speaker output rather than the normal ear speaker. This not only means the user has no privacy, but it also means they will likely be bothering everyone around them who just wants to travel in peace and quiet.

This is a very real challenge for AR content and something that is still being developed and improved on by all the major wearable device developers. AR has tremendous potential as a format, but it could quickly be seen as an undesirable product if everyone that is using an AR device is annoying everyone around them. This has immediate and direct consequences for audio, for what we plan to include for audio content within a project and for how we implement it.

Choose Wisely

Because of the need to mix AR audio with real-world audio I think we will need to select the audio content we present very carefully. The user is already going to have a mix of the audio we provide them as well as whatever sound exists in their world space. So keeping the AR content simple and clean is going to be vital.

If we are presenting a narrative game experience, in traditional formats or VR, we might also add environmental sounds and underscore the scene with some music. But for an AR experience our audience already has the environmental sounds of their real-world space and this may even include music in the background somewhere. AR is designed to blend and enhance with the real world, so anytime the AR content clashes with the real world it risks losing its effectiveness.

Because of this I feel we will need to craft new and unique experiences for AR that are vastly different to the methods we have used for entertainment in other formats. Later in this chapter, I will discuss an example of the type of experience I think could work very well in AR by utilizing its strengths and even turning some of its weaknesses into narrative functions.

Frequency Range

Because AR devices do not cover the ear and require small speakers to transmit the audio content, there is another very real challenge to the content we can produce—the available range of frequencies we have to work with.

The smaller the speaker, the harder it is to generate low-frequency content. There is a reason why the low-frequency speakers in a sound system of the subwoofer in a theater system are large diameter cones. To generate the longer wave forms of low frequencies, we need larger diaphragms to generate the sound waves. Ear buds can produce reasonable base because they are very close to your eardrum and so they do not need to generate very much energy, and also because by placing them inside your ear they create a sealed chamber, which also assists this process. AR devices have the speaker set back from the ear canal so the proximity advantage is lost and so is the sealed chamber.

This means that the audio signals that can be produced on AR devices have a greatly reduced frequency range for the lower end of the spectrum. Content below 100 Hz is very unlikely to be heard and in some cases even higher frequency content could be lost. This of course is only an issue if you plan to create audio content that utilizes those low-frequency areas. The simple solution is—don't. This might sound like I am oversimplifying things, but if a device cannot do thing X, then the easiest approach it not to try to do thing X.

The issue with this simplified suggestion is that much of our modern media has become very reliant on low-frequency content to spice things up. We all seem to love making things go bang, rumble, and *bwaaaarm*. Maybe this is the problem, as audio producers we have all become too reliant on low-frequency content to make an impact on our audience. It might be that AR creates a renaissance in audio production where we more fully explore what we can achieve with the higher end of the frequency range.

Booming explosions aside, it is a very real limitation and something that does need to be considered carefully. If your experience requires that you represent a large truck in front of the user, then it is going to be extremely difficult for you to create audio that will accurately simulate that virtual object. So while we may be able to create a virtual object and really make it seem like it is right there with the user, the lack of low-frequency audio content is going to seriously undermine the immersion of that experience.

I have worked on a variety of different solutions for this problem both in my own personal research and also working for other teams. Devices like rumble packs and bone conducting headphones, I have personally found to all be extremely unconvincing and in the case of bone conduction it was unpleasant and uncomfortable as well as not sounding very good. This does not mean that an alternative solution cannot be found and it may even exist already, but my personal experience of these solutions was always disappointing. It is a complex issue to try and overcome and we need to keep working at it.

mixed reality challenges

Right now, MR seems to be being used as a label for anything that does not quite fit under the banner of either VR or AR. As with all these terms I think we may still be a few years away from being clearly able to define which is which. From what I have seen about MR and from various discussions I have had, I think MR is going to pose some very real challenges to the audio content of these types of experience and that the blending of various formats needs to be approached carefully so as not to lessen the impact of the experience.

MR: Contamination of Content

The idea often suggested for MR is that it can be a blending of the formats to get the best aspects of each format and combine them to create an engaging experience. The issue with this of course is that combining formats can also double the number of issues and create unexpected conflict that would never have arisen from any single format workflow.

One example of this is the idea of using an AR headset such as HoloLens and combining it with a cinema experience. So in the same way, 3D movies might provide the illusions of an object moving out of the cinema screen, AR glasses could allow a virtual object to really move out of the screen and for each audience member to experience their own unique version of the narrative where the transitioning object can relate personally to them. So even though each audience member gets to see a virtual object pop into their world, the exact behavior of the virtual object can be tailored to be unique for each participant.

This all sounds like fun, until we have to put sound to it. AR devices can provide a private visual experience to each member of a group audience. We can all see the screen and all see our own virtual object or character emerge from the screen and interact with us. We can see the original screen through our device and share that with the whole group, and the virtual aspect can be private and unique to each viewer. The needs of audio make this scenario very difficult. If we are enjoying a shared cinema experience then we all need to be able to hear the audio in the cinema space; most likely through the speakers in the auditorium. To do this, we need an AR device that does not obscure our ability to hear the cinema speakers. Then if a virtual object comes into view each of us will need audio that matches our private version of the virtual experience. So we need to be able to simultaneously hear what is played through the cinema speakers as well as being able to hear audio for our virtual content.

If we provide our audience with any type of headset that allows for the cinema speakers to be audible as well as for private audio to be played then we will likely have a significant issue with contamination. If I can hear the cinema speakers then I will most likely also be able to hear the content playing from the speakers of the person next to me. Open-backed headphones or similar technology do not obscure the sound from being audible by people other than the headphone wearer. So a group of people sitting in an auditorium will likely be able to hear sound bleeding from the headsets of those around them. Anything we do to reduce that unwanted crossover of the audio will either make each individual private audio stream harder to hear for the individual or else make it difficult for all audience members to hear the main speaker output. If we provide everyone with closed-back headphones and route all audio through them then we have effectively created a VR project from the audio point of view.

This may not be such a bad approach as the limitations of how audio is transmitted in the real world and how easily it can be contaminated means that MR experiences that may work for visuals may not work as cleanly for audio.

Let's look at another example of mixing the formats, combining VR or AR visual content with room-based speaker audio output. I have spoken with a few people who describe how combining VR or AR visual content with purely speaker-based audio could be a cool way to share experiences with a larger group of people. On the surface, this seems to be a valid format for many people, but for me it instantly breaks the whole concept of VR and AR. In my mind, these formats are mostly about placing the audience into a virtual world or placing virtual objects into the real world. In both examples, the delivery of audio is a critical aspect to completing the visual illusions. If the aim of the experience is to present some interesting visuals that are disconnected from the audio and do not rely on it for localization then this could work as an experience format. So if it was like a music video style of experience where the music might sync up to the visuals from a timing perspective, but had no requirement for localization this could be an effective MR event. If, however, there is any content that needs to be localized then the combination is unlikely to work.

The complex nature of spatial audio and most of the reason for this book existing is because it is very hard to convince people that a sound is located at a specific angle and specific distance from the viewing position without using very tight control of the audio content and how it is delivered. As soon as the audio is taken away from headphone delivery, synced to a viewing headset, then the ability to position sound objects is dramatically reduced or removed entirely. You simply cannot have everyone sitting in an auditorium and play audio through speakers with any sense of accurate 360 spatialization; the audio would just revert to a traditional surround format. This is a completely acceptable way to present content as long as you realize that is what you are creating.

Speaker output removes the ability to head-track audio, it removes the ability to spatialize audio, and it removes the personal sweet spot that everyone can access via headphone output. You could create some interesting effects by combining headphone audio and speaker audio as long as the limitations of the headphones are understood. Open-backed headphones will produce the bleed issues discussed earlier and closed-backed headphones will obscure and frequency-filter content played through the room speakers. Low-frequency content from speaker output is less likely to be obscured and frequency content below 70Hz is very difficult for people to localize so this content is less likely to interfere with the localization of spatial content coming from the headphones.

Humans use a considerable range of the audible frequency spectrum to help localize sound sources. So if an MR experience has a combination of spatial audio presented through headphones as well as audio played through speakers, then it is important to mix that content carefully. If a specific spatialized sound needs to be localized for the experience to be effective then playing content of similar frequencies out of the speaker at the same time may confuse the listener and reduce their accuracy in localization. It's like asking someone to accurately describe the colors in a picture in front of them while shining a bright light with a red filter attached onto the picture. The addition of the red light will make it very hard to distinguish details.

Much of this information is important at the early planning and design phases. Avoiding the issues by designing around them is often a better approach than trying to fix the issue once it has been implemented. These are all issues that we have previously not had to deal with and yet another example of why the new realities provide a great many challenges as we work our way to better understand their potential and limitations.

hyperreality (HR)

I have added this as an additional category after seeing and interesting conference presentation by Chance Thomas. A live venue experience that referred to their production as a HR event sounded like some clever marketing spiel until I saw exactly what they were creating. The room-based experience combined a real-world space where audience members were immersed into a virtual experience with VR headsets and headphones. But this experience took things one step further by utilizing real-world wall and scenery objects to provide accurate object feedback to the audience. The audience could actually bump into walls and feel certain objects in the virtual world. But more than that, this experience included jets of compressed air and objects that would interact with the audience haptically. The added touch sense looked like it added a significant aspect to the experience and so I think the term "HR" is an appropriate addition to the new realities group.

In general, I think HR would be much like virtual reality in how you would produce assets for it, except that any elements that produce sound in the real word would need to be accounted for in the virtual presentation. So a door opening or a jet of compressed air would probably need to be represented by a sound through the headset that was loud enough to obscure the real-world sound, otherwise there may be a risk that the real-world sound feels out of place.

Any real-world sound will be filtered passing to the audience's ears through the headphones and so may sound muffled or muddy. Triggering a virtual sound to coincide with the real-world movement and actions I think would provide a more consistent audio presentation. I suspect certain elements of a HR experience could also include speaker-based vibration or low-frequency content for haptic feedback in the form of rumbles and other mechanical vibrations. So an HR experience may contain elements of VR, AR, and MR depending on its design.

4 what we're doing now: analysis of existing projects

VR project analysis

One valuable way to improve any skill set is to observe and analyze existing projects using that skill set and then assess what could have been done differently. By evaluating the good and bad aspects of completed projects, we can explore various approaches to creative challenges.

This chapter will not only include various virtual reality (VR) and alternate reality (AR) experiences and critique their effectiveness but also suggest alternative approaches to the challenges they faced.

Criticizing any project is a difficult thing to do. It is a valid way to discuss aspects of production but it can be misinterpreted as being only negative about a project. I want to make it very clear that I have nothing but admiration and respect for all the teams that are working in the new realities right now. Not everything will get every aspect of production perfect, but these are the teams that are helping us all learn and all improve our creative skills by forging ahead into the unknown. So even when I am critical about some of the content, I do so to help raise awareness of all of us with no intended disrespect.

broadcast

BBC Special Binaural Audio Broadcast
Doctor Who Series 10, Episode 4, Knock

The BBC has long been both an advocate and a leader in the research, design, and implementation of audio technology. Recently, the BBC have established a department for research and creation of spatial audio in Cardiff, Wales and this team has utilized spatial audio for a number of projects. *Doctor Who* is one of Britain's most popular and loved (as well as longest running) television series, and so it is significant to discuss how spatial audio can enhance the experience of such a well-known show.

From the team's description of their work, the experience is described as a binaural version of the fourth episode of the series. The tools designed by the BBC allow for the spatialization of sound elements into broadcast content. As a typical 2D television broadcast, this is a logical evolution of the linear stereo mix that would commonly be implemented. In this case, the BBC have realized that many of their viewers these day watch their content on mobile devices via headphones and so binaural content is a way of adding a significant point of difference to their content as binaural sound works best through headphones.

The episode itself is quite interesting. There is no doubt that the binaural mix provides a richer and "broader" sonic experience. The content can be positioned across a larger listening field than traditional stereo content. I found that this enhanced the mix as it had excellent spatial separation which made the mix clearer. The sounds were not fighting for the more limited space of a stereo mix and so it just felt easier to listen to. At this stage, I am not even thinking about

The sound of hope.

the actual effectiveness of the spatial positioning, but just that the overall sense that it was easier to hear and discern all the sonic elements in the episode.

Spatially there were some key points I noticed and enjoyed. At one point, Bill, the Doctor's companion, says a single word off screen to the left. We know from the previous camera cut that she is standing very close to the Doctor; when she speaks, the spatialization places her extremely close to the listener, as though she is practically speaking quietly into our left ear. This effect was very well done and created an excellent sense of proximity. I think this is where we hear the first evidence that the BBC team is not simply using a standard head-related transfer function (HRTF) data set as HRT does not deal well with close proximity content. This was a subtle but key element in the early part of the episode.

As the episode develops, there are numerous environmental layers that are spatialized in various ways. Overall these are low key and just add to the openness of the mix. But they also serve the purpose of maintaining the audience's sense of the surround nature of the audio. In general, another reason why this is a good example of how to approach a new technology is that it is dealt with in a sensitive manner. The spatial content doesn't beat you over the head with its presence. At one point, there is a series of knocking sounds and each is positioned around the listener; this is a key part of the narrative and at this point the extended use of spatial positioning highlights a key point in the episode.

One observation I found personally I think is worth mentioning. I found I got a good sense of sounds to the side and sounds to the rear. But I did start to wonder if it was because of the way humans hear sounds that I could perceive those rear positions so convincingly. As has been mentioned elsewhere in this book, humans have a tendency to often confuse sound sources positioned directly in front and directly behind. If we don't have a visual object to associate a sound source with, then our brains will often just decide on our behalf that the sound must be behind us. In *Doctor Who*, often the sounds behind were environmental sounds or events that never had any presence on screen at any time, so I wonder if this lack of visual cues helped to trick the brain into making the rear positioning more convincing to us. It is absolutely valid if this was the reason. Utilizing our own senses against us to enhance the narrative is a clever way of implementing assets into your project.

Overall, I found this an excellent example of how audio content can be used in our more traditional media forms in a way that enhances the experience for our audiences. Spatial audio is going to evolve in many different directions simultaneously and I think some of the applications are going to have some very interesting results.

vive

Earthlight

Earthlight is an astronaut simulation experience, released in 2017. At the time of writing this book, it was still not fully released, but I was lucky enough to be able to arrange a demonstration of the experience at the developer studio. The experience has been developed for Vive and utilizes the two Vive controllers to interact with the virtual world.

The *Earthlight* experience has three main sections and I got to try out two of these as part of my investigation. The first section simulates being in a training pool inside an astronaut spacesuit and getting used to navigating, then performing a simple equipment repair. This was a very interesting experience for me as the simulation scenario was all about training the character to operate in the environment. I was adjusting to the feel and controls of the experience to the narrative, which aligned very well with my own feelings and experiences. Interestingly, I think spacesuit experiences work really well in VR because you have a headset and headphones on your face that you can feel and that restrict your movement, so in many ways the physical sensation of wearing the VR gear actually adds to the experience of being in a spacesuit.

From an audio point of view, this experience is also interesting. You are enclosed completely in a spacesuit and maneuver underwater to get to your target. I immediately noticed that all I could hear was the air circulation pumps in the suit. As I moved through the water, I expected to hear the clichéd sound of waves from an underwater perspective. When I mentioned this to the dev team they informed me that they expected the same, until they spoke with real astronauts that had done this exact thing in the real world. Apparently once in the suit the air circulation system is the only thing that can be heard. The devs even have reference recordings taken from a training scenario that they based their sound design on that confirm this.

While I was visiting the developers of *Earthlight* we had a conversation about this exact topic and that we all felt the need for the water movement sounds we had expected. We agreed that an accurate simulation without the water sounds was worth preserving for the sake of those users who want to experience as accurate a simulation as possible. But it was also acknowledged that for the general public, providing a more "Hollywood-style" experience was also relevant.

This returns us to the concept of creating fun. We have all been trained by the standard formats of most action films to expect audio that is larger than life and often our enjoyment is enhanced by this element. I have met many people who, when they first hear a real firearm being fired, will comment on how flat, lifeless, and boring the sound is. They have been conditioned by movies to expect all guns to explode like artillery pieces. So a game that is likely to offer a hardcore simulation mode as well as a general mode can certainly tailor the audio content to reflect an accurate simulation of reality, or a stylized or "enhanced" mode for the audio content.

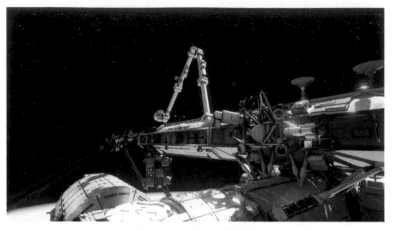

Opaque media's earthlight.

Apart from the air supply system, the other main sound in the experience is from contact with your hands on various surfaces. If you bang your hand on the surface of the space station you can hear a resonant but filtered thud as the vibrations travel through your suit. This was a nice touch, but I did notice and note that I didn't hear any sound from my hands grasping at the hands and cables as I moved around. Again, I am uncertain if these sounds would be present in the real world, but I felt in this case audio feedback was not only a good stylistic choice, but that it would significantly enhance the users sense of grabbing and releasing various objects. Essentially these sounds were like user interface (UI) button press acknowledgments. "Yes, I did grab that handrail, I saw my hand close and I heard a dull sound as the contact vibrated through my suit."

The 2013 movie *Gravity* set our expectations for this kind of thing and I see no issue whatsoever in emulating what I think is an excellent example of sound design for film, set in a very unusual environment.

The main audio content for the *Earthlight* experience is the communications dialogue between the character you are controlling and the person in charge of the mission and mission training. This dialogue is the narrative element of the experience combined with instructional content and it blends quite seamlessly between the two. Interactive experiences often blend instructions into the narrative content and when it is done well, as it is in *Earthlight*, it provides a nice method to ease the audience into both the experience and the story that is being told. The character you control in

Earthlight is voiced by a young female voice actor and just as in the *Star Wars Battlefront* VR experience, I found no disconnect or break in the immersion of the experience being in a VR experience controlling a VR character. In both instances this surprised me quite a bit.

Earthlight is quite a sparse experience from an audio point of view, but I do not say this as a criticism of its design. I think the sparseness of the audio does very well to enhance the isolation of being in a vacuum. I doubt there is much to be heard when you are floating in the void of space and in this instance accurately following reality provides excellent support for the narrative of the experience. There is a sense of scale and awe when you leave the station and find yourself hanging onto the hull above the entire planet. Silence is perhaps the best accompaniment for a sensation that leaves you feeling very small and fragile. Silence is also something that is used too seldom in modern media because I think many of us fear our audience will not understand its application and our project may seem incomplete. But for *Earthlight* this limited audio palette helps to provide a clean environment and a real point of difference to many games and media that cram in lots of content.

gear VR

Dark Days

It is important for me to continually play and assess content created in the industry in which I work—obviously for the reasons of producing this book, but also to continually assess the kinds of content we create, to find inspiration, and also to ensure I am aware of what people are doing with the new technology. I found the GearVR to be a useful tool for rapid prototyping of work and a great way to demonstrate VR content to others. I wanted to make sure I was also aware of the types of content people were creating for the GearVR and a quick Google search told me I should check out *Dark Days* as it was one of the best examples of content for this mobile platform.

Dark Days is essentially a spooky point-and-click VR adventure. Generally, I found it an experience that relied on jump scares more than anything else. Jump scares work very well mainly because of a human's fight or flight instincts, and for this reason I don't really like them. It's a little like shooting fish in a barrel, and not really an example of how to create an excellent experience. *Dark Days* does, however, have some nice environmental dressing that does a good job of establishing an eerie place to explore.

What I discovered about the audio was very unusual. The entire experience appears to be at best plain stereo and possible even mostly mono, not mono sounds spatialized in the experience, just simple mono. The first moment of significance in the game I didn't even register for a few seconds because I was looking in the wrong direction and the sound cue did not sound like it was in the environment I was in, it was just a noise. So even though there was something significant I was supposed to see, there was nothing in the game to draw my attention to the event itself. Even basic 3D sound in a 3D game engine would have provided some directional guidance to the location of the event.

This is why I believe the audio may have been in mono as there was no head-locked stereo panning to these objects; all the environmental sounds just seem to exist inside your head at the point where you would hear a mono sound. I am not sure if this was intentional or a technical issue with their project. With the new reality tech being so early in its development stage it is possible that either the spatial audio process had an issue, or the dev team decided to avoid potential issues by keeping the audio very simple and so adopted a mono mix.

This mono mix, however, did provide a very interesting opportunity to analyze other aspects of the audio for this title and also a general approach to audio production for VR. So the very first danger cue, as I mentioned, did not alert me to the narrative moment I was supposed to notice. As my character was sitting in a moving car I would trigger the intended event eventually—that was unavoidable, but I think it was really significant how the audio cue here not only failed to draw my attention, I also barely noticed it at all and this is worth exploring.

The sound used as a cue to this event was a kid of scratching sound, I assume to represent the creature that was positioned to startle me. But with spatialization not present this sound blended into the overall "stack" of sounds all in the mono position. The environment of a moving car had a generic car engine sound, some music playing on the radio and the narrative internal voice of the main character. I was looking around the car and just checking the visual perspectives as I turned my head. Then the scratching sound commenced. The issue is, it was a generic scratching sound that the developers either recorded themselves or sourced from a library, but the sound had none of the reverberant qualities that would have existed inside that car.

So I am in VR, sitting in a moving car and I hear a sound that sounded like it was originally recorded in a much larger room, without the absorbent materials of a car interior. Even fairly old cars, like the one depicted in this experience, have fairly muted interiors as they are sound proofed against their own engines and other external sounds. So a sound file triggered that has the qualities of a large reverberant room, simply sounds wrong—out of place. I was not really focusing on the sound at this stage because the game had only just started, so I was caught off guard by it, which is good, because that means I reacted to it more like a regular audience than as a sound designer. My brain just said "nope, that sound doesn't belong" and the analysis I present here is from the thought process afterward.

In many ways, the removal of spatialization contributed to the exposure of this sound effect. Without spatialization the sound in this experience needs to utilize other qualities of sound behavior to help position the audience into the environment. I suspect that if this scratching sound had been recorded inside a real car then the matching of reverberant qualities would have had a much more significant effect. My brain would have thought "oh, what's that sound? There is something scratching WITHIN the car!" and as a result I would have looked around. This is an excellent example of how matching the reverberation behavior of a space is important when placing a sound into that space. Our brains have a certain level of disconnect with VR. We know we are not in the real world, but our brains can fool us in multiple ways to accept certain aspects of a virtual environment.

In this experience, we already had a handful of sounds. The internal monologue does not influence our interpretation of a space, because it is occurring inside "our" head (or the character's head that we are inhabiting). The radio sounds like it is coming from a speaker, which is appropriate for any radio and my guess would be the recording of the radio may have been made inside a car, so it did include a reasonably accurate level of reverb. Of course, the sound of the car itself would obviously has been recorded inside a moving car of some sort. Importantly, the sound of the car is the first environmental sound we are exposed to in this experience, and it is a continual looping presence. This is important because it not only sets the reference for the space initially, but also is a constant reference

Samsung gear VR.

to which all other sounds can immediately be compared. So referring back to the scratch sound, my brain simply does an A/B comparison. Scratch sound triggers, my brain thinks "oh, new sound ... hang on, it doesn't match the car engine sound! It must not be a sound from inside the car."

After the scare in the car, the experience switches to you being at a roadside motel and you must go through the steps of checking in. But you have some freedom to wander around a little and explore. This is not only where the next series of audio content was exposed by the lack of spatialization, but also a solution that the developers had utilized was also apparent.

As part of creating the environment, the developers had included a series of sounds that depicted things in the parking lot. As a point-and-click style experience, movement was achieved by looking at a region and if an arrow appeared you could teleport to that spot. The point-and-click functionality essentially meant you teleported from one static VR minienvironment to the next static VR minienviron-ment, so the developers could craft each little cell of the environment to have specific content. In one place, there were a handful of flies buzzing around to enhance the sense that this location was not very pleasant. The flies were implemented quite effectively by the fact that you could only hear them when you were standing on the exact spot next to their little swarm. So even though not technically spatialized to that location they had a type of spatialization in that they acti-vated and deactivated when you moved into their proximity or away from them. While a very simple method this was a very clever way to implement a very basic spatial mapping for various sounds.

For larger scale sounds, however, the lack of spatialization did become noticeable. When I first appeared in the motel parking lot I could hear a metallic creaking sound. I immediately recognized this as the sound of a watermill, as I have recorded these exact sounds myself. But initially I couldn't see the spinning fan wheels of the mill. The issue, of course, was there was no spatial information to use to help me work out which direction it was in. The creaking sound seemed like it should have been fairly close as it was loud enough to be within only a few meters. I eventually found it behind a telephone booth at the edge of the parking lot. Being hidden behind the phone booth was why I had issues seeing it (the experience is set at night), but again the audio not only didn't help me locate it, but also it actually provided false info to my ears and my brain. The mono mix stacked all the sounds into the same central "inside my head" position so it made it difficult to get clarity for each sound.

This project highlights why certain aspects of sound behavior are really important to creating narrative media. I do not think *Darker Days* is a terrible product, but I do think the audio could have been implemented more effectively. But I am also very happy that this project exists as it is an excellent vehicle to discuss various aspects of audio production in general and specifically for VR experiences. The ability to isolate certain aspects of the sound because there is not true spatialization makes it an excellent case study.

playstation VR

How We Soar

How We Soar places the audience onto the back of a giant phoenix as you fly around a magical realm full of floating objects. As you guide your mount through a series of rings and try to pick up glowing objects, the narrative unfolds and aspects of the environment change. This game utilizes a clean and simple visual style with some wonderful bold and saturated colors. The sense of being mounted on the back of a giant bird is quite effective.

From an audio point of view, the music that accompanies the experience is light and has a nice ethereal nature to it, appropriate to the content. The sound design is sparse, which I think was the right choice for an experience such as this. It is a clean, open, and vast world where the sense of freedom through flight is well matched with a subtle treatment from the audio. I think the choice of sound content is good, but I think it is let down in some regards by its implementation.

Being a Sony VR title, the developers would have had access to the Sony VR spatialization tools which I know from other experiences are solid and effective. So I will go through the various points of my experience with the audio and then describe methods that might have helped with some of the issues I encountered.

Environment

The first thing I noted was the ambient wind sound. Essentially, it is white noise that accompanies the audience for the entire experience. This is basically what wind is, a natural example of white noise. The problem is I think too many developers implement it like that as well. Wind exists almost all the time in the real world. Sometimes it is soft and subtle so we can barely perceive it and at other times it can be huge and dramatic. But it is something that we are all used to experiencing and something that is so familiar to any listener that it should not be implemented carelessly.

I found the wind sound in *How We Soar* to be flat and lifeless. As I tried to focus on it, I could not perceive anything beyond a simple mono sound set to equal output from all directions. It was as if an emitter had been placed above the listener with a mono sound looping from it. The entire point of this game is to experience the sensation of flying, and the wind is a critical element of this that I feel that they missed an incredible opportunity with. So how could they have produced a better result?

World Objects

As I played through some of *How We Soar* I noticed the sounds for the world objects as they animated—giant books floating in the sky and interesting architectural shapes that moved as you progressed through the level. All the actual sounds for these worked really well; the movement of the paper and the various objects as they unfolded all had appropriate sounds. But again I think the implementation had a few shortcomings.

Often as I flew around I would see an object start to move or a page in one of the giant books would move. The issue was that the sound I heard for these objects sounded like the object was right next to my ear—it was a sound position for an object within my arms' reach, not a massive object 100 m away. As has been mentioned in this book multiple times, accurate spatialization in 360 spherical surround is really tough and I suspect the issue I raise here is going to be a very common one over the next few years of new reality development. It was not the location of the sound that was the issue. If the sound was to the left I heard it to the left, if the sound was around to the right and the rear it seemed to localize pretty well. It was just that the sounds felt too close.

If we do not have the functionality or the resources to calculate accurate spatial positioning via reverb, there are other methods we can adopt. *How We Soar* had a significant challenge in that the entire experience happens way up in the sky in a totally open environment. So they could not have relied on the help of room reflections even if they had wanted to. But even outdoors, sound has a few characteristics that could have been utilized to help with depth placement.

Using both volume attenuation and frequency filtering could have significantly helped in pushing the sounds of the objects further away, so they felt like they were emanating from the objects in the world. Volume attenuation can be difficult, especially with an experience such as this. "Make the book sound softer because it is further away," is kind of what I am saying. But softer compared to what? These are massive magical books floating in the sky animating of their own accord. Who is to say how loud these objects would be when they do make a sound? So just dropping the volume to represent distance may not be the best approach.

Sound over distance does change in other ways though. Generally, higher frequency content drops off sooner than low-frequency content. So, for example, if there is an ocean in the distance we can hear the low rumble of the waves and it is not until we move close that the sound resolves and "opens up" the upper frequency aspect of the sound. Each of the page movement sounds in *How We Soar* had a beautiful crisp clean sound of the parchment moving. That was kind of the problem. The crisp high-end frequencies made me perceive those sounds as though they were right next to my ear. A bit of frequency filtering to cut out the top end should work quite well in pushing those objects further way to the player's perceptions.

These are just two aspects of a VR experience and in both instances the solutions are not complex ones that require powerful tools to achieve. This is an important point that I will make again and again throughout this book. We are still in the early stages of tool development and workflow design for the new realities, and there will be new technology and advances for us to work with over the next few years. But much of what we do and what we can do comes back to our use of stagecraft. Our knowledge and understanding of how sound behaves in the real world, combined with the inspiration techniques that our colleagues in film, television, games, and live theater have been using for many years can provide us with many solutions to various challenges for creating our audio worlds.

In Chapter Five, I explore various production techniques for creating new reality content. I also explain some of the techniques I used in a recent PS4 game that could have been applied to a game such as *How We Soar* and might have created a more dynamic audio environment. There is never a "right" way to design creative content, but there are certain approaches that can produce results that might make the

Sony playstation VR.

audience feel more engaged. The process of evaluation, trial and error, and exploring new approaches is how we all develop our craft.

playstation VR

Star Wars Battlefront: Episode One X-Wing Mission

I need to be somewhat cautious with an analysis of this experience. I am a long-time *Star Wars* fan and a VR experience such as this one is something I have wanted for many years. However, I have played this short mission multiple times now, so the initial wonder of it has mostly worn off. I played it again to analyze the audio for this chapter and so I performed many actions and movements specifically to test the audio performance.

The first thing I did was to test the effect of elevated positional sound. In the very opening, there is an object that moves across the screen slowly. This is the perfect test for spatial positioning. It is a single object making a strong clear sound as it moves and it is the only thing creating sound. This allows you to turn your head and assess the effectiveness of the spatialization. I dropped my chin down to my chest to see if I could perceive the sound of the object coming from "above" my head. I also rotated my head left and right slightly to further test the elevational effect. The main impression I had when I did this was "I am not sure."

This is actually really significant. "I am not sure," is not a failure by any means. When I lowered my head, specifically trying to detect if the sound was positioned above my ears, I could not really tell if it was or not. I was looking for failure, I was testing for a negative and I could not find that negative. An average audience will simply listen and in most cases accept what the experience presents to them, but when I specifically tried to detect an elevated sound I was left uncertain.

It is worth explaining in more detail why this is significant. Through my own tests and those of industry colleagues many of us have discovered that humans in the real world are often not great at detecting sound sources positioned above. If they are directly above us then sometimes it can become easier, but angles of 45 degrees and below we often cannot detect clearly. I have mentioned several times in this book that we may often need smoke and mirrors to compensate for not only the limitations of the technology but also the limitations of the human brain.

When I have tested other VR experiences and done similar tests, I have clearly detected no sense of sounds being positioned above the head. So a result of "I do not know," I think may actually be the most desirable result. If the sound I heard was "yes, absolutely I can clearly hear that above my head" it might risk standing out too much. Remember we are trying to create an overall blended audio environment. So in regard to elevational positioning this experience was one of the best I had encountered. I did the same test a few moments later when there was an R2 astromech droid wandering around in front of me and again I got the same perception.

The second aspect of the audio that I noticed the very first time I ran this experience was a simple but very clever use of the technology. The X-wing is positioned in an empty white space. Not a crowded cluttered hanger environment, but a white void. It has a few pieces of machinery around it but it is otherwise endless white space. When I first loaded the experience, I saw that and said "oh cool!" and I heard myself. My own voice was played back to me through the headphones, but with a reverb added to it to make it sound like I was standing in a hangar space. This was so simple and yet so incredibly effective at dragging me instantly into that virtual space.

This is related to a second use of spatial reflections in this experience that I think is important to discuss. When you click to enter the cockpit, the screen fades to black, but the audio continues and "narrates" the action of the cockpit closing. You go from the open space of the hanger to a sealed, tight space. The reverb in the hanger is obviously not based on accurate reflection calculations because the "hanger" is an endless white void with no walls. Equally, I doubt the reflections in the cockpit are mathematically accurate to the space either and the important thing is they do not need to be. The critical component here is the change itself, not the specific values of space A versus space B. For the audience, they receive a suitable representation of moving between two different spaces and the reverb reflections match that change.

Once the main mission loaded, I constantly moved my head around and steered the ship to evaluate the spatial audio I was hearing. Again, when I flew past the giant capital ships and listened to their roaring engines I got a nice subtle blend as the sound moved from my front to rear perception. It felt like it was transitioning cleanly as I moved. Even these engine sounds were pretty subtle. They were a part of the environment and not a key feature. But all the positional movement as I moved past sound sources held up very well even as I specifically focused on them.

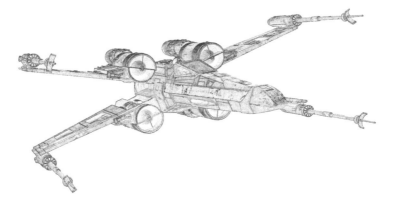

Being inside the X-wing cockpit in VR was far more
immersive than any other X-wing game.

When it came to the combat sections there was one aspect that
was noteworthy. There were a lot of TIE fighters and they were all
around me. And this is another aspect of effective audio implementation. By the time, I was surrounded with dozens of wailing TIE
fighters zooming all around me in different directions at different
distances a lot of the work was being done by my brain. I don't mean
to say that the audio team didn't do a good job, in fact they did an
excellent job, but once you have implemented a single fast-moving
object so that it can move past the player in a convincing manner
and sound accurate with good amplitude attenuation and frequency
filtering, then at least a portion of the effectiveness of the mix is dealt
with by the audience's brain.

Sound designer Walter Murch refers to the concept of keeping
track of 2.5 audio sources. If we hear a set of footsteps we can focus
on them and track them. If we add a second set of steps, we are still
able to isolate and differentiate between them. Once we hit three sets
we start to struggle. The same applies to people speaking or—to TIE
fighters screaming around our cockpit.

So once we have a few objects moving around us, our brain kind
of gives up and accepts there is a lot of sound and a lot of movement.
So we perceive considerable spatialized movement without focusing on any one object. This means we can apply an audio level of
detail. Sure, accurately track the TIE fighter closest to you and then
maybe two or three others, but the rest almost don't need to make
any sound at all because we simply perceive there are lots of moving
TIE fighters around us.

One final aspect of the X-wing VR experience that is worth mentioning is the voice-over (VO) content. Before launching the mission, you can select either a male or female pilot. I selected a female pilot. What you experience is the voice of a character that represents the person who is flying the X-wing. It is her story. And yet I was flying the X-wing in an immersive experience. This was an interesting design decision. I was able to look down and see my body in the cockpit, and yet I could hear a voice interacting with the other characters. Strangely, instead of this having a negative impact on the immersion I felt, I found it enhanced it significantly. This short experience had a very tight storyline and the narrative was a core of the whole experience, but even though my "existence" was kind of like a ghost inhabiting the pilot's body, I found it really compelling. The writing was excellent and the voice acting very enjoyable. I instantly liked the character and enjoyed following their adventure.

The audio for the main character was treated so it felt quite a lot like it was inside my own head and the radio VR from the other characters was also very close, but different enough to be obviously not inside my head. LU 2, the astromech droid for my X-wing, could be heard chirping away behind me. I felt like I was INSIDE a *Star Wars* story and this was a significant and enjoyable experience as a result. I will also say that the success of this experience for me was significantly influenced by the quality of the audio production and implementation. This is still my favorite VR experience and that is very much because of the audio and highlights my belief that VR will live or die based on its audio.

The perfect counterpoint to my thoughts on the *Star Wars Battlefront VR Mission* is to hear directly from one of the creators.

Developing the Sound of the *Star Wars Battlefront: Rogue One X-Wing VR Mission*

Jay Steen Audio Lead: Criterion

When starting development of the *Star Wars Battlefront: Rogue One X-Wing VR Mission*, Criterion Games' aim was clear—to put the player at the heart of a *Star Wars* story. VR as a storytelling medium has the potential to be more immersive than any other, and the *Star Wars* universe is rich with personal stories played out across an epic backdrop, so combining these gave us the opportunity to create an amazing experience of fantasy fulfillment for the player.

The audio team approached this from three directions: allow the player to roleplay as a hotshot rookie pilot, make space combat feel tangible and dangerous, and underline dramatic moments with a powerful score. To do this, we had to explore the new ways of rendering spatial audio made available by the Playstation VR, figure out how to combine these new methods with more traditional audio rendering tech, and help solve new game design challenges such as directing player attention and keeping the experience comfortable.

Before delving into the three main pillars of the experience, it is important to outline the different tools we had to output sound. The most important and utilized output type was the object output, which provided a way to output a mono signal as a binaurally spatialized 3D point source. To complement this, we had a direct output, which ensured that it was possible to play multichannel sounds direct out to the headphones. This signal flow bypassed binaural processing as we found this worked best for nondiegetic sounds. The title was a PSVR exclusive, which meant we needed to keep the mix of the social screen (the screen the PS4 normally outputs to) in mind. We used a mixdown of all object outputs and the direct output bus to a surround mix, which needed extra attention and tweaks to ensure it matched the headphone experience. Finally, we implemented support for playback of ambisonics-encoded sources, and experimented with new ambisonics microphones, but due to project time constraints we were unable to make use of this technology in the shipping game. This was unfortunate, as we believe the relatively old format could have new potential in the current generation of VR.

Our first pillar was to build a character-driven narrative that would allow the player to roleplay the journey of a pilot from rookie to veteran, something that we as *Star Wars* fans have always wanted. To achieve the level of immersion we wanted, we felt strongly that the player would need a self-voice and should interact in characterful ways with the rest of the cast. We were concerned that this would detract from immersion and that the player might be unaware that the voice was supposed to be their own, so we felt it was important to clearly differentiate it from other voices. After some experimentation, we found that using the direct output to play back the self-voice made players feel like the voice was emanating from themselves. Object outputs were used a short distance in front of the player for all other voices gave them a sense of "otherness." Some radio processing was applied to the object output and its position was locked to the control panel of the X-wing. This meant as the player looked around in the cockpit, the position of the radio voices changed relative to the listener, whereas the self-voice remained fixed. Alongside this, a clear, neutral condenser mic was used to record self-voice performances, whereas radio voices were recorded using a dynamic mic. The differentiations between self-voice and radio voices meant we did not have any problems during development with players not understanding the self-voice was supposed to be theirs. As a team, we were surprised that none of our playtesters found it strange to have someone else's voice as their own.

With these tools, and through our collaboration with Lucasfilm, we were able to immerse the player in a *Star Wars* story that tied into and featured characters from the *Rogue One* film timeline, let the player join and fly with Red Squadron, and had a memorable and fun cast of characters.

Our second pillar was to make combat feel tangible and dangerous. We achieved this by having an X-wing that felt responsive, powerful, and fast from a first-person perspective, while maintaining the sense of fragility that would result from having a thin pane of glass between you and space.

The mission largely takes place within the cockpit of an X-wing, so this part of the experience merited a lot of attention. We had a lot of excellent source material to work with in creating this from both Skywalker Sound and DICE's work on the X-wing in the base game, but we quickly found that the content that sounded great with a flat screen experience was underwhelming in VR. It didn't feel like the engine was coming from all around the player, and it didn't feel fully diegetic due to the content being baked into a stereo loop that played back direct through the LR channels. We experimented with how to spatialize the different loops, with our first attempt using object outputs positioned on the engine turbines and in front of the cockpit. This was a slight improvement, but we found that as we spread the turbine roar over more of the soundfield (by increasing the size parameter of the object outputs) it became more difficult for the player to spatially resolve at all, and lost some of its impact. There may have also been some interaction between the noisy, wideband content, and the impulse responses used for HRTF that contributed to this effect. Our next attempt tried to combat this by baking the source content in a quad format, and playing it back direct out. This allowed us to control the spatialization fully and avoid any interference from the HRTF and object spreading algorithm. We also implemented a twist panner that was linked to the opposite of the rotation of the player's head, which made the sound appear to be coming from a consistent part of the X-wing as the player looked around. We were much happier with the result of this, and we improved on it by splitting the source content into layers with different spatial weights that responded to different physical properties of the X-wing handling. We would have liked to use ambisonics-encoded content to improve on this even further, but as mentioned before, time constraints precluded this.

We did not completely remove object outputs from the player X-wing, however. For discrete, percussive sounds such as the cannon fire, objects worked perfectly, and changing the cannons to objects spatialized to the tips of the wings started to add depth to the soundscape of the cockpit. Another area where objects excelled was in creating a diegetic UI for the X-wing's cockpit dashboard. Each button had a spatialized sound associated with it that the player could interact with, with more meaningful interactions like opening and closing the S-foils and switching on the targeting computer having bespoke spatialized sounds. In doing this, we succeeded in giving a sense of personality to the X-wing (helped by the astromech unit that sat directly behind you) as well as making the cockpit UI feel more solid.

Building the soundscape out further from the player's point of view, we made heavy use of Frostbite's high dynamic range (HDR) mixing system. As well as mixing and prioritizing more important sounds, in VR it had the additional effect of directing the player's visual attention to louder sounds, for example, a loud explosion or impact behind the player would generally make them turn their head to look at the source of the sound. We made use of this in scripted moments, as it's very inadvisable due to nausea to force the player to look in a certain direction in a VR game, but you can direct their attention with clever use of loud sounds, as we did during the Star Destroyer arrival scene. This effect also works excellently during dynamic dogfighting combat, and we put it to best use when the X-wing's shield is up, which not only prevents you from taking damage but also spatializes the sound of hits that would have damaged you to the direction they arrived from. This allowed the player a chance to turn and locate their pursuer before maneuvering the X-wing to fight back. The shield also helped to control the intensity of the dogfighting experience as we applied a snapshot mix which ducked and applied a low-pass filter to most combat sounds. This gave the player a break from what could be a fairly chaotic soundscape.

Music is an incredibly important part of any *Star Wars* story, and as such our third pillar was to underscore the dramatic moments of this experience with a powerful score. We worked with Gordy Haab, Battefront's composer, to create a score that drew on the music of *Rogue One* to add authenticity and familiarity to the mission. We wanted to treat the music as "space ambience" that rises in intensity to match the action, so we decided to treat the music as a nondiegetic source and play it direct out, without spatialization. We were worried about taking this approach as we had heard from other VR developers that this could seriously detract from presence and immersion, but we found that it did the opposite: it increased the player's sense that they were at the heart of a *Star Wars* story. Perhaps this is because players expect nondiegetic music from a cinematic experience, and this overrides the need for all sounds to be spatialized to increase presence.

Overall, the Criterion Games audio team's time working on the X-wing VR Mission was a fantastic experience and opportunity to explore an emerging platform and start to develop a whole new vernacular for audio. It reinforced our belief that you should continue to experiment, not try to "solve" VR for all cases, and focus on what works best for the game or experience you are making.

location-based experiences

Chanel Summers provides a detailed insight into her work creating live experiences for VR and AR.

Creating Immersive and Aesthetic Auditory Spaces for Location-Based VR Experiences

Chanel Summers

Introduction

I am going to discuss specific immersive and aesthetic auditory design techniques as applied to the creation of full-motion, multiparticipant virtual reality (VR) game experiences for live, commercial, and location-based entertainment (LBE) installations. Location-based, or out-of-home, VR experiences are typically more social than at-home consumer content and can provide much more elaborate and immersive experiences not possible in an average consumer's home. They can also be a powerful partner to in-home gaming VR and AR experiences and even possibly accelerate the adoption of VR by consumers by exposing consumers to VR content, perhaps for the first time, and acclimating them to the new technology. These experiences utilize many of the same audio techniques as consumer VR software but there are also significant differences to consider when designing and implementing audio for LBE VR.

I will introduce fundamental design considerations and emerging best practices used in spatially responsive VR audio design and implementation, and complement these with the practical examples that embrace the complexities of immersive and aesthetic audio design in VR.

VR System Description

The audio design examples I will use are drawn from content developed for commercial application by a leader in LBE VR development: VRstudios, Inc. As of the time these applications were released, the company's VRcade installations were the only full-motion, multiplayer, untethered system which did not require a backpack computer or mobile phone to provide the computing resources to render the VR experience and as such afforded players a wider range of movement, without a loss of visual fidelity, than other early LBE installations. These advances also required adaptation and further refinement of then-current VR techniques based on real user feedback, business objectives, and customer requirements.

Typical VRcade installation.

In this section, I will highlight some of these adaptations and refinements as applied to three VRcade projects: *Barking Irons*, *planktOs: Crystal Guardians*, and *VR Showdown in Ghost Town*.

The standard VRcade configuration supports two simultaneous players in the same virtual and physical space and allows for a full range of player motion in physical spaces ranging from 225 to 900 ft^2 (approx. 21 to 86 m^2). A picture of a typical VRcade installation is shown in the above figure.

The VRcade system allows games to run on dedicated high-powered computers, and then streams the content wirelessly to the players' HMD without the need for wires, mobile phones, or backpack computers. The HMD is a display with essentially no processing. This unique architecture provides a state-of-the-art, crystal clear, and completely untethered experience. It also defines the capabilities that can be utilized in the development of the content. Furthermore, multiple capture volumes can be networked together to support even more simultaneous players in a single game world.

Audio and the VR Environment

It has been my experience that those elements that make a VR environment so immersive and compelling are created more in the audio space than in the visual space, for several reasons.

First, audio can represent all of space rather than just what the viewer is seeing, including sounds that emanate from behind the user, not in their field of view, or ones where sources have not been graphically rendered.

Second, the perceptual complexity allowed for by the human body in audio reception is greater than that allowed by the eyes for the visual reception.

The auditory system can simultaneously process multiple frequencies with a variety of amplitudes whereas visually each bit in an image corresponds to a specific color, but cannot represent multiple colors simultaneously.

Audio can be received through vibrations, and therefore physiologically, by several parts of the body simultaneously in addition to the ears. Thus, audio can affect us on a subconscious, psychological, and physiological level.

Very early in the design process, we need to consider how we approach the creation of the spaces we are building and throughout the process we need to create spaces that are coherent, consistent, and cohesive within the story and game space.

The narrative of the game and the desired gameplay set the foundation for the visuals of each setting within the game, but adding the audio brings them alive, making the experience effectively real in the player's mind.

What follows is a discussion of some thought processes, audio design techniques, and production decisions that VRstudios, my team at Syndicate 17, and the professionals at Hexany Audio used to advance story and gameplay in each experience's virtual environment.

Nondiegetic Music and VO in VR

Before diving into specifics, I want to explore one general area of consideration that crossed all project boundaries. Special consideration must be given to music and VO if they are to be included in a VR experience. Nondiegetic music, which is music that does not appear to emanate from any apparent "source" within the game, is common in traditional (i.e., non-VR) games and experiences and is often referred to as "underscore." However, in VR the use of underscore is still being debated, with many disagreeing how this should be treated in VR. Some argue that nondiegetic music breaks immersion while others put forth that it actually helps to create immersion by guiding the players' emotional states and aiding in the interpretation of the actions and events they see unfolding before them.

One example of this ongoing debate that I have previously described elsewhere, centers around multiple iterations of the *Leviathan* property. Unlike in the original *Leviathan* AR experience that I had worked on for release at the 2014 Consumer Electronics Show, there was no music in the encore *Leviathan* VR experience first shown at the 2016 Sundance New Frontiers Festival. Even though the world of *Leviathan* is fantastical, it was also a goal to have it be "realistic" in nature. This required that music would need to emanate from a diegetic source rather than being part of a nondiegetic underscore. For instance, originally plans called for the design of an elevator inside *Leviathan* where players would hear elevator music but that idea was ultimately not implemented in the design due to time constraints. Similarly, all VO emanated from the characters within the experience. The scientist in the experience gave participants instructions on what they needed to do; there was no "voice of God" VO narration. This piece was specifically designed without "voice of God" narration and a nondiegetic score to create a more "realistic" space. The use of VO and nondiegetic music in VR should be based on the desired look and feel, scenarios, and project objectives.

Barking Irons

Barking Irons, an arcade style shoot-out set in the Old West, was launched at the CVR conference in Vancouver, British Columbia in May, 2016. This was the first VRcade game to support multiple simultaneous players occupying the same physical and virtual space in a completely wireless environment. The game is designed for physical spaces up to 30 ft by 30 ft with two users moving across the entire area, enabling them to move around, even run and jump around, within the physical capture space more actively than in a smaller space or a consumer's home. In addition, multiple capture volumes can be networked together for additional players to play in the same virtual space.

In *Barking Irons*, players start in the desert just outside town, where they can test their guns on destructible targets like bottles and barrels (see the below figure). Players see each other as futuristic robot avatars and are equipped with a Western revolver with a sci-fi twist. When ready, the current sheriff of the town introduces the rules and loads the players into the center of a Wild West town.

Animatronic bandits spawn throughout the town and start shooting at the players. The player who can dodge incoming bullets and shoot the most bandits will be crowned the new sheriff. This experience was specifically designed to be a fun and easy-to-play arcade experience for participants of all ages and skill levels.

As with most VR games and experiences, some mechanism must be present in the game to indicate to the player when they are "going out of bounds" or

Barking irons game environment.

moving beyond the allowed play area. Visible gridlines are commonly used for this purpose. *Barking Irons* was the first game in which VRstudios experimented with placing natural limits in the game space by utilizing elements in the story world, such as barrels and wooden boxes as capture volume barriers thereby theming the grid walls with the experience. Audio cues can also be utilized and naturally built into an experience to indicate game boundaries.

Game Environment and Environmental Audio Design

For the ambient Western audio, I wanted to ensure that we created an immersive, believable, and organic space that had some dynamic variation to it. This was accomplished by creating a seamless game world through the use of "acousmatic" audio: sounds whose sources are intentionally not visible.

To truly be immersive, it was important that players felt like they had stepped into the Old West. The right balance and a cohesive combination of environmental and gameplay audio was required. Additionally, in order to have a more believable and complex soundscape, the sounds that comprised the environment needed to not seem repetitive and on a "cycle." With any type of shooter in VR, players are extremely sensitive to the sounds associated with guns, shooting, explosions, and impacts. This introduces a heavily weighted opportunity to elevate the player's experience. To that end, we wanted to make sure that we had extremely satisfying impact and gun sounds with many variations to each.

The organic nature of the environments in Western-themed video game *Red Dead Redemption* is impressive and the environment in *Barking Irons* was modeled after this type of organic design. The goal was to create something at least as subtle, putting the player in the middle of a very personalized experience. This subtlety is even more important in immersive VR than in a traditional video game, as you are actually inside the experience.

Balancing Audio for the Environment and Gameplay

The main objective for *Barking Irons* was to strike a balance between creating effective audio that satisfied basic gameplay requirements, and building a soundscape that worked well and cohesively within the world, supplying the players with auditory cues so they can play the game while also making them feel like they're truly in some futuristic world drawn from the Wild West.

The soundscape/ambience incorporated sounds like wind, tumbleweeds, birds, horses galloping by, rattlesnakes, coyotes in the distance, and a train going by on train tracks even though the development team was not going to render any of this out graphically. One of the awesome things with audio is that we don't need to see any of these objects to make them real for the player; we can just imply them through audio. And we set each of them up to trigger appropriately, so for instance, you wouldn't hear a train traveling by you every few seconds.

The "appropriate" audio was then spatialized and attenuated in the VR environment. An early reflection model was built in conjunction with a Wwise real-time parameter control (RTPC) for player_height. This project was built in the Unity engine using Wwise from Audiokinetic and Two Big Ears' 3Dception.

Not all sounds need to be spatialized in the VR experience, hence the term "appropriate." There may be sounds that are static or head relative. For instance, the sheriff VO is attached to the sheriff robot in the lobby scene and attenuates as you move your head and walk around in the space. But in the game level, since you don't see the sheriff when he alerts you to the start of a new round, his VO announcements are in simple stereo as they are just there to communicate info to the players. However, for the individual environmental sounds mentioned earlier such as the coyote sounds, the rattlesnakes, birds, horses, train, and tumbleweeds, user-defined Wwise 3D positioning was used. This enabled the definition of the "spatial positioning of an object in a surround environment using animation paths" [2] that follows head tracking, so you can place things in the world without even needing to anchor them on a game object in the world. Hence, the individual ambient world sounds are always positioning as you rotate your head, and therefore you always feel a sense of direction and depth within the world. A more natural and immersive environment was created as a result of this design.

At this point, 2D looped stereo ambiences such as general ambiences that we did not feel required spatialization were mixed in with individual 3D mono spatialized sounds which worked quite well and felt very natural. The wind and general ambience was not designed as a quad array with emitters placed around the listener in all directions, as we didn't find that necessary with this experience. All these environmental sounds also played a key part in immersing the players within the space since these subtle sounds blended with the environment in a dynamic way. As a side note, people who played the game remarked that the nondiegetic music also really made them feel like they were in the space, as it set the tone for them.

While the environmental sounds induced emotion and helped to create a truly immersive experience, it was essential to balance the environmental sounds with the sounds that were essential for gameplay. The effectiveness of the gameplay is greatly reduced if the players don't look where they need to look at any point in time during play. Great care was also taken to not overwhelm and distract players with too much sound.

Iterative Design and Testing

It is important to test and see where people are looking and responding with regard to your audio cues. Then, adjustments can be made based on that data. It is very difficult to theorize and predict people's responses in such a complex soundscape. Multiple iterations of the design/test/modify/test process is mandatory to achieve a high quality and effective experience.

Because of this, we ended up doing some experimentation with the animatronic bandit spawning sounds, as having effective and well-positioned audio cues was key to the gameplay. The original spawn sounds which were reminiscent of futuristic transporter sounds, while very cool sounding, were just not reacting well with all the gun shooting between the two players. The spawning sounds were too subtle and were getting masked and overwhelmed when players were shooting rapidly and new animatronic bandits spawned in. So, the team had to think about a better sound that would be more attention-getting. It was imperative that the sound be very clearly positional, alerting the players to look in that direction. It was suggested by the development team that perhaps a grand whoosh could be interesting for the new spawn sound, however that idea was eliminated immediately as that sound would be too nontransient since it would be very similar to the current spawn sound in the game. As a result, the sci-fi sounds were changed to be strong whip cracks which were very satisfying sounding. This was a win–win as it worked well with the story, environment, and gameplay. It was crucial that these bandit spawn sounds be very prominent audio cues and not subtle, like the environmental sounds.

Sounds that are too quick or too soft can be challenging to locate. Wide band or broad spectrum sounds will spatialize better. With low-frequency sounds, it's harder to tell where they are emanating from. Low end is good for the feeling of a sound and affecting physiology and great for giving an object weight, presence, and size. Sounds that are primarily low-frequency like an energy pulse or a rumble are well suited to being stereo sounds.

During testing, it was agreed that projectile whiz-bys on the bullets would be very helpful and effective in providing a more immersive experience. As mentioned previously, an early reflection model had been created so that players could hear the enemies when they shot at them and to assist with further localization of the audio sources by getting more reflections from the animatronic bandits. An occlusion prefab that filtered out certain sound frequencies when players ducked behind barrels and boxes was also put in place. The resulting effect was quite subtle, but very effective.

The Enemy Take Damage sounds were originally one single sound that would get triggered, but as that seemed too repetitive, the team changed these to have several variations. We also removed the initial electrostatic audio layers from these sounds and kept them as "successful" sounding metal hits. This was due to the testing we performed and noticing that we couldn't distinguish whether the player was being hit or the enemy was being hit, as both incorporated electricity sound layers since both the players' avatars and the bandits were robots.

In addition to this, the Player Take Damage variant sounds were modified due to testing with various people. It was noted by several participants that they could not tell when a bullet hit them. In response, the bullet impact sounds were made to be more visceral so that players would get a physical feeling and effect when hit by the bandits' bullets. Originally, the sounds started out as metal sounding hits, and while they sounded great, no one was really feeling impacted by them. Another sound layer was created that had more of a negative quality to it that would signify deep consequences to make people feel even more immersed in the experience and to motivate and incentivize them to move to avoid being shot. Electricity sparks were added on top of the metal sounds for when a player got hit and we created variations for this as well. The static-like sound was reinforced and some low-frequency content was also added in, so players would feel the sound in addition to hearing it.

Experimentation became a key element of the design, development, and testing processes. Again, the driving philosophy for the sound design was to make sure that the participants felt like they were in the space and that they had clearly localized sounds in order to play the game effectively. Testing and user feedback allowed specific areas needing improvement to be quickly identified and then validated as to the effectiveness of improvements once made.

Music

The team incorporated nondiegetic music into the game. There are different schools of thought regarding whether nondiegetic scores can be used in an immersive VR experience. As mentioned, I strongly believe that how you approach VO and music in VR will be based on the scenario you are creating and what your objectives are for your project.

For this project, the team determined that a nondiegetic layered score would be an important aspect of the game as it would set the tone of the game, lend to the ambient environment, and contribute to the game playing mechanic, as the music layers were driven by a parameter indicating how well you are doing (player success), with the music transitioning to higher intensities as you succeed in the game.

Everything was built in layers that loop so the track would play indefinitely in a particular intensity level until a parameter told it to move on to the next mood or intensity. It is important to point out that it was also essential to make sure that the sound cues were never masked by the music.

Per the request of the developer wanting to experiment, the audio team even built a real-time fader—"head volume fader" RTPC (player_ducking_musicvolume) to explore the idea of having a fader dial attached to the players' heads in which the music would change based on ducking activity, but we ended up not using it as we deemed it could sound "wrong" and disruptive to the experience if we kept changing the music based on the players bobbing up and down to dodge the bandits' bullets.

Headphones

Another factor taken into consideration in the audio design was the Bluetooth wireless headphones as the ones used for this experience also utilized virtualization. 3Dception is designed to be in a stereo field, that is, it relies on a stereo experience. The headphones had to be tested in combination with 3Dception to see if the concatenated effect would be detrimental to the audio. Is the virtualized software "hurting" the sound or are the effects benign? The testing resulted in adjusting the virtualization software settings for the Bluetooth headphones, as the virtualization software, while making the experience seem fuller, was ultimately affecting the precision of the localization.

In general, it is never a good idea to have headsets that perform sound virtualization when there is already real-time/dynamic sound virtualization that you are doing within the engine.

Furthermore, the design had to account for Mumble, an open source, low-latency voice chat software that allowed the players to communicate with each other in the experience. As Mumble, like most voice chat solutions, attenuates all other audio in an application to 50% by default in order to be heard, the developers needed to adjust the Mumble ducking settings to leave more headroom for the game's audio middleware engine (Wwise), and also to adjust all other in-game volumes to ensure the appropriate sounds cut through the Mumble ducking.

The attention to detail, trial and error, and sophisticated audio design contributed substantially to the commercial success of the game and the quality of the VR experience.

PlanktOs: Crystal Guardians

Many of these same concepts were then applied in very different ways to a very different title. Launched at the Immerse Technology Summit in October 2016 in Seattle, WA, *planktOs: Crystal Guardians,* is a beautiful and immersive undersea bubble blasting game that emphasizes the themes of adventure, wonder, and joy, and sets a new standard for family-friendly VR experiences (see the below figure). Like *Barking Irons, planktOs* is a multiplayer game with players either cooperating to maximize a group score or competing to get the best score in the group. In the game, players find themselves in a beautiful underwater reef, a fantastical stylized environment in which they see each other wearing big metal scuba suits equipped with a bubble gun and charged with protecting a precious crystal from incoming attackers that happen to be "corrupted" fish, or fish covered in an inky black cloud. Players use their bubble gun to "cleanse," not shoot, the fish from the evil inky blackness released by Planktos Corp and the Weatherbird II.

PlanktOS game environment.

These fish spawn around the players and move toward the crystal to pass on their corruption and destroy the crystal. The player's goal is to protect the crystal, save the fish, and cleanse the ocean.

Game Environment

In adapting the original PC game, developed by Blot Interactive, to VR, we set out as one of our key goals to create an incredibly immersive but "good feeling" environment through audio. We aimed to create an immersive, stylized, natural, and organic space with somewhat realistic and hence, "serious" underwater ambience, which would then leave room for the bubble gun and all the related impact effects to be wonderful and fun.

Since part of the game is wonder and exploration, other interactive aspects were included that were separate from the main gameplay, but allowed for unexpected delight: shooting a starfish with a bubble made it giggle while shooting a clam caused it to release bubbles and to jump.

This project was built on Unreal Engine 4 (UE4) and was a shorter scope project than *Barking Irons*. In the interest of time, it was decided to avoid middleware completely and go with Unreal's native audio controls. There was enough new development and a multitude of operational questions with this project, that the distraction and hurdle of implementing audio middleware was just not practical.

As *planktOs* did not use HRTF filtering, UE4 attenuations and spatializer were used instead of the 3Dception product which was used in *Barking Irons*. Interestingly, the development team initially thought the spatialization was more positional in *planktOs,* before we created the environmental model for *Barking Irons,* that is, and that's because HRTF filtering reduces the hard stereo panning, which can often be assessed as sounding less positional.

Music

This game included nondiegetic music as well and was a major contributor to the soundscape and environment. The design was centered around a *Finding Nemo/ Thomas Newmanesque* styling, as this type of style provided the perfect elements of wonder and excitement, yet still had a bit of a serious side to it. The ambience and music were more on the "serious" side with the gameplay elements having more of the fun effects with really fun sounds.

Three music layers were created from that foundation and were designed to escalate in additive intensity between the three stages in the game. The musical framework was designed such that Stage 1 would go from 0 to 30, Stage 2 would go from 20 to 50, and Stage 3 would go from 40 to 100. These musical segments were then connected by the bubble particle chamber sequence which is the sound-based level transition with no music. The challenge here was to make this music ramping while ensuring that the intensity layers didn't feel disjointed with only a few seconds in between. We utilized the nondiegetic music to heighten emotional impact, set the mood, tone, and pacing of the environment, and as a game design mechanic with transitioning intensity layers as indicators of player success.

Finally, as in *Barking Irons*, we needed to adjust the virtualization software settings for the Bluetooth headphones, as the virtualization software was muddying up the mix a bit.

The resulting game was exciting and fun, and based on user comments the audio was the key factor that drove the very favorable player response to this game. Indeed, many players remarked that the environment was so comfortable and relaxing that they just wanted to stay in the experience.

Less Is More

In both titles, *Barking Irons* and *planktOs*, I took a deliberate "less is more" approach with the audio design. The team didn't want to overload the environment and suffocate the story. We wanted to be subtle. So, we were extremely careful about filling the space up with too much sound. Even though we would be dynamically mixing the assets and prioritizing sounds, we knew that too much sound would saturate the spectrum and the experience would end up losing clarity and focus. It could be overwhelming or too distracting to the listener. But worst of all, the story would become "suffocated" with sound. The result was in both cases a wonderful balance of environmental and gameplay immersion.

Knott's Berry Farm VR Showdown in Ghost Town

A very exciting and very large-scale VR project that we worked on was the result of a creative collaboration between Cedar Fair Entertainment, Knott's Berry Farm, and VRstudios called *VR Showdown in Ghost Town*. It launched on April 1, 2017 and is the first permanent installation of a free-roaming, multiplayer VR

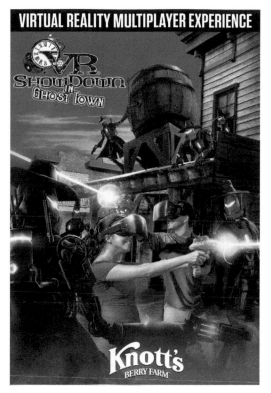

Knott's Berry Farm *VR Showdown in Ghost Town.*

experience in a US theme park. The experience was custom built for, and is exclusively available at Knott's Berry Farm (see the figure above).

In this immersive and interactive VR attraction, players are transported to a futuristic version of Knott's Western town of Calico, where they have to defend the town from swarms of attacking robots. *VR Showdown in Ghost Town* is a 3-minute experience that ties into preexisting Knott's Berry Farm's lore of Professor Welles' time machine while also capturing the likeness of iconic buildings from Knott's Ghost Town. The experience features intense gameplay, cinematic moments including a cinematic train explosion through a time distortion where players must dodge the incoming debris, and a dramatic finale.

The core gameplay of *VR Showdown in Ghost Town* is destroying various robots and avoiding getting hit, but there are additional complex story elements at play around the Wild West town. Each story element features a miniboss robot that is trying to destroy the town. The Big Boss robot appears at the end of the mission and controls a tractor beam that pulls the bank's safe toward a portal. Players must destroy the boss robot before he steals the safe and compete for individual high scores while striving toward shared team goals.

The Installation

The game was also designed and developed specifically for the VRcade custom hardware platform, described earlier, which includes incredibly accurate positional tracking sensors, a proprietary, wireless VR HMD, and a custom gun peripheral. Beyond the standard VRcade hardware, the gun peripheral was modified specifically for the *VR Showdown in Ghost Town* installation to match the gun model in the experience and to heighten immersion. This modification also helped to provide a seamless transition from reality to virtual reality. The software content was developed in Unreal Engine 4 using Wwise from Audiokinetic and the Oculus Audio SDK.

The *VR Showdown in Ghost Town* installation features design work and theming from Knott's hardware and décor teams to theme the entire user experience as a time travel adventure, including a themed preshow video and scenic decoration throughout the VR play space. The Knott's installation includes eight capture spaces of roughly 20 ft by 17 ft with two users playing simultaneously in each space. Players are encouraged to move around the room to dodge incoming enemy projectiles and pick up useful power-ups, and there are both physical hardware indications and virtual software barriers that indicate to players the limits of their physical play space. Up to two capture spaces are networked together to allow anywhere from one to four players to play together in a single game instance with two players located on one side of town and the other two on the other side of town. This means that depending on which pod you are in, you will have a different perspective on many elements of the game.

Audio Design Objectives

Similar to *Barking Irons*, we needed to be able to use audio to create a truly immersive environment and make the players believe they were actually transported to this future Western town. But we also had to supply players with very strong audio cues so they could play the game in this super sound-rich environment.

Audio-wise, our primary focus was on the big actions and cinematic moments in the game. As the main gameplay sequences were taking place in one large environment, we really had to walk that fine line between creating an aurally rich and immersive world without overcrowding the space with audio elements and ending up with a dense "wall" of sound without definition or nuance.

Some of the key things we had to focus on aurally were:

- Go big on the effects.
- Create very satisfying and varied sounds for all the explosions, as there would be many in the game.
- Focus on cause and effect.

- Players do something and need to receive satisfying feedback sounds from their actions.
- The various story elements will need to be indicated by some kind of audiovisual cues.
- Aurally, pay more attention to having the enemy robots inflict damage.
- Place less importance on the robots spawning in and more attention to their firing at players.
- Before the core robot enemy attacks, have some kind of charge-up audio indicating that something bad is about to happen.

Authenticity

In order to get players fully immersed in the setting, each sound in the game world needs to feel true, to sound authentic.

Create a "sense of place."

Create an immersive, natural, and organic space.

A guiding philosophy that the team discussed was this idea of dramatic divides and departures in which it would be essential to aurally capture the melding of a world of futuristic technology with the dusty grind of the Wild West. Perhaps somewhat similar to HBO's *Westworld*, there would be two different "worlds" in existence here between players starting in the futuristic lobby scene and then teleporting to the futuristic version of Calico: the lobby world being similar to the fictional *Westworld* laboratory with clean, light, minimalistic ambiences and Calico being similar to the fictional *Westworld* theme park: gritty, grimy, and very sound rich. This philosophy even applied to the music in which the team from Cedar Fair and Knott wanted us to think about having traditional Western topes meet hi-tech electro stylings. But with all of this in mind, it was absolutely imperative that the audio give the "vibe" and familiarity of Knott's Berry Farm's actual, real world ghost town area.

This was VRstudios' first project to utilize the specific combination of game and audio engines that had been selected (UE4/Wwise/Oculus Audio SDK), so our first priority was to conduct a technical test with implementing the plasma ball projectiles that emanate from the ranged robots' guns into the game engine and make sure that all worked properly. As we had already created the initial sound palette and the plasma projectile was all about being super positional and utilizing Doppler, it was a great test candidate (with the notion that the specific designed sounds and any attenuation settings would be adjusted as the game world got built). We needed to make sure that players could tell exactly where these projectiles were coming from, whatever the direction might be.

We also needed to decide what was absolutely important to be tightly spatialized and what could be in simple stereo. As I have mentioned previously, not all audio in a VR environment needs to be spatialized in a VR experience.

Audio must take kind of a hybrid approach, where some audio is spatialized and others can be rendered in simple stereo.

This was our first project utilizing the Oculus Audio SDK as we had used 3Dception in the past until the company, Two Big Ears, was acquired by Facebook, so I also had the team conduct a comparison test with the enemy projectiles with one test utilizing non-HRTF spatialization and the other utilizing Oculus. I had members of the development team listen to the comparison test and they reported a preference for the test that did not use the Oculus Audio SDK. They could tell that the Oculus test was more positional, but disliked the murkiness of the HRTF filtering. Our approach to "brightening" this up and making the sounds clear was to be selective about which sounds we put through the Oculus engine and which we did not. Plus, since many of the sounds that were going to be built would have multiple layers, the plan was to only use it on elements that were more critical to be spatialized. Certain layers would be spatialized through the Oculus engine and certain layers would not.

The Environmental Audio Design

The lobby is where the players start out prior to being teleported to Calico. It was imperative that we create a very satisfying and significant sound to mark the players' transition from the lobby to Calico. It needed to be "cinematic" so that you could really tell the transition was taking place, as well as being seamless and "swirly" with the accompanied animation. Additionally, in the lobby experience a little robot or "training bot" flies around the lobby space for players to shoot prior to being transported into the Western experience. This sequence was to help to teach users what to do and realize that it's a full spherical 360-degree space. So, audio was essential right from the beginning of the experience, as there had to be highly positional sound on the robot to encourage players to look all around as it flew around the lobby space.

Similar to *Barking Irons,* with regard to the Player Take Damage sounds, it was essential for the team to create very visceral sounds so that players could get a physical feeling and effect from being impacted from the enemies and the exploding train debris in the game. The requirement was that these sounds needed to signify deep consequences in order to make people feel even more immersed in the experience and motivate and incentivize them to duck from being hit by projectiles, rockets, lightning clubs, or debris. We took a similar approach to the sound design from *Barking Irons,* creating negative sounding electrostatic audio layers reinforced with some low-frequency content to provide that physiological effect.

And finally, we needed to develop the sound of the players' gun: a futuristic double-barrel laser-based weapon, rather than a realistic Western revolver. What was essential here was that the laser blasts needed to have a good amount of variation to them, as all four people would be constantly shooting. We definitely did not want any listener fatigue.

cinematic moments: the train and the finale boss battle sequence

While there were other cinematic moments in the game, the two really big ones were the speeding and exploding train, and the final battle against the Big Boss.

After the first wave of core robot attacks, the robots commandeer Steam Engine 41 in an effort to destroy the bank and expose the safe. The robots run the train too hot and end up creating a time distortion as the train steams into town. The train explodes through the time distortion and players must dodge the debris flying off the train (see the figure below).

Cinematic train explosion through a time distortion.

The first and foremost challenge we had to address was the creation of those initial train entrance sounds. Not only did we need to really get those iconic Knott's Berry Farm's Ghost Town and Calico Railroad sounds like whistles, chimes, and steam dialed in, but they had to be really attention-getting and highly spatialized. We had to make players turn their heads. The team also had to make the train "angrier" and aggressive sounding as it was running hot and going to explode. Low frequencies were utilized to reinforce the weight, mass, and feel of the train, as well as to reinforce the train explosion.

Next, in order to execute the big payoff for the sequence successfully, it was absolutely critical to use audio to sell the slo-mo effects, which made possible the perception of a distorted different timeline, as well as the effect of time returning to normal. The initial entrance into the time distortion was handled through a very cool bass drop effect. Initially we weren't quite getting enough of the slo-mo distortion effect from the sound, but ended up making it bigger, sharper, and more exaggerated, which led to a very satisfying "warpy" and distorted experience.

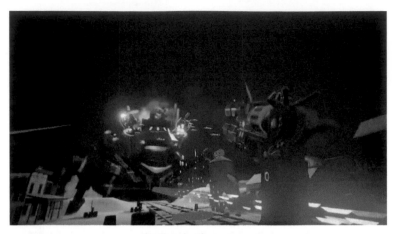

Big Boss battle sequence.

The Big Boss battle is the dramatic gameplay climax in *VR Showdown in Ghost Town* in which players must destroy the boss robot before he steals the safe (see the figure above). A critical objective was to make sure players connected with the Big Boss and its immense power. The sound needed to really create and emphasize a sense of scale and size, weight and mass, and to give the Big Boss its presence. The Big Boss robot entrance needed to be dramatic and cinematic: loud and attention-grabbing. After all, this was the big dramatic gameplay climax. Since the Boss was dropping out of a time portal with a heavy thud, the Boss itself had to sound heavy. The creative direction for the Boss was to think more like big sheets of metal moving into themselves and grating: giant and clunky.

The creative direction from the development team emphasized that great importance had to be placed on the positional projectile sounds of the Boss's rockets going past the player, the Boss rockets' impact sounds, and the sound of players shooting and destroying the Boss rockets: explosions which would also have to serve as very satisfying and clear success sounds. Projectile and impact sounds were to be very exaggerated. When the Boss' rockets hit the players, there needed to be slightly more intense static sizzle take damage sounds versus when the core robots hit the players.

Challenges Overcome

Because the environment was so sound rich, it was essential to set the priorities for the audio tracks. We had to think, "what are we missing in this environment and what are the important sounds the players need to hear? What needed to be huge and more cinematic, and what could be pushed back in the audio mix?"

For example, there are these enemy robot types called "melee robots" in the game. These characters spawn around the town and run up, carrying lightning clubs, to storm the players while lots of other things are going on around them in the environment (see the figure below). Specifically, when they get onto the train platform that the players are standing on, they activate their lightning clubs and charge at the players. Every time the melee robots' lightning clubs hit a player, they lose points, so players are required to dodge incoming attacks or shoot the robots before they get the chance to swing.

Melee robot attack.

Getting the makeup of the sounds just right for these types of robots, so people could actually hear them sneak up on them and not be overwhelmed, was crucial. We needed to create sounds that would be a big identifier/audio cue that would attract the players' attention. As the melee robots carried lightning clubs and then featured an exaggerated wind-up with their clubs prior to their attacks, it seemed a natural fit to create lightsaberesque activation and lightning crackle and sizzle sounds.

However, one of the biggest pieces of feedback that internal Knott's playtesters were reporting is that they couldn't detect when the melee robots were sneaking up behind them or out of their field of view (FOV). We tried adding footstep sounds which I was initially concerned about doing as there could be the possibility that the footsteps would get irritating for the players, and that perhaps melee identification/localization might have to be handled through the lightning club activation and wind-up. But because the melee robots appear so suddenly and we needed a more advanced audio cue warning, we thought it would be a good test to see if they worked or not. While the addition of the footstep sounds helped somewhat, they would get lost in the mix when action really started to ramp up. So, both the footsteps and the wind-up sounds for their lightning clubs weren't cutting through the mix with all the sonic blaster shooting between the four players. Those sounds were too subtle and were getting masked and overwhelmed when all four players were shooting rapidly. The team had to think about what would be a better sound that would be more attention-getting. The requirement for the sound was that it needed to be very clearly positional, alerting the players to look in that direction. I recalled the team having a similar issue in *Barking Irons* where we changed out the animatronic bandit spawning sounds to whipcracks so they would cut through the mix and players could locate them. We ended up going with these sort of robotic growls which ended up doing the trick. We also took the gun sounds down a bit in the mix in order to assist with highlighting the melee attacks even more.

As mentioned earlier, not all sounds work well as audio cues and not all sounds spatialize really well. It took a trip back to the drawing board to create the right kind of sounds that could spatialize well and cut through this super rich sound mix. That was a learning process which required experimentation in order to achieve success. This also goes back to the point I made with regard to *Barking Irons* in which it is essential to constantly be testing and iterating, particularly when it comes to your audio cues.

Music

Unlike the music system for *Barking Irons* which was designed as a layered intensity system, this system was designed as a branching one in which each track branched to a different track.

As there would be no physical source of the music in the game world, the music would be nondiegetic underscore and sit as a 2D stereo send that enveloped the world. This left room for the "appropriate" environmental audio to be spatialized. Also, the team from Cedar Fair and Knott's preferred the music not to emanate from an in-game source like the saloon, as they didn't want distracting and potentially irritating volume attenuations based on player movement.

I worked closely with Christian Dieckmann, Ken Parks, and the rest of the team from Cedar Fair and Knott's to determine the creative direction for the music. Our thoughts were to set the locale quickly with a more traditional Western styling and then transition into a modern mash-up of classical Western tropes with modern musical elements for the main gameplay sequences as the action picks up. Then we would go off into an electro, industrial, techno styling with orchestral elements for the Big Boss and Boss Battle sequence. The Boss music would actually go in the reverse direction of the main gameplay music, with the focus more on the techno and metal than on the classical instrumentation underneath. We also wanted the Boss music to be more sinister than the main gameplay music, but the general philosophy was to start with the traditional and go off with the new.

As per my usual practice, I like to start off with a short musical concept in order to make sure we were capturing the thoughts of what was discussed, particularly since when it comes to music, even when you have clear direction and reference tracks, there is still room for different interpretation. So, I first had the team create a 50-second draft musical sketch for the main gameplay environment music to demo how the music might play out, as well as its potential stylistic makeup which represented the blend of styles of pure Western and modern elements such as techno, electro, and rock. The sketch started with a sparse Western intro to set the tone of the Old West environment and to give players a sense of place and atmosphere for when they teleported in. It then transitioned to a more driving mash-up/blend of the old with the new modern musical elements that were more driving and epic, with a techno beat underneath for when the waves of robots begin attacking the players. The mash-up was a hybrid of epic Spaghetti Western and driving techno/synth elements. Adding in the electro elements versus just rock ones gave the sketch a more sci-fi mechanistic feel that would tie in better when we did the Boss music sketch.

Furthermore, I suggested adding a "galloping" beat, as Ramin Djawadi had done so skillfully in his adaptation of the Rolling Stones' "Paint It Black" from the HBO adaptation of *Westworld*, to our track to increase the intensity, drive, and tension, and invoke the feeling of the Old West. For me, it was essential that the team provide an emotional impact and connection with the main gameplay music. As in the reference track of Ennio Morricone's "Frank's Theme" from *Once Upon a Time in the West* that I had provided, the lead melodic line is quite emotive, lyrical, and expressive. This is something I absolutely wanted the team to achieve. Once Knott's was happy with the sketch, we would wait to fully develop that music out in conjunction with the gameplay mechanics.

For the music that would play during the Boss finale, I wanted to make sure that the team incorporated lower register instrumentation or ones that have a "heavy" presence to them like timpani and double bass, as I wanted to portray who the Boss is musically, as he is this big, bad, menacing gargantuan of a robot. So, the music had to be bass-heavy and resonant. Also, he's not super agile so the initial concept sketches needed to be not quite as driving as the main gameplay music sketch. I instructed the team to keep some of the Western essence in the Boss theme/Boss Battle sequence music, as the Western phrasing tied the two pieces of music together. I didn't want this dramatic departure with the Boss so now you think you are in a sci-fi game. So, I wanted the Boss' music to be distinct and not like you are just hearing a variation of the main gameplay music, but it also is not so vastly different that now you think you're in a totally different game altogether. Hence, why I wanted to share some elements from the main gameplay theme with the Boss' theme. So, I advised the team to identify the unique Western motifs and phrases from the main gameplay music sketch and to use them in the Boss's music, but have them show up on different instrumentation and/or make them even more sinister sounding by using more minor or diminished chords.

One of the things I wanted my team to do was to add a fuzzy lead guitar mirroring the main melody to bring out some of the rock elements against the orchestral elements. Based on further conversations I had with Knott's, I instructed the team to add in some more electro and rock elements to enhance the track while keeping the orchestral underpinnings to maintain the track's power. I wanted the team to punch up the "futuristic" angle by perhaps adding an additional electro synth line, not a lead but something highly present in the mix. We had to keep the track a little less orchestral and a little more guitar/industrial/gritty, as while the main gameplay music should emphasize more of the orchestral, the Boss music flips that around/reverses direction and should emphasize the electro/fuzzy guitar/gritty combo. The two are sort of mirror images of each other.

Once the sketch was approved, we built out the Boss's music in parallel with the actual gameplay. The team also had to create two different branching ending musical stingers based on whether you defeat the Boss or the Boss escapes.

Music needed always to be complementary to the events in the game, "directing" musical moments to accentuate the game play experience for the player (see the figure below).

Just as the emotional arc of a game's narrative structure can be visualized and mapped out based upon the intensity, emotion, and feel of player interaction, those same elements of the audio design can be mapped out, creating a meaningful and dynamic emotional state. Narrative audio maps are graphical tools and techniques that provide a visual foundation or roadmap for crafting deep emotional resonance, great drama, smooth transitions, continuity, and flow within a game level or environment. They also help develop the structure and pacing of the gameplay's narrative and action and aid in the creation of smooth changes in intensity and musical styles, as well as natural transitions to other narrative moments. The process of detailing the narrative arc of a level's audio follows the exact same steps as mapping the story and gameplay elements within a level.

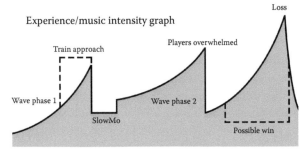

VR showdown in ghost town experience/music intensity graph.

In my experience, the team must answer critical questions that will shape the direction of the musical score: What are the roles that music will play in this world and game? What is its purpose? Most importantly, how are we effectively conveying the narrative through the music? We had to be thoughtful of how the music represented the narrative and gameplay within the game, while taking into consideration the pacing of narrative and gameplay: peaks and troughs, levels of tension and relaxation, conflict and resolution. These would represent elements of great drama through the musical choreography of the level or environment: the journey, exploration and discovery, obstacles or challenges, conflict and resolution.

Conclusion

Audio can and should be an integral design element from the start, conveying elements of narrative, characterization, or gameplay by itself and in concert with other game elements. Audio must be more than a list of assets to be compiled and assembled like the items on a shopping list. Rather than just coupling each of the visual elements of a game with a corresponding functional sound element, audio should always further the goals of story, characterization, and the creation of a holistic ecosystem.

Well-executed sounds and a brilliantly composed soundtrack have minimal value when accompanied by nothing more than surface meaning. The techniques discussed provide ways for an entire production team to work together in order to create a cohesive, holistic unit of all the elements as well as a "rhythm" within a game experience.

Games can and should aspire to delivering more impactful experiences by taking into account that sound enhances the underlying meaning of the experience in a very personal way and contributes to a deeper meaning within a game.

Further Reading

Audiokinetic Wwise Documentation, 2017. Retrieved March 2017 from https://www.audiokinetic.com/library/2015.1.3_5488/?source=Help&id=position_editor_3d_user_defined).

C. Summers, V. Lympouridis, and C. Erkut, "Sonic interaction design for virtual and augmented reality environments," presented at the Sonic Interactions for Virtual Environments (SIVE), 2015 IEEE VR Workshop, 2015.

C. Summers, M. Jesse, "Creating immersive and aesthetic auditory spaces in virtual reality," presented at the Sonic Interactions for Virtual Environments (SIVE), 2017 IEEE VR Workshop, 2017.

C. Summers, "Chapter 7 making the most of audio in characterization, narrative structure, and level design," *Level Design Processes and Experiences*, CRC Press, 2016.

creation and implementation: putting it into practice

working with the new realities

So far we have defined concepts, presented issues and challenges, and observed how other practitioners have dealt with some of these challenges. Here I want to start to discuss solutions and processes that we can use in creating sound for the new realities. Key to all of this is thinking and designing spatial content.

One of the key aspects of spatial audio is designing and creating an audio environment that has a sense of presence all around the audience and elements to focus on. This adds to the audience's agency by providing more content to interact with. As the audience decides where they will place their focus, the world responds to create a unique perspective based on how the audience chooses to interact and position themselves in the world. Looking left instead of looking right results in the elements of the audio world being perceived differently.

Agency comes from the choices the audience makes and how much they are able to influence their own experience.

As sound designers, we need to populate a virtual world with sounds that highlight the environment and support the narrative elements of the experience. Sometimes this will require sparse and subtle content and at other times it will require masses of sounds that mix and blend in what may seem like a cacophony but must still be considered and well planned. We know of the various weaknesses of both the current technology and of humans' hearing so we must accommodate those weaknesses and create an experience that still engages the audience.

Placement

Where you choose to place a sound source defines how it will be heard in a virtual world. But, as with all things we can exaggerate and enhance the content we create. We might place birds at the top of a tree and crickets at the bottom of a tree and then if the experience shifts to represent the summer months we might swap the bird sounds for the sounds of cicadas at the top of a tree. If you want cicadas to really feel like they are up in the tree-tops then maybe the best solution is to position them even higher than the tree. This may really sell the idea of the cicadas being positioned above the listener and create the sense of elevation. This is the theater craft approach we can take to enhance what we do. So in the same way a stage actor wears overdone face makeup and a stage whisper is closer to a soft shout, we can utilize a level of exaggeration and extension to help convey certain messages to our audience.

A string quartet in real life is placed in a loose semicircle so the sound emits from one group; the musicians can all communicate but at the same time they are all facing toward an audience. This comes from a balance of factors that presents an interesting experience for the audience. In VR we can position the audience inside the quartet and position the musicians all around the audience in a full circle. This placement would be impractical in the real world where the quartet must play to a larger audience, but in VR everyone can be in the optimal position. This layout would allow more separation and may enhance the spatial effect in a desirable way. The only way to be sure would be to try it and see what happens.

Obviously, we need to place sounds close to where we would expect them to be in real life. Birds sing from the tops of the trees and crickets sing from under the ground beneath the tree. So unless we want to create a completely fantastical environment where real-world rules and expectations are ignored, there is a level of realism we will usually work toward. We can however balance how we implement our sounds and where we place them to maximize the spatial effect.

Implementation

If you were to add the sounds of birds to the top of a 3D tree model in a game world and the sounds of crickets at the bottom, then each time you placed a tree you would have a sound source positioned in your world in an acceptable location. Birds and crickets often place themselves in and around trees so it is a natural concept to link them to the tree models and propagate the world in that manner. Where there are trees there are birds, where there are fewer trees there are fewer birds, and so on. I have done this for traditional screen-based video games and I know it works. Using this process for VR and AR would also work. We expect a dense forest to be more populated with birds and insects than an open plane, so the association with the tree model and the sound emitters is logical and practical.

If you find in certain areas the density of trees creates a massive overload of birds and it sounds unrealistic then with most audio tools it is fairly simple to dial back the number of sounds playing. There is usually a weighting, or "chance to trigger" function in most audio tools. Set this to 50% and then only one in every two trees on average has sounds emanating from it. These are very simple implementation techniques, but they give effective results.

Min and Max Distance Functions and Attenuation Curves

Many audio tools designed to position sound sources into a 3D world have functions called min and max distance. Short for minimum and maximum distance, these functions allow you to tune the behavior of attenuation over distance for your positional sounds. Minimum distance defines how far a sound will travel at

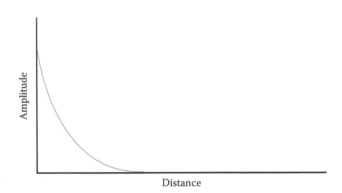

Normal attenuation curve with no minimum distance defined.

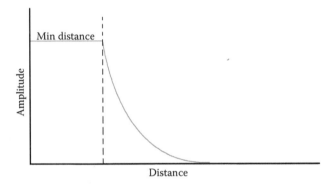

Minimum distance increases how far the sound plays at its set volume;
this pushes out the overall distance the sound can be heard.

the amplitude you have defined before it starts to drop off (attenuate). A min distance of zero means that a sound will immediately attenuate from the point it is played from. If the min distance is set to 10 meters and the playback volume is set to 10dB then the sound will emanate in all directions at 10dB and sustain that 10dB value all the way out to 10 meters (in game meters). Beyond 10 meters the sound will attenuate based on the drop-off curve shape you have defined. In this example, maybe the sound is for a giant piece of machinery and you want it to be very loud and for that sound to carry for 10 meters before it starts to get quieter.

Max or maximum distance is the point at which a sound will stop attenuating and from that point on will maintain the volume it has reached forever (unless there is a hard distance cut-off that sometimes is used for resource management). The combination of min distance,

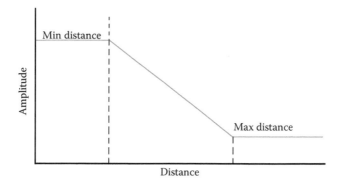

Applying a max distance value defines where the sound will stop
attenuating. This image also has a linear drop-off applied to the sound.

max distance, and drop-off curve type allows you significant control
over how sounds behave. This is an excellent set of tools for tuning
any 3D environmental sounds, but for spatial audio these tools can
significantly affect the overall effect.

Min distance is a useful tool for making a sound carry further,
without having to increase its base volume level. Any increase in the
min distance value will push the entire attenuation curve further
away from the point the sound is emanating from and as a consequence the sound will travel further and be louder at each distance
point than it previously was. So if a sound is too quiet at 100 meters,
but is the right volume at 1 meter, you can increase the min distance,
push the entire attenuation curve further out and the 100-meter
point will be louder.

Alternatively switching from a logarithmic drop-off curve to a linear drop-off curve would also increase the amplitude at the 100 meter
mark without expanding the initial maximum volume region. The
choice of which method to adopt depends entirely on what you decide
provides the best results for your project. Each of the different possible attenuation curves will shape how your sound behaves over
distance. With many tools the values for min distance, max distance,
and curve type can be set per sound source so you can shape each
and every sound if you have the need.

For spatial audio though, adjustments to min distance values can
have other consequences for your environment. Spatial audio relies
on point sources of sounds being positioned around the listener.
As we turn our heard we hear the sound at 2 o'clock and the sound
at 6 o'clock relative to our position. If we turn our head back and

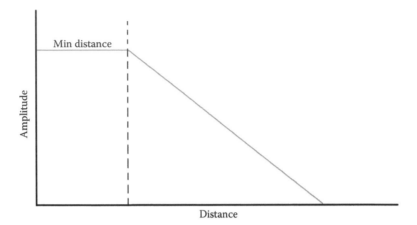

Different drop-off curves will also alter how the sound changes over distance.

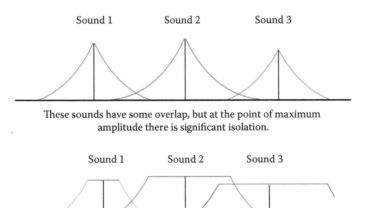

These sounds have some overlap, but at the point of maximum
amplitude there is significant isolation.

Sound 1   Sound 2   Sound 3

The significant overlap of these sounds will likely impact
the spatial separation for this scene.

forth those positional sounds provide anchored points of reference.
We localize where they are and our brain becomes comfortable that
we can hear two sounds from two locations. If we need to significantly increase the min distance of one of those sounds we are effectively expanding how much area that sound occupies. Its circle of
maximum volume gets bigger so the sound starts to be a volumetric
sound. The problem with this is that it can overlap with other sounds
and then we may start to lose the sense of spatialization.

In the above figure, we can see three sound sources. The verti-
cal lines indicate the position of each sound and their maximum
volume level. None of these sounds has a min distance defined and so

they attenuate immediately. The drop-off curves indicate how the volume drops as you move away from the position of each sound. There is some amount of overlap between sounds 1 and 2, and sounds 2 and 3, but in both cases the sounds have attenuated so much that if you moved from the sound at position 1 toward the sound at position 2 there would be no ambiguity as to the positions of each sound.

When min distance values are defined for all three sounds each of the sounds now covers a greater area at their set volume before they start to attenuate. This results in significant crossover between the sounds. But it is not just that there is crossover as the sounds are attenuating. In this diagram sound 2 and sound 3 share a region where they are both at their set maximum volumes. From an audience's perspective as they turn their head left and right there is no clear line where sound 2 ends and sound 3 starts. They bleed into each other. Sometimes this may not be an issue and ensuring the sounds are audible across the environment is a higher priority, so the sacrifice of spatial isolation is an acceptable payoff. But this illustrates that the technique of working with min and max distance to balance volume levels can have a significant impact on the openness of a spatial mix.

Reverb

Achieving accuracy in spatialization is something that has been discussed in several parts of this book. The cost and difficulty in calculating accurate room reflection is something that is going to be a challenge for spatial audio for some time. But this doesn't mean that we should avoid using reverb. In fact, reverb is a critical method of grounding an audience into an environment. I am playing a console game currently and the reverb applied to the character voices is really strange. All the environment sounds seem to match the world space pretty well but the character dialogue all sounds like people are speaking from big echoing rooms. It is distracting and reduces the feeling that the characters are actually in the same room you are. So if reverb can do this for a regular screen-based game, then it can have a significant impact on virtual experiences.

Our goal as always is to create content that is engaging and enjoyable, and sometimes it needs to be accurate and carefully crafted. So the math is the basis for our decisions. We rely on programmers to effectively apply the math to create the tools we can work with. When it comes to crafting an experience, we also use the math as a basis for what we create. But just because I am building the audio for a 10 × 10 room does not mean I set the reverb to a 10 × 10 space and leave it at that. Often there will be a variety of factors that will influence how the sound for that space needs to respond in the experience. As I craft the sounds and apply reverb, many of the decisions come down to how it all feels and importantly how it makes the audience feel.

I mentioned earlier that often all we need is a point of difference. We need the audience to understand that we have stepped inside away from an open environment. Accurate placement of sound objects within a space that allows a human to localize the position of the sound is a desirable result for spatial audio. Sometimes that accuracy is critical to an experience and we just need to achieve an appropriate sense of space. If all we need is that sense of change, then any reverb that matches the feel of the room we have entered will provide the desired feedback for the audience. More often than not the math will result in the best sound being the reflections for the 10 × 10 room we have just created. At the very least those are the best values to start with.

If our project does require absolute localization accuracy, then that is our goal. If a project is designed for a serious purpose and the user must be able to accurately locate a sound source as often as possible then our task is to utilize the functionality we have to achieve that (as much as it is possible with any particular technology).

Our audience may not understand how reverb works,
but they can feel when something sounds wrong.

This however does not affect how we approach our sound design. We may start with absolutely accurate physics modeling and values designed to achieve accurate spatial positioning, but the end result is what matters. If we find that the best result is to add reflections as if the room were 100 × 100 and 9 out of 10 people who listen to the experience report these values make them feel that the object is positioned correctly then the end does justify the means. As we have discussed multiple times, there are so many factors involved, so many challenges to overcome, and quite a few weaknesses in human perceptions to account for that we may often need to approach certain challenges in unusual ways.

Reverb can also be a costly effect to apply. How you set up your specific software and project can define how efficient it is, especially for real-time processing. If you have a complex room environment with multiple sound sources and lots of furniture and other objects, it could be practical to apply various reverbs to the different sound sources. Instead of trying to calculate all the expensive math to account for the room size, the multiple surface materials, and the many objects, you could apply a muted reverb to the sound sources that are positioned near the bed and the curtained window and more live reverb to the objects emitting sound near the open door to the bathroom and mirrored closet. A set of reverbs based on objects and their immediate environmental circumstances may provide a convincing result without needing to try and calculate all the reflections for all the objects within the room.

The nature of new reality technology and the fact that we all need to relearn many of the creative methods we are used to working with also means we have a certain level of freedom to try out new and unusual techniques and see what might work. Applying reverb on a per sound source basis rather than as a blanket effect on a room may not work at all, or it may work some of the time. I am about to try this process on a new VR project. Unfortunately, I may not have time to report my findings before this book is finished. I can say with certainty that many of the people I know working in various areas of production for the new realities are trying out all sorts of techniques just to see what might happen.

Breaking Our Sounds for Better Implementation

Spatial audio provides both challenges and opportunities for audio designers to create new types of content. Often our approach to audio for spatial implementation is going to be very different to what we are used to. The idea of cutting up sounds from their traditional format to implement them better in a spatial domain is a new concept that I am still experimenting with.

As is often the case, this concept came about mostly by accident. Through a process of having to compensate for something I thought I had done wrong, I discovered that in fact the process had been done in the best possible way, I just didn't realize it at the time.

The initial idea came from recording firearms. For this project, I traveled to collect the raw material, so I was recording live military firearms on an open range. Most people have heard a gunshot either in a film or in a game—the usual bang sound followed by the long tail echo as the sound travels in the environment. I was very used to this sound as I had been trained in firing military weapons as part of basic training when I was in the army, but I had forgotten exactly how it sounded from the shooter's perspective.

When you hold and aim a rifle it is essentially right next to your ear. Hopefully you are wearing some kind of hearing protection, but even so, the sound of the rifle going bang is extremely loud. It's a single sharp point of focus for the shooter. It also has an extreme proximity because of where the gun is in relation to your ear. This means when you shoot a rifle the tail of the sound is far less notice-able because your brain is still processing the initial bang. There is also an element that you are concentrating on where you are aiming, so your focus is not on the overall complete sound, your ears still hear the tail of the sound, but you may notice it less.

When we represent a gunshot in a film or game, we tend to trigger a sound file and attach it to the location of the gun. The gun is in 3D space, we attach a sound emitter to it, and it goes bang. The sound event itself may often be made up of multiple layers or elements, but they are usually all located at the position of the weapon. In VR or AR, if we are trying to immerse the audience then I think we can improve the results for many sounds by splitting the elements apart.

If I fire a rifle, the bang is right next to me, so in VR the bang impulse should be located on the virtual rifle I am holding. But the echo tail should be located off in the distance, possibly at several locations and it should wrap around and envelop me as the bang echoes off the surrounding environment. This contrast between a loud sound at close proximity and then a fading tail positioned off in the distance I think would produce an effect that would really high-light the open space the audience was in when they fired the rifle.

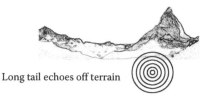

Long tail echoes off terrain

Short impulse from firing

The immediate impulse of firing the rifle is close,
but the tail can be very distant.

A similar effect occurs when you are driving a car. The sound of the engine emanates from the front of the car you are in as the engine is positioned in front of the driver. But if you drive past a wall or a series of posts you can hear the sound reflect off those surfaces. The reflection sound is a distorted version of the engine sound, but it comes from the surface it has reflected from, not from the engine bay.

If we have correct physics modeling of sound behavior then our system would simulate all of this correctly. But if we do not have that capability we can still simulate this behavior in several ways. Utilizing dynamic sound emitters to broadcast echoes from any location that might bounce back various sounds is one approach. We may simplify the exact physics behavior to provide a simple feedback echo, but in many cases this is likely to convince the audience that they are experiencing the echo as it might sound in the real world.

Gunshots, vehicle sounds, and characters yelling across a valley, instead of just adding some reverb to a sound effect we should consider how that sound would behave in a certain environment and plan for how we could divide the sound up so the reflections can be spatialized in a more convincing manner. I have suggested in several places in this book that if the physics and math cannot be fully utilized in our projects then the use of smoke and mirrors techniques is completely valid. Whatever it takes to make our content sound as good as possible and enjoyable to the audience is our primary goal.

"Observation" of Audio

This observation activity is based on an exercise that many teachers of sound design and location recording set for students. It requires careful and analytical listening of your environment. I have heard so many students say "oh yeah, we've done that, it's easy." Hearing is easy, listening is a skill many of us have either forgotten or never developed in the first place. The very first instance when I discussed this exercise with some students is probably the best example of why this is so important.

I was guest lecturing at a specialist institution for advanced film and television students. These were postgraduate students who had mostly done some audio production during their studies. I had heard about the listening test and so I thought I would try it out with this group. So I asked the question:

What can we hear in this space right now?

It was a standard classroom in a large building, so it was mostly quiet, with very few reflections in the room and glass windows thick enough to remove most outside noise. But after a couple of minutes I got the following responses from the students:

- Air-conditioning fan
- Voices from adjacent classroom

  From all six students present that was all they could "hear" within their classroom. I asked them was that all? They stopped for a second, looked at each other and told me that "yes, that was all they could hear." So I updated their list with the sounds I could hear in that exact same space.

Do not underestimate what you might hear from an empty room.

- Air-conditioning fan
- Voices from adjacent classroom
- Ride-on lawnmower outside the window
- The very quiet, but audible classroom clock
- Student A tapping their pencil
- Student B's squeaky chair as they moved around
- Student B's rustling pencil case
- Student C's zipper moving on their jacket
- Student C tapping their foot gently
- Student D's felt tip pen writing on their notebook
- Student D's jacket "creaking" as they moved
- Faint footsteps down the hall
- A door opening somewhere down the hall

Once I listed all these sounds the students agreed they could hear all of them, but they realized they had been blocking them all out. These were "nothing" sounds. Everyday sounds that we remove from our thought process as they are not important. This is understandable as we are constantly barraged by so many sounds that we need to block many out just to be able to concentrate on the ones most important to us. But it was revealing that even when asked to note all sounds in their environment, the students still blocked out so much. It was even more surprising when dealing with advanced students who had worked with audio before.

So why is this exercise useful or even relevant to the study of audio for the new technology formats? Listening is always relevant for audio people. It is our most critical sense and like any other skill it is something we must maintain and develop. But further than that, analyzing different sounds in different spaces can help us evolve our understanding of spatial audio, how we react to it, and how it reacts to our environment.

Standing still and closing your eyes for a few seconds when you are out shopping, at the movies, or out to dinner can reveal how audio propagates and behaves within the environments you are visiting. How strong are the reflections in this café full of people eating? Can you understand exactly what the people at the table next to you are saying? What about two tables over? Three? Is that group in the corner booth with all the mirrors on the wall really louder than everyone else or is the combination of walls and materials artificially amplifying their conversation across the café? How does the sound change each time the waiter comes out of the kitchen and the doors open? How do the sounds of the kitchen from the serving window blend with the door opening when the door swings open?

These are simple concepts in many ways, but if you were to try and accurately recreate this environment in 3D space using object-based audio and HRTF plugins it would be an incredibly complex project.

As I type this, I am sitting in my studio space. It is a small room with a desk and a computer. There are some acoustic panels on the wall to reduce reflections. I can hear the fan operating behind me because it is a warm summer's day. Occasionally I hear a creak of the wooden floorboards as our house shifts and creaks. Often I can hear the footsteps of one of our cats walking into my room. It is so quiet where we live that I can hear the soft pads on the cat's feet on the wooden floor. I can hear cicadas outside my window. They must be in just a single tree because they appear to be localized to only one point in space, not across a wider area outside. I can hear a bird call; it sounds distant, further away than the cicadas.

The fan sound is interesting because it is blowing air in my direction. Does that mean it is blowing the sound waves as well? Does the sound of the fan at the front project further than from behind? The fan is also the loudest sound in my studio right now, apart from my typing on the keyboard. If I listen carefully, I can discern the combination of direct sound of the fan from behind and slight reflected sound from the walls. The behavior of sound in my room would be quite complex if we analyze it.

My floor is wooden floorboards. The walls are standard plasterboard but I have added some acoustic treatment. In some regions there are corrugated foam panels and in other places material screens. Two of the four walls are entirely windowed from half way up the walls, but these windows also have roller blinds that can be pulled down. There is a desk, a work bench, a cupboard, a glass display case, a hanging rack for audio cables, my office chair, and a table made out of an old upright piano. I mention all of these elements because accounting for all of them to accurately model sound behavior would be incredibly complex and costly.

The listening exercise I mentioned earlier is a way that you can analyze a space and target the important elements. My room is small, but not very reverberant because of the acoustic treatment. The significant number of plants and trees outside the windows means there

Studio space.

will likely be the sounds of birds or insects. These sounds would be audible, but quiet and frequency-filtered due to sound passing through the window. Specifically, spatialized sounds could be placed to represent a sound source outside the window to recreate this or a more general ambience could be applied from that general direction.

This is where we can target specific creative decisions. Is there a need to go to the trouble of creating specific and accurate spatialization for the outside sound sources to recreate my studio space? Does this accuracy and the effort it takes benefit the project of recreating my room sonically? If there is a reason to draw the audience's attention to something important to the narrative outside my window, then the answer might be yes, but if the only purpose of those sounds is to add a level of authenticity to the environment that we can hear something of the world outside the window, then the time, effort, and resources put into accurately modeling the outside space could probably be better spent elsewhere.

This applies to every aspect of my room in this example and every aspect of any project in the broader sense of this example. To achieve 100% accurate modeling of sound behavior would be an awesome outcome for every project, but only if it is possible to achieve this within the constraints of budget, processing resources, and within the person hours available for development. Right now it is not possible at all to have 100% accurate sound behavior, so we must decide as part of the planning process which characteristics we can utilize and where we will apply them to achieve the best results. In many ways nothing has changed from when film was limited to a single mono recording with no editing or mixing possible. There were limitations then and there are still limitations now. How we manage those limitations defines our craft.

working analysis

Take a look at this photo of a road construction site. In this next section I will use this scene to demonstrate some of the elements that

Road construction in Sannohe, Japan.

you may need to consider and different approaches to recreating this scene in a 3D virtual environment.

The construction site pictured above is in some ways a very simple environment to discuss as there is only a single vehicle operating, but do not underestimate the challenge even this simple environment presents.

Sannohe is a small country town in Aomori, northern Japan. The curving road that is being repaired is the main street; the road on the right-hand side of the photo is a small road that crosses a nearby bridge over the local river. In the middle of any weekday this street has little traffic and in general this is a small, quiet farming town. This information will determine the additional ambiences in the space and also indicates that there are no large buildings of any sort just out of shot. The buildings on the left are typical of all other buildings around this scene.

To recreate this as a 1:1 scale VR experience the asphalt roller is obviously the main source of sound in this scene, so we will start with that. The 1:1 scaling is the most critical aspect of creating an accurate sound model for this experience. As we are trying to recreate a real world realistic experience, it allows us to gather data in a few ways.

Amplitude Drop-Off

In some ways this is the easiest aspect to figure out. If we have just taken that photo with the aim of recreating the scene in VR we can calculate the drop-off of the machine's sound by simply walking away. Turn and walk down the road in any direction; how far can we travel and still hear the roller? Is it still audible when we turn the corner up the road and the buildings are blocking direct line of sight? If we walk in the other direction where the road is straight (off to the left of the photo) are we able to walk further and still hear the roller?

If we really wanted accurate information we could do the same thing and carry a decibel meter to record precise drop-off information over distance. This would let us model accurate attenuation behavior for our virtual street scene. I suggest this method for two reasons. Obviously, we could just measure the output level of the roller and then apply physics and calculate that the sound will drop off to X level over Y distance. That's what physics tells us. Except that the physics of sound attenuation is affected by a great many factors that in the real world can complicate things significantly. The process of measuring every possible factor at this location and how they contribute to the sound attenuation would be a massive undertaking and only really useful if our purpose is an absolutely accurate modeling of this space for scientific purposes. To create a virtual environment for a game or video experience what is more important to us is how the sound behaves in the environment and how we can recreate that. So the practical approach of literally walking down the road and listening and maybe measuring the output at various locations is an easy way to map out the behavior you are about to recreate.

In many ways it does not matter WHY the attenuation might be far more than estimated if you walk left down the road and far less than estimated if you walk right. What is important is that for some reason a factor within the environment has influenced the behavior of the sound to achieve that result. We know the sound is behaving in this fashion because we can hear it. So a practical approach is to accept the behavior we hear and model it into our virtual experience. The alternative of trying to figure out what characteristics of physics is causing this behavior and then trying to accurately model it into a simulation is unlikely to be worth the effort.

So the listening test seems fairly straightforward, but there are more than a few variables to consider. The first is how we address the virtual model of the roller.

There is no visible exhaust pipe in that photo, so we could assume the exhaust pipe is at the back of the machine facing the rear. This is important for a couple of reasons. Firstly, as our project will be 1:1 scale, we should really add an emitter to the 3D model of the roller that plays the exhaust sound at exactly the same location as the real exhaust pipe. So if we walk around the roller as it operates, the sound of the exhaust is emitted from the exhaust pipe's location. Most games do not include multiple emitters for an object, opting to simply place a single emitter somewhere around the center of the object. But representing a model at full scale means the audience can lean down or even kneel next to the exhaust pipe and listen to exactly where the sound is generated. So every aspect of the roller that we want to produce sound should have those sounds emitted from the location where those sounds would be produced on the real-world roller. It doesn't matter exactly where the exhaust is located, more that we need to account for that point as being the emitter for exhaust sounds and that it may project sound directionally.

This positioning is also directly relevant to how the sounds are perceived and their attenuation, and many other aspects of sound production. If the exhaust pipe faces to the rear then it emits a direct sound focused to the rear. So standing behind the roller is like standing in front of a trumpet player. The sound source is pointing directly at you and so will be loudest at this point. The sound will also travel further to the rear of the roller as it has a direct path. If you move to the front of the roller, you will likely still hear its exhaust sound, but it will be quieter and almost certainly the frequency content will be filtered in some way. So in this case the output sound of the roller is being affected by the roller itself. This means if you walk away from the roller to its front the attenuation will be different, the volume will drop faster and the overall sound will be different. If we move to the sides of the roller we will have a different result again, and each side should be unique.

So far we have not even considered environmental reflections or absorption, nor how the weather and humidity may be affecting the sound over distance. Just dealing with the physical shape and design of the roller alone for one aspect of the sound has exposed a variety of challenges in simulating this scene. If we add in the environment, we have the hard road surface behind the roller that will reflect the exhaust sounds, but in front of the roller we have the newly-poured road surface. The asphalt will be hot, porous, and generally more absorbent of sound waves than the aged hardened road behind the roller. So this is an additional factor that may influence how the sound waves to the front of the roller are affected. This would also change the sound to the rear of the roller as it moves forward.

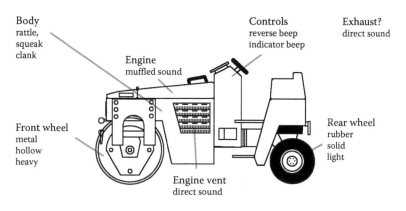

All sounds influenced by road surface

Diagram of roller with potential sound sources marked.

As the exhaust moves over the fresh asphalt the sound emanating from the rear of the roller would probably change.

The large concrete building to the rear is more likely to reflect sound back as echoes or reverb than the lower wooden buildings to the sides and front, and the curving street provides a very interesting echo "canal" along which the reflections can travel. The shop windows at street level on the wooden building would also result in some interesting reflections of high-frequency content. However, all these reflections will likely disperse quite quickly as the open sky will allow a lot of the energy to escape the immediate location. So in general this is an outdoor environment with the typical outdoor reverb you might expect with a few buildings that may generate some reflected sound waves.

In a few short pages we have only dealt with the sound of the roller's engine exhaust. The roller itself will also be producing sound from the engine hidden under the front end. This sound is less direct than the exhaust and is shielded by the structure of the roller, but will include more of the overall mechanical elements of the engine operating than the exhaust output. With many vehicles the engine sound may change significantly as you walk around the vehicle. There is the obvious difference between the engine at the front and the exhaust at the rear, but many engines will have more subtle changes as you position yourself around the vehicle. A fan belt or other drive element on one side, pistons more clearly audible from a specific angle, turbines, fans, and other mechanical elements that may be clearly audible from one angle and almost inaudible if you take a step in either direction. I am potentially being overly detailed here in my description, but all of these elements can combine to create a more convincing and accurate simulation of a real-world environment.

The roller wheel will produce different sounds depending on the surface it moves over. The rollers are often partially hollow and so will resonate internally as they roll. When rolling over the hot asphalt there will be much less resonance as the asphalt will dampen both the internal resonance of the roller as well as any external vibrations. If the roller is traveling over loose gravel the surface will constantly shift, crack, or shatter under the weight. These sounds may reflect off the bottom surface of the vehicle and also off the road surface if the gravel is laid onto a hard road surface. So in this case we have a vehicle that is creating multiple sound sources within its own structure—some of these which resonate within it before they are affected by environmental reflections.

This analysis could be applied to any vehicle or piece of machinery. I chose the roller because it is an unusual device and in this photo it is in a setting that is slightly familiar but also different enough to get most people's attention. This makes the analysis easier as we often tend to overlook the objects that we see each day. We all know what a standard passenger car sounds like and how it is built, and sometimes this familiarity does breed the "contempt" of us thinking we know what we are hearing. An industrial roller has a functionality and design different enough that we can look at it and ask ourselves "what am I hearing?" But when we do sit back and ask that question it can be surprising just how complex a device like this is, and how many factors in the environment can affect its sound behavior. In most cases all those factors contribute equally to the sound produced by our family car.

I am taking this analysis to extremes for a reason. We would seldom ever want or need to accurately model an industrial roller in a VR experience. If our goal was to entertain then anything that sounds a bit like a roller would probably be enough for most people. If our goal is to educate then the only sound behavior that is really important is that specific to the education topic. If our goal is to sell an industrial roller to a client then does the sound matter at all? The quality of any content depends on the purpose of the product and often on the budget. There will be times when simple audio content will suit the purpose of a project, but in many cases high-quality audio can be a significant differentiator.

Lots of time and money has been spent over the years to improve graphics and interaction functionality for computer programs. As the content gets better and better the money spent results in smaller improvements in the experience. The quality curve reaches a plateau and more and more money needs to be spent for smaller improvements. Audio is still one of the key areas where an overall improvement of the experience can be achieved by moderate spending. So the level of detail used in the example of the industrial roller experience would create a detailed and engaging experience for the audience. So whether it is for sales purposes, entertainment, or education, applying this level of detail to the roller audio will make the entire representation of this piece of machinery more realistic and more convincing.

When applied to a game experience the sound of the roller could be used to significantly impact the narrative of the story. Does it hide the play by covering their movement sounds? Does it interfere with the play as they try to track an opponent? Does the sound of the roller indicate life in an otherwise abandoned town? In all of these examples the accuracy of the sound could have a direct impact on both gameplay and narrative. For a serious application, the accurate modeling may be useful in informing local government if planned equipment purchases align with town noise regulations or allow direct comparisons between models. While it is unlikely that a council would care how noisy a piece of machinery is, it might be relevant.

Regardless of the purpose, a detailed analysis of a piece of equipment and its environment provides considerable information that allows for more accurate design and modeling of that sound behavior. Exactly which aspects are utilized in the design and how they are implemented is always up to the team and what works best for their needs.

creating a VR clock

Feel free to use the following analysis as a practical tutorial for how to approach the creation and implementation of audio of a new reality project. Choose an object relevant to your own interests and apply the theory as you go through this section.

Creating a physical sound source in the real world is easy. I can place a ticking clock onto a table in front of me and suddenly I have a continuous sound source. But what does that exactly mean? Only by understanding the characteristics that make up a "real" object can we precisely model how that object needs to function in a virtual space. So let's take a look at each of the elements of my clock and consider how we would address them in a virtual space.

The Actual Sound of a Clock

A clock is a good example for us to work with in a virtual space. It is a perpetual looping sound, but also one made up of shorter, transient sounds. To recreate the sound of our clock we could probably get away with a very short sample and setting it to loop. A correctly functioning clock will have little to no difference to each cycle as it functions. So each tic-toc is essentially exactly the same. To create a virtual clock, we need to record our real clock, trim our sample to ensure it loops cleanly, and then set it up to loop endlessly.

Accuracy and Detail

For a project where the clock is important I want to ensure I record the clock sound with a sensitive microphone, placed as close as physically possible. It is not just the tic-toc that is important. In the real world, I can move right up to the clock, place my ear almost against it and hear all the details of the inner workings, the gears and springs all combining to produce the clockwork action of the clock. From a distance of a few feet it may only sound like a simple tic-toc sound, but up closer I need to include a much more detailed set of sounds.

This level of detail is more important than it may initially seem. It depends on how the clock object in your experience is going to be

A wind-up clock.

utilized, but because many new reality experiences are often at 1:1 real world scale it allows the audience to behave in the same way they would in the real world. So, just as I described being able to pick up a clock in the real world and place it against my ear a VR experience may allow the user to lean down right to the point where they are virtually right up against the clock. If this is possible then a very close detailed recording of the clock is an important aspect of creating a believable simulation. If there is no noticeable difference in the sound between being three meters away and three centimeters away the illusion of the virtual clock is lessened.

This possible scenario defines our approach to content creation right from the point of capturing source material, and has implications throughout the entire production and implementation process.

Sidebar

One thing that even experience sound recordists can forget is the effect of proximity on any sound source. We are used to hearing certain sounds in the real world without examining how those sounds can possibly change based on proximity. A good example of this is a basic set of drawers that you might use to store clothes in, a square cabinet with three or four drawers made of wood that slide open and closed. We would all instantly recognize the expected

Clockwork mechanism.

"whoosh" sound of a drawer being slid open or closed and an average recording of such an event would be suitable in 99% of instances for most media. But if the experience requires the audience to move extremely close to the drawer as it is opened or closed the experience alters significantly. A wooden set of drawers produces quite a textured sound as the wood of the drawer slides across the wood of the cabinet. Both surfaces have a certain roughness that means up close, the scraping of wood on wood is quite unique. The textural quality of the sound quickly becomes inaudible as you move away from the sliders.

The point here is that many sounds have multiple aspects that combine to make the overall sound. A car engine has many moving parts, and a footstep is a combination of the impact of the whole foot as it touches the ground over time as weight is transferred from heel to toe. From an "average" listening distance we collapse many of these sound elements down into a single "footstep" sound or "car" sound or "drawer" sound. The more textured or detailed elements sometimes do not carry as far as the overall combined sound. It's like trying to hear just the second clarinet in a fortissimo orchestral tutti passage. If you sit next to the second clarinet you can probably hear it, (unless the trombones are directly behind you), but from the audience's position it is all part of the blended mix.

For the new realities we will often provide the audience with the freedom to wander among the orchestra and to experience what it is like to sit next to the second clarinet. So the material we capture as raw source recordings, how we process and then implement that material will have a major impact on our end product. If all we have is a stereo recording of an orchestra from two microphones placed 20 feet in front of the ensemble, then there is no way we can spatialize our experience and allowing the audience to walk among the musicians will expose that limitation and likely undermine the immersive nature of the experience.

This needs to be accounted for from day one of production as it impacts every aspect of the design of a project. The orchestral example alone would require a significantly different approach to acquiring the raw material. It might be necessary to record each instrument in isolation to facilitate individual positioning and mixing. From an implementation point of view to create a virtual orchestral experience is no small task. Correct placement of a 70-piece orchestra would utilize 70 channels for simultaneous playback, the mixing of such an experience would be incredibly challenging and the final output platform would require some incredible CPU power if you wanted to accurately spatialize the entire experience with room reflections.

Best workflow practices for this type of project will only become fully apparent once we start to try and do these kinds of projects and I suspect there will be a significant number of challenges that we may not even think of until we try it. By starting with a much simpler project idea we can imagine the challenges a little more easily and from there discuss how it might be approached.

Physical Placement

Back to the clock—to use it a virtual world I need to define my clock sound as a 3D sound source. This will most likely be attached to a 3D model of a clock in our virtual space. Our sound is now a looping sound, defined as a 3D sound source so that in the virtual world it occupies a specific location relative to the rest of the virtual space. How big is our virtual clock, and how big will it ever get? If there is a possibility of our clock growing to a gigantic size (or conversely the audience shrinking) then the relative position of every aspect of the clock has to be able to change. So our single homogenous clock sound may need to be split into individual components. If the clock can now be interacted with as if it was relatively the same size as the internal workings of Big Ben, then each cog, spring, and working mechanism that produces sound will require an isolated sound source so that the audience can now stand within the workings and hear each sound source positioned accurately. This applies to any and all virtual objects that may scale up or down as part of the experience.

Simulating Sound Wave Properties

Reverb

The details of how we implement the clock sounds are what really determine how convincing our environment is. If we do not plan to move either the clock or the listener's position, we may be able to apply a single reverb solution for the entire space that will help sell the simulation. A convolution reverb created through an impulse response from the room in the real world helps us create accurate modeling of the reflections in the virtual room.

If we assume the clock is in the exact center with the listener close by we could capture an impulse response in the same way by placing

A virtual clock requires virtual sound.

a microphone in the room where the audience will eventually be placed, and trigger sound source at the exact position of the clock. This may provide a reasonable simulation of the clock's sound waves reflecting on any surfaces within the room and returning to the listener's position.

This method has quite a few "ifs" involved and so would only provide a very basic solution that limits movement around the virtual space. The issue here is that moving the audience, clock, or both can get complicated from a reflections point of view. This is most easily demonstrated graphically.

Observe how even just one new object changes the reflections from the listener's perspective. If the audience is allowed to move around freely then the reflections would need to update in real time for all surfaces. This quickly gets complex.

One way to do this could be to tell the program to "ray trace" each possible sound wave and any surfaces it might reflect from. The program would calculate reverb using live updating to create a far more

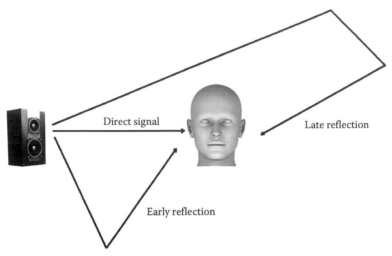

Direct signal, early reflections, and late reflections all reach the ear at different times.

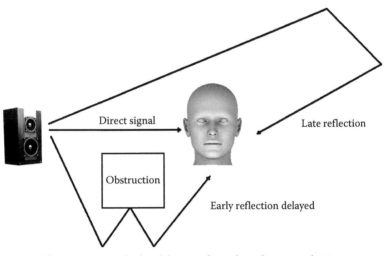

Obstructions may further delay sounds reaching the ears so the time
between early and late reflections may be almost nothing.

accurate model of exactly what the listener would hear as they moved around the space relative to the ticking clock. The problem here is that ray tracing uses a huge amount of resources, which limits its practical application.

Many of the technology and plugins will provide possible solutions for simulating reflections in a virtual space. Some will try to accurately model reflections and others will provide template solutions for rooms approximate to your virtual space. Reflections are a complex issue and the technology is constantly evolving. Often your choice of plugin to use for spatialization will be based on how well it supports certain features and simulates real world behavior. By understanding the aspects of what might be important for your project you can make a better choice as to which technology will suit you best.

Using the orchestra analogy and suggesting the possibility that our perspective of the clock's size may change will influence our approach to crafting our clock audio. If the clock will never change size in relation to the audience a good quality recording of a clock will suffice. A very close-in recording with lots of detail could be blended with a cross fade over distance to a more "traditional" recording of a clock, so the audience can listen right up close if they desire. Then implementation is about positioning the clock correctly and setting up accurate behavior for attenuation. Defining that behavior with your spatial plugin is part of your implementation step.

If, however, the clock may grow in size relative to the audience then it may be necessary to record various isolated elements that allow the user to walk around inside the clock in the same manner as our orchestra. This may not mean recording the actual clock or any other real clock. As the elements within the clock grow larger each of those elements will likely take on the characteristics of any large object or device. As a general rule, larger mechanical devices generate louder sounds and often produce sounds of a lower pitch. So capturing recordings of other pieces of machinery to represent our giant clock could be a good approach. This is a common aspect in sound design—when things get larger, or smaller, or faster, or slower we create suitable versions of how we think they would sound. Think of the lobby scene from the original Matrix movie and the excellent sounds for all the firearms in slow motion. These were not real gun sounds slowed down; they were uniquely crafted sounds designed for that scene.

From an implementation point of view it would be likely that the single sound source for our regular-sized clock would expand into multiple emitters within the clock positioned to represent each of the sound-generating elements within the clock's mechanism. Once placed, all internal elements would need to be mixed and blended, and individual attenuation behavior defined to create a believable experience. If the experience allows the audience to zoom in from our normal-sized clock and enter into the huge clock the implementation of the dynamic changes in sizes would add even more challenges to the project.

Smoke and mirrors

This exercise can be applied to any object or device that you might ever need to create in a virtual world. If you do not have access to the exact real world object, such as a battle tank or airliner that you can get near enough to analyze, then utilize something suitably similar that can provide you with useful information. It may be easier to access a piece of construction machinery and it will have similar characteristics to a tank, for instance.

The point of this exercise is to allow you to examine sound behavior for an object and then use that analysis to extrapolate what the object would sound like if it were implemented into your virtual project. It shows what might be required if the object is going to behave in an unusual manner such as growing larger or morphing into a different object. Real-world observation can provide insight on how the sound behaves in various locations such as in an enclosed garage and then out into the open air. Capturing some reference recordings, even at low quality, is a great way to give yourself a guideline for implementation.

Gaining access to some objects, locations, or equipment may be hard or impossible.

serious audio design for serious purposes

In the previous tutorial talking about the industrial roller, I posed the question of why we would or should care about the quality of audio for such an experience and if it was worth the effort to model careful and precise audio content. In this section I want to discuss a very real and important example of why and when careful and accurate sound design is both critical and valuable.

VR and AR are already being used for many nonentertainment purposes, such as education and training content, as well as industrial engineering, medical procedures, and research. In the future, I think the new technologies will be used for as many serious purposes as they are for entertainment. Audio is often not seen as critical and sometimes not even used at all for some of these applications and I think this is a possible oversight that misses an important opportunity for serious applications.

If I ask a simple question I suspect I could guess the answer for the experiences of many people.

What is the first indicator to you that the car you are driving has a potential problem?

In the vast majority of cases the answer would be, "it sounds funny." While certainly a vehicle may display issues through a loss of power or that it feels unusual in its handling, in a great many cases the first indicator that something is wrong is that the sound it produces is not what we are used to.

Every piece of machinery from our family car, up to a multimillion dollar steam turbine in a nuclear power plant has an optimal way of operating and when operating in that optimal manner will produce a particular sound, a signature sound that everything is working properly. VR and AR provide the opportunity to create applications that can monitor the performance of machinery as it operates and provide feedback to staff to check for potential issues.

When a piece of machinery is first commissioned and assessed to be running at peak performance a series of sound recordings could be made at various locations around the operating machinery. The exact location of each recording is logged and a simulation is built in either VR or AR. Then at periodic intervals staff can return to the machinery and either record new samples for comparison or simply listen to the original reference samples while standing in the correct location. A simple A/B test for how the equipment sounds. If there

Simulating equipment failure as part of training can save lives.

are any notable differences, recordings could be analyzed in greater detail.

The testing application shows the staff exactly where to stand in either VR or AR to ensure the perspective the user is hearing is correct and the archived recordings should match the sound currently being produced by the machine. Differences in pitch would immediately indicate if any cyclic operation was running either faster or slower and any irregularities in the cyclic nature of the sound could indicate operational problems. The key benefit of this method is that is permits a quick and easy way to check equipment without having to shut it down, which can be very costly for many industries.

This methodology is essentially applying the stethoscope method to machinery in the same way we listen to the human heart. We know what should sound like and so any deviation from that could be an indication of an issue. The key function of VR and AR in this example is the ability to orientate the user to the exact location and perspective that the initial calibration samples were recorded to ensure the test are performed accurately and the capabilities of special audio allow us to simulate the behavior of the machinery as it should be in real-world operations.

Audio diagnosis could be a useful method of analysis for many stress-test types of situations, from high-performance cars, to industrial machinery, and even military equipment. Our sense of hearing is our key danger sense and we rely on it every day for basic survival with something as simple as crossing the street. For serious applications, it could and probably should be used for training as well as diagnosis.

Simulating Survival

If we take things one step further in the serious application of new reality technology I would suggest that audio is a critical aspect of many simulators that has been overlooked for far too long. The example of an issue with your family car takes on a whole new level of importance when that unwanted sound you hear is from the attack helicopter you are flying.

I have spoken with companies that create content for various flight simulator programs and the common thread I hear from many of them is that the quality of the audio is poor to fair at best. Again, I find this quite surprising as it costs a significant amount of money to develop a serious flight simulation program for training and these are designed to save lives. Overlooking the sound element, which would likely be a very small percentage of the overall budget anyway, seems an odd choice to be making.

Any number of scenarios could be run through a simulator to test a pilot's ability to deal with dangerous issues. How many of these would start with an indicator that something was wrong

For a combat pilot, all their senses are critical to their survival.

because the equipment did not sound the way it should, or a turbine was slightly out of sync with its partner, or the fuselage made an unusual creaking sound as the vehicle was operating? I am well aware that many aircraft and also many surface vehicles produce very loud sounds while operating so it can often be super hard to hear anything above the roar of the engine, but humans are surprisingly good at noticing frequency elements that are not usually present. Even mixed in with loud engine noises operators will often notice something hidden within all the noise that just seems out of place.

So our flight sims designed for training and critical situation simulation would likely benefit significantly from the advances that have developed from VR and AR production. Any training material could help to develop their user's sense of audio awareness that may save lives in crisis situations. Exactly how these applications develop will depend on the approach taken by the teams creating them. But the technology certainly supports a wide range of possibilities.

the James Bond adventure in AR

A good way to have a discussion about any of the new realities is to base that discussion on an actual project. All the technology, concepts and ideas we consider and discuss are more thoroughly tested when we apply them to an actual project. Even if the project does not really exist, the process of planning and executing its design on paper is an effective way to expose potential issues in the way we consider design, in the limitations of the technology, and forces us to ask questions about how we would make such a project into reality.

Because AR is still very much under development as a format, discussing a hypothetical project is also an excellent way to foresee how we might design future projects and the types of challenges waiting for us in the future.

As a self-confessed geek, I am also a bit of a James Bond fan, and I think that AR could be an amazing platform for a really engaging experience set in the James Bond universe. The technology is still a fair way off what I would consider ideal for the concept, but the audio side of things provides some interesting challenges. So, let's discuss an imaginary experience, for technology that does not yet exist as a basis of analyzing how audio for AR has a unique set of challenges. Oh, and if this project does ever get made, I so want to work on it!

The core idea behind this concept is that using an AR headset you would play through a James Bond adventure where you would be accompanied by a virtual version of 007. The experience would insert James Bond into your world and as you walk, drive or run around the real world our favorite MI6 character provides elements of the narrative that you must react to. So there might be conversations with virtual secret agent contacts, virtual baddies you have to follow and hidden locations you need to discover. The idea here is that you are moving within the real world enjoying this private adventure that only you can see and hear.

One of the principle requirements with true-scale virtual objects is how we assign sounds to those objects. If we create a video game where the player can run around, interact with other characters, and move through a virtual world, there are significant limitations to what the character can do and so it reduces the level of complexity for the audio design. If we add footsteps to a character, then as long as they come from the same general location of that character the audience will be happy with the result.

If we create a full-size James Bond character, then we must create a far more detailed audio model. Bond is usually over six feet tall. The sounds of him walking need to emanate from his feet and need to emanate from each of his feet correctly. So, we would need to place a sound emitter into each foot. Any sounds created by his hands need to emit accurately from the hands and of course his speech needs to come from his mouth. All of this may seem obvious, but these are not requirements we have previously had to worry about. In a traditional game you cannot usually get close enough to a virtual character to know if the sounds come from the specific body parts, but with true-scale AR you could lean down and listen as the character walks and if the sound does not emit from the correct location it will instantly break the illusion of reality. In fact, you might even need to go as far as placing an emitter for heel impact and another for the front of the foot is it touches the ground.

Related to a virtual character's core sounds we have the issue of surface types for footsteps. Traditionally we can drop sounds into a game to cover a few of the major surface types—rock, sand, grass, water etc. But the instant we bring a virtual character into our world this becomes trickier. As an audience member for this type of experience we have a direct and instant reference to footstep surfaces;

our own footsteps. We can walk, listen, and compare the sounds of our feet with those of the virtual character. The sounds do not need to match 100% because different shoes do produce slightly different step sounds, but the sounds do need to align fairly closely to match surface materials as well as the quality of other sound behavior such as sound reflection and absorption. There are various procedural algorithm methods of creating impact sounds, and it is possible one of these might provide a useful solution, or assist in a custom solution, but the problem is not a trivial one.

This is a good place to pause and dig deeper into our first real challenge to better understand how an AR project may differ from what we have previously created. If we were creating an AAA console game then the likelihood is there would be a large team of developers including artists, programmers, and sound designers who would spend months or years building up a virtual world, populating it with virtual creatures and ambiences, and in general performing the task of "world building." An AR project such as we are discussing here does not require that step as we experience the game within our own world. This is why AR projects will be very different to create from the more traditional forms of media we have previously experienced. The things that are important to the audience will be very different to traditional media and will require very different approaches.

It is not unreasonable to consider a team of audio personnel having to spend months on perfecting the footstep sounds for an AR experience such as this. In the same way that the world ambiences for a VR game are critical to help place and ground the audience into that virtual world, the footsteps of a virtual character are critical in grounding them into our world. So while it might seem very strange to obsess with something as basic as footstep sounds they are the sonic equivalent of ensuring a character's animation has weight and balance so they really look like they are moving and behaving realistically. It is also true that if an audio team absolutely perfected 007's footsteps to the point where they perfectly matched your own across any surface inside and outside, the average audience member would not even notice. However, if you get it wrong, EVERYONE will notice. Such is the role of the audio team.

AR is going to provide an almost completely different series of challenges for production teams compared to traditional media. Obviously we would hope that all the dialogue was professionally acted and directed, and produced to a very high technical standard. Any voiceover would also need to match similar environmental behavior as the footsteps, so as Bond speaks to us he sounds like he is in the same type of room we are. We will analyze some more of the technical difficulties with environments in a minute, but there is a major performance issue that needs to be considered.

If you and I are walking along a busy city street, we will speak to each other in a specific manner. In general, we will speak in a louder voice; we will project our words specifically to overcome the sounds of traffic, other people, and any other noises within our environment. We do this to make sure our companions can hear what we say as we walk and talk. Often, we will even turn our heads toward our companions so that our speech has a more direct path from our mouth to their ears. If we suddenly walk into a shop as we are talking, we are likely to immediately drop our voice mid-sentence. We instantly recognize that our environment has changed and that it is inappropriate to be projecting our voice at outside levels. This would be the same if we entered a taxi or other vehicle, or went from an office space into an elevator.

Living in busy, built-up, crowded cities, we have all unconsciously adapted to our changing environments and how we need to alter our speech behavior on the fly to appropriate levels. If we wish to create AR experiences where a character can be walking along with us holding a conversation, then we need to acknowledge this behavior and attempt to reflect it in our virtual characters. Much like the footstep challenge, if we get it right most people may not notice, but if we get it wrong we will end up unable to hear our virtual characters as they speak too softly outside, or being knocked over by their loud voices as they project too loudly when inside.

Again, it is the challenge of how we can effectively draw virtual characters into our real-world space without them seeming completely false and comical in their behavior. The technical side of detecting our location is not that complex. Most wearable devices and even mobile devices have some form of camera. The camera can at the very least detect changes in lighting that may indicate an inside or outside environment. More advanced systems may be able to detect walls and calculate that you have changed your location. The real challenge is how we use this information.

When we speak outside it is far more than just a louder voice. We project from deeper inside our body cavity; often, this involves using our diaphragms. This significantly alters the tonal quality of our voice. It is not a simple act of altering volume or even filtering certain frequencies to match our inside voice and our outside voice—they are very different sounds. A drum is a good analogy for this. When you play a drum louder it is far more than just more volume. The impact of the drum stick is far greater, so there is a sharper attack when the stick initially hits the drum, the drum skin stretches far more as the increased impact pushes it further, then the decay of the sound will be longer as the strike rings longer as more air is displaced from the greater impact. Human speech is a different system but the level of difference between loud and soft is similar.

The consequence on an AR project is that you might need to record all dialogue to cover both states. Since for an AR experience such as this the realism of the main character dialogue would be one of the principle assets for the entire project, it would be critical to maximize the impact that dialogue has on the audience. So in a movie or game the quality of the script and acting is essential for an engaging experience, in AR both of these factors are also important, but accounting for the environmental changes would equally contribute to the immersion of the experience.

I have not yet spoken about accurate modeling of environmental spaces because this is a significant challenge for all content created for the new realities. The same issues we have with matching room reflections and real-world obstruction and occlusion apply to VR and AR, and even MR experiences. We are still experimenting and evolving the technology that allows us to accurately localize sounds in space, and whether it's a virtual space or placing a virtual object into real space, the challenges are significant. Calculating and then simulating a full set of reflections and sound absorption behavior is a major aspect in creating the simulation of positioning an object so we hear it at a specific location. This issue comes up again and again in this book, in group discussions, in project meetings, and in conference presentations. It is something that is being worked on by many groups and the technology changes almost weekly as teams try to overcome the challenge.

Psychoacoustics can be extremely beneficial in this regard. Using the weaknesses we have as humans to improve the illusion can be quite effective. If we place the 007 character into the room in which we are sitting and he is standing or sitting a few meters from our position, as long as the volume of his speech is not too loud or too soft then the realism of the experience may still be quite convincing. Even without accurate room modeling of perfect reflections there is a critical factor that works in our favor and that is the human brain. If we see an object in front of us and we have an expectation that object will make a sound, then our brain will process the sound and assign it to where we expect it to be. As humans are more sensitive to human speech over almost all other sounds this further enhances the experience.

If we are enjoying a James Bond experience, and Bond is sitting across from us speaking, then our brain will actually do a lot of the work for is in convincing us what we hear is real and that the sound is emanating from the virtual model of Mr. Bond. It gets less easy once 007 moves around behind us if we need to know exactly where he is. Again, our brain will help us a little. We cannot see the object we are hearing and so our brain will assume it is out of sight and will probably assign it to our rear, but exact localization of that sound source can be very different. In this regard, the design of the experience can also go a long way to helping make things convincing to the audience. If we design the experience so that absolutely accuracy in localization is not a requirement of the experience, we significantly reduce the stress on any weaknesses within the current technology and the weaknesses we have as humans. So James is in front of me when I can see him and "somewhere" behind me when I cannot.

All forms of media and communication have limitations. Limitations are often excellent motivations for creativity. The design aspect of how we utilize the different realities will be the most crucial issue initially. As an industry, we need to explore and develop different genres of experience and develop those that work best on any specific platform. First person perspective, for instance, is problematic for VR as many audience members find themselves feeling nauseous from that type of movement. Similarly, since AR as a platform is designed to add virtual elements into our world, it is less effective at transporting us into other worlds. I suspect AR will be an interesting platform for narrative experiences and more suited to that than to action-based experiences, but only as we develop these formats will we figure out the best type of content to deliver on each platform.

Working with 360 Video

Although 360 video may not have the same level of interaction possible in a VR game experience, it has many factors that are similar to VR content and has far more agency for the audience than traditional film or television. All of this means that there are new challenges we need to address, and interesting possibilities for creating engaging content.

So let's try to answer some of the questions raised in Chapter Three as I think they are significant.

What microphones should I use?

I was literally asked this question a few hours before writing this paragraph. It is a logical and reasonable question regarding the production of 360 video. Most 360 cameras have a microphone of some kind built into their structure and so the camera can capture audio as you are filming your 360 scene. However, in most cases I would only ever use the recorded content as a reference to produce my own audio. Unless you have access to one of the top-level professional 360 cameras the reality is that the built-in microphones are not really suitable for quality production work.

Many 360 cameras only have one or two microphones. This means they are recording either a single mono sound field or a stereo capture of the environment. Neither of these provide a decent spatial representation, they do not support head tracking, and will generally sound very flat. Also, as a general rule they will be small and inexpensive microphones so the general quality is probably going to be very basic.

One of the key issues with recording sound anywhere is the ability to deal with wind noise and vibrations. Almost all microphones are susceptible to wind creating unwanted noise against the diaphragm of the mic and to capturing general vibrations from handling and movement of the user. This means your recorded sound may be full of low-frequency rumbling and noise. There are a wide range of solutions that can be combined with microphones to reduce or remove these unwanted sound elements. The most common being a wind sock or "fluffy" that is placed over the microphone to disperse the unwanted energy from the wind. Most 360 cameras have a single tiny access hole for sound to reach the inbuilt microphone and so it is either very impractical or completely impossible to protect this area from wind and vibrations without interfering with the lens of the camera.

What format should my 360 video be in?

So if the recorded sound from a 360 camera is seldom usable for production how do you add sound to your 360 video? What format should my 360 audio be in?

When you are assembling your assets to use in creating your 360 video you can pretty much use all the same audio content you have

Samsung Gear 360 camera 2017 model.

used previously. Mono and stereo sound files not only work for 360 video, they work very well and in many cases mono sound files are the best solution for creating a 360 spatial mix. Mono sound files are ideal as they can be positioned spatially in the exact same way they would be implemented into a video game's 3D world space or even into a traditional linear film and then panned as needed. Mono sound files are used in almost every production line of audio content. From mixing the various mono mics of a drum kit together, to creating fully immersive Dolby Atmos environments out of multiple mono streams. For creating 3D video game worlds or engaging VR experiences the mono sound file is the perfect raw building block to start with; 360 video is exactly the same. Using mono sound files and positioning them with a spatial panner into your video will allow you to create an engaging and immersive environment. It is more about how you design and implement your project than it is which sound file format you use.

This does not mean that binaural and ambisonic content cannot be useful. Both of these formats can provide very interesting options for producing 360 video spatial audio content. But they seldom can provide all the content for your project as they both have limitations to how they can be implemented. So these formats will often function as a layer within your overall mix, but much of your content will be mono source material.

How do I encode my project and what is the best delivery method?

I have combined these two questions because I think they are directly linked. The choice of encoding methods is directly linked to where you want to share your video. If you plan to release your video on YouTube then you need to check the YouTube recommendations for the best formats for their delivery platform, and this applies to Facebook, the Oculus menu system, the Gear VR format, or Vive's network. Each platform developer has defined their preferred method of delivery. Each platform has its own hardware and software specifications. When you encode a video or piece of audio the settings you chose should reflect the optimal settings for the platform you want to deliver on. But there are a huge range of options for audio and video encoding and this can be super complicated, so let's have a look at some of them. Not all of these are directly related to just the audio, but they are an important aspect of producing 360 content.

Video file container

This is related to the file extension that your produced video will have, think .mp4 or .avi. But this is not always directly related to the codec used to encode and decode the video. It is possible to have three videos that are all .avi and they can still have different codecs.

Codec

The codec is the algorithm used to combine all the frames of your video, sync the audio, and compress the entire thing into a single file. Different codecs permit different qualities of playback and ratios of compression for delivery. To create and play back a video of a specific codec you need to have that codec installed on your computer. There are also codecs for audio content and sometimes a video codec will include audio compression, or a video codec may combine with a specific audio codec to create the final video file.

Frame rate

There are a wide range of different frame rates that can be used to produce videos. Often it is best to match the frame rate that your video was captured with on the video camera. Changing frame rate can affect the quality of the video, but should not affect syncing to the audio as the program will account for that.

Bitrate

This affects playback quality and compression size. The higher the bitrate the better playback will be, but this will also make the file larger in size. Often there is a trade-off between file size and playback. Bitrate will affect audio quality, but often there is a separate bitrate setting for audio playback. A low bitrate for audio playback is like poor quality mp3 and can make the audio sound tinny and thin.

Audio format

This is where you need to define if your audio is going to play back in stereo, surround, or spatial audio. Ensure that whichever program you are using for encoding your video it supports the audio format you require. This will often take trial and error tests to get the desired result. It is not uncommon to have to produce your project in one format, render out a video and then use a second program to rerender the video into the best format for your final delivery platform.

Remember that each time you render a video it is likely to lose some quality so keep rendering to an absolute minimum. Sometimes multiple rendering steps are unavoidable as different formats are supported by different programs and you need to work through a process.

The linear nature of 360 video allows for some aspects of audio production to be simplified compared to more interactive media, but other aspects become more complex. Because of the fixed perspective, it is possible to readily utilize all types of audio content. Mono, stereo, binaural, multichannel, object-based, and ambisonic assets can all be useful in the production of 360 video content. Some of the tools already available allow for both spatial and nonspatial audio content to be rendered out and then combined when encoding the video. While this makes the workflow more familiar to traditional linear media producers it is also possible to create complex object-based spatial audio products that utilize many of the same technology and functions as interactive spatial audio.

When working with spatial audio panning for 360 video, one primary difference is worth keeping in mind. A spatial panner works differently to a traditional surround panner even though they will both look similar.

Usually a spatial panner has a circular area with the center representing the listener position and output arrayed around that central listener. However, with a traditional 2D speaker-based panner the positions are representative of panning relative to speaker positions. So if you place a sound at the 2 o'clock position it is representative of positioning the sound somewhere between the front right and rear right speakers weighted more toward the front. If we move the position to the left, closer to the listener, this represents shifting the panning from entirely on the right-hand side and will blend content into the left-hand speakers.

The Audio 360 Spatialiser adjusts spatial positioning not channel-based panning.
(Copyright © 2017 Facebook, Inc. All rights reserved. With permission.)

A spatial panner works quite differently. A sound positioned at 2 o'clock should sound as though it occupies that point in space, around the 60-degree point of the circular radius. If we move the sound closer to the center position, then the sound will get louder as the distance from the listener affects attenuation. If we move the sound further away it will attenuate downward. With a surround panner as we move away from the central position to the right the sound will get louder in the right-hand speakers and quieter in the left-hand speakers. So this distance attenuation is a different type of behavior in spatial audio.

This type of positional mixing is more familiar to interactive audio developers because it is similar to how 3D games work; this is another instance of where the new realities are becoming an excellent merging of the slightly different skill sets of linear audio professionals and interactive audio professionals.

The 360 video system also has a fixed positional perspective. While you can rotate your head and look around a scene you cannot move freely through the scene as you could in an interactive experience. This provides some huge challenges for 360 video narrative production, as the 360 view makes traditional film editing techniques a challenge to work with. That said, the 360 audio perspective provides a whole new range of possibilities. The head tracking functionality allows the artist to produce an experience where the audience is aware of the sonic world around them and can experience that world from different rotational perspectives as they turn their head back and forth. In the case of audio, the fixed positional perspective means that ambisonic content can also be used. An ambisonic recording provides a spherical capture of a sonic environment. It's like placing a glass bowl over the listener that creates a bubble of environmental content. In interactive experiences the audience can often move around and so ambisonics will not always work. Effectively the audience can walk up to the edge of the fishbowl and even pass through it so sounds need to be positioned spatially to avoid this occurring. But for 360 video the ambisonic bubble is an excellent way to create a spatial room tone or atmos layer.

Attention focus

Some production and encoding tools for 360 video provide a function for attention focus. This can really enhance the experience for the audience if used well. The attention focus function allows you to define a region of your viewing space that the audience is looking directly at and attenuate the audio for content outside of that focus cone. So if the focus region is set to 45 degrees the process will register the central point of where you are looking with the headset and then expand from that point by 45 degrees to create a viewing cone. Anything in the video that falls outside of this cone is reduced in volume by the defined amount. So if the attenuation value is set to −12 db all audio content outside of the focus cone is reduced in volume by 12 db. The Facebook Spatial Workstation is one of the programs that includes this feature.

This is a very powerful tool in creating immersive 360 content as it allows you to define and control the cocktail party effect. So as the audience looks around their environment in 360 the audio responds to their point of focus and enhances that point by reducing all other sound objects in the mix. This is an excellent way of enhancing the separation of sound objects in the mix and significantly increases the audience's agency in the experience.

INSERT (THE COCKTAIL PARTY EFFECT)

One key aspect of how audio works in the real-world vs. how humans process audio is referred to as the cocktail party effect. If you and a friend attend a noisy cocktail party then you need to compensate and adjust for the various noise levels within the room space. If the two of you are having a conversation, then you are both constantly focusing tightly on each other's words. You look at your friend's face and watch their mouth and you position you own head to be in the best position to be able to hear what they are saying in the noisy space. This might require you to lean in or angle your head to be able to hear them clearly. It also requires you to active filter out other sounds as your brain prioritizes them lower than the sound coming from your friend's mouth. If a third person were to join the conversation you would then all three adjust your position, focus, and concentration to allow a three-way conversation.

This term applies to any scenario where you actively apply concentrated attention on one sound source and try to minimize focus on all other sounds that may interfere.

The "focus cone" function for 360 spatial audio attempts to simulate how we use our brains to overcome the cocktail party effect. By controlling the spatial mix based on where the audience is looking we can create clarity and separation in a spatial audio mix. Instead of sounds just bleeding across each other, the focus function can raise specific sounds above the overall mix. This means the audience is controlling

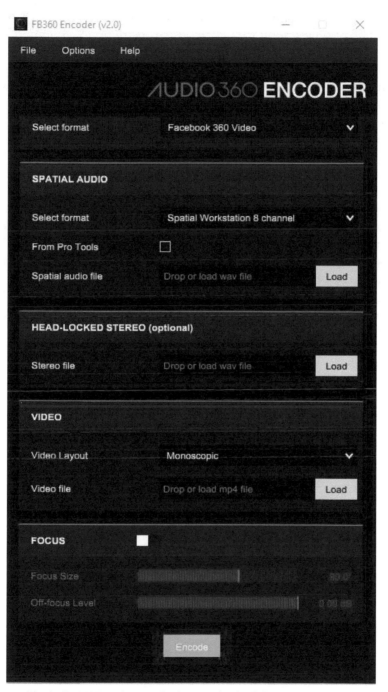

The Audio 360 Encoder provides functionality for defining a focus region.

which sounds are more prominent based on where they are looking. The degree of how strong this effect is can be defined when you create the project. Attenuation of 15 dB outside of the focus cone is a significant drop and could work really well to achieve spatial separation in an environmental experience. However, this level of difference would likely be too extreme for a 360 video of an orchestra playing.

In this example you might want a point of difference as the audience looks from the horns to the flutes, but a 15 dB drop will significantly alter the overall experience of listening to the music being performed. A 3 dB–6 dB attenuation may be sufficient to highlight the instrument group being looked at without making the overall performance fluctuate too much as the audience turn their heads. The exact values will depend on the desired overall effect and the content you are working with, but being prepared to play with the values and trying different settings to see what you can achieve is a critical part of finding the perfect balance for your project.

The 360 linear content can combine the best aspects of all the possible file formats to create some truly unique results and as the techniques of filming and editing 360 videos evolve I think there will be some very interesting audio examples created to support this evolution.

content creation

Once we understand some of the core concepts of how the new realities are different to existing media it places us in a good mindset to start working in the new realities. So if we want to create content for a VR or AR interactive experience or a 360 video do we approach this step differently to more traditional media? There is no single right way to do anything creative. The right way is the way that serves you best. However, having said that, there are a handful of techniques I have used over the years for game audio production that translate very well to the new realities. Even though my previous work was usually for traditional interactive content it can be relevant and useful to linear 360 formats as well.

New Realities: New Creation Approaches

Game developers have long been used to working in 3D space and dealing with object-based spatialization. The final delivery format has almost always been channel-based panning, but within the game engines themselves the audio is positioned within a 360-degree spherical world. Because of this many game audio designers have found the move to the new realities less of a jump than people working in traditional linear media. There are still many game developers that have relied on traditional media implantation methods. These methods do work, but that can limit the dynamic nature that can be very effective for interactive content and these methods also may not translate across to the new technologies as easily.

World Building with Audio

As I write this book I am also working on an open-world game called *Yonder: The Cloud Catcher Chronicles*. The game is beautiful to look at and allows the player to explore a fairly large open-world environment with many different biomes and a yearly season and weather cycle. It is also the first open-world game I ever worked on, so for me, getting the foundations of the world environment as good as possible was important. I had already been doing research into a variety of design and implementation techniques for virtual world environments when I started working on Yonder. I realized that many of the techniques I had developed were as useful and relevant to a traditional console game as they were to spatial audio for virtual reality. I will describe some of the techniques I used working with the Wwise audio toolset. Many of these techniques are not limited to Wwise, but it is a good basis for the discussion of this design.

I wanted to establish a strong sense of the openness of the world the player can explore. This was not a VR experience, it was a regular Playstation 4 game, but spatialization of audio is something that has interested me for many years. I adopted some techniques for spatial wind sounds that I had developed for VR and AR projects. I asked the programmer to create what we would later refer to as "the weathercock." This was an object positioned on top of the listener object in the game. Initially this was directly on top of the camera, but because the game is a third person perspective we later adjusted it slightly forward of the camera position. This would be where all our world ambient and weather sounds would occur.

Building a weather system

The idea behind the weathercock is that it accompanies the player wherever they go. Think of it this way. In the real world, you experience the sounds of the world through your ears. You hear the wind as it moves past the side of your head and your ears pick up the sounds. You hear rain and thunder from the perspective of your ears attached to your head. So even though all these sounds occur all over the real world, from your perspective everything occurs sonically right next to your head. So when we create a weather system for a game or interactive experience we need to make sure the audience experiences the weather right next to their head.

So instead of having to create weather sounds and place them all over the virtual world we position these sounds attached to the player and they follow them wherever they travel. This is a simple concept, but the key is in how you implement it. Using the Wwise audio tool set I created my wind event. The event itself was made up of four sound sources. They were actually the same single sound file, but for each sound source I set Wwise to start and loop the source at a different point in the main sound file. The result was four unique wind sound sources.

Then using Wwise's custom defined 3D positional tool I positioned each of the four wind sounds at cardinal points around the listener position, basically at north, south, east, and west around the listener. So in the game, the player would hear unique wind sounds all around them. I set the entire array to not lock to the camera rotation, so those sounds were fixed and as the audience rotates the camera the wind sounds would stay fixed. Essentially the player would have

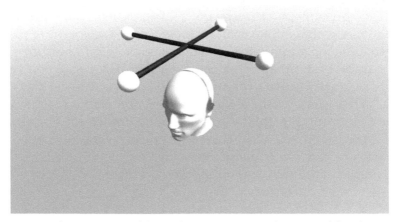

A visual representation of the weather emitter system. The emitters follow the character and create a bubble of weather sounds.

an experience very close to turning you head in the real world in relation to the direction of the wind. You would feel the wind sound change as you turned your head. All of this required a single mono sound file of wind set to looping, but it was implemented in a manner that more accurately simulated how wind behaves in the real world. I will refer you back to the basic listening test and the value of that exercise. By really listening to the real world around you, you can better understand who to approach implementing even the most basic sound elements to maximize their impact.

One last point on the implementation of the weather system; when I placed the wind sounds at the four compass points around the listener I did so at irregular distances. The distance I selected for implementation was 5 meters from the central listener position. But I adjusted each position to vary slightly. So north might have been 8 meters away and south only 3, east 7 meters, and west 4. I had set a simple attenuation on the wind sounds so that the sound attenuated over distance. When I implemented the weathercock system the distance variation between each point was very small and so any perceivable difference due to the distance attenuation would be incredibly subtle. But subtlety is how we emulate sound behavior in

Sounds placed in a 3D world can be further offset individually.
This process offset the four wind sounds positioned above the listener.
(Copyright Audiokinetic 2017. With permission.)

the real world and if every single layer you add to your sound environment has some small examples of subtlety, over the course of building your entire world audio you break away from the repetition and predictable behavior.

In the new realities, spatialization of something like wind can be so central to the immersion of the audience. One of the first things when they enter the experience will be the environmental sounds and the slight subtle changes in wind as they turn their heads really helps to sell the immersion.

Applications for immersive audio

As I was finishing this book I started working on a VR project with lots of different interior spaces. I applied the same approach to implementing room tones to create an immersive spatial audio effect. The exact same approach, using a room hum, or air-conditioner sound instead of wind, positioned at the four compass points creates an excellent sense of space for a VR experience. So the method of building the weathercock sound array can be just as effective for all kinds of ambient layers for traditional games as well as the new realities.

Another aspect of the audio environment for *Yonder: The Cloud Catcher Chronicles* was a changeable weather system. Essentially the weather could change dynamically to add rain and thunder. The weathercock system was designed to blend between multiple different wind layers, all set up in the compass point array with offset values. A game parameter defined wind strength of 0–1 with 1 being the strongest value. I used the system to blend between several wind sound files, each set up in the same way as the basic lowest level wind. As the values picked up, initially the first wind sound file would continue to play, but I would increase the volume and also adjust the high-pass filter. At its most gentle the wind sound was passed through a high-pass filter to remove a significant amount of the low-end frequency content. The lightest wind was airy and sparse, but as the wind picked up the volume would rise and some more of the lower frequency content would be audible. At a certain point it would then blend to a stronger wind sound and then ultimately to a stormy wind sound with the volume and low-pass adjustment being utilized across all three sound file groups.

Getting the details right

The visual effect for rain starts and a sound file of rain is triggered.

That is all we need, right? Wrong.

For quite some time games have understood that it is good to provide feedback as the character moves around the world. So as they walk on gravel or wood or metal the sounds of the footsteps change as the different surface types are registered by the game engine. But for some reason a single sound for rain is adequate.

In an open-world game it is likely that the audience will move from forest to grasslands, to sandy beaches and snow-covered mountains. Now go out and listen to how different rain sounds as it hits all those different surfaces. In fact even in a forest the rain will sound different in a clearing where it is hitting the ground to when you are under the leaves. If the forest has giant thick leaves like a rainforest then each impact resonates as the water drops impact those leaves, but in a pine forest the impact of the rain is quite different.

All of this is about differences and the point of difference for the audience. If they are running across the grasslands in the rain then their journey will be accompanied by a light swish of white noise as the rain hits the grass, but as soon as they enter the forest the rain shifts in two ways. First, all the rain impacts are now happening above the audience's head as the rain hits the leaf canopy, but also each rain drop is now hitting a leaf which will produce a vastly different sound than when hitting the grass. All of this can be achieved by creating appropriate rain sounds and then using a parameter to switch as you move between environments. In most games, you are likely tracking this data for various reasons anyway, so there is no requirement for lots of code changes and the sound files do not need to be huge. The lack of this attention to detail is something I often do not understand. As game projects try to improve the quality of their products for their audience audio is still something that is undervalued for the impact it can have on a player's experience. For new reality experiences this attention to detail can significantly increase the immersion for the audience.

The same process can be applied to wind as you move from open plains to closed-in mountains and of course rain, wind, thunder, and other weather sounds can all be combined to create a wide range of weather states.

Creating a Virtual Environment

Here I will take you through a step-by-step process for creating some of the elements for a dynamic environment that can be implemented into a new reality experience to provide spatial audio. I have used many of these techniques in the past for regular video game environments. Some are adapted slightly to make the best of spatial audio formats, others work without needing any changes. In all cases it is the attention to detail and the intent of the implementation that can allow these techniques to work well for VR or AR content.

Creating a forest

I have used this example more often than I can remember over the years, but for the new realities it is more relevant than ever. If we take the example of creating a generic forest ambience for a piece of narrative media, there are a few ways we could approach it.

In a standard film or television show the most common approach is to record some content at the actual location of filming or to drop in an ambient track to add the desired feeling. The ambient track could be simple stereo or a multichannel recording if the final format is to support more than stereo. This method is an old and reliable way to add the environmental feeling of wildlife and create some life in your scene. Often a track is added that has a different sound than what was really present on location. This allows the creators to present the illusion of lush wildlife for a location that might have been fairly quiet in reality when the filming was done.

While this technique works well for linear media it can fall flat in an interactive environment. If I am able to walk around inside an environment in a 3D video game or I can walk around and turn my head in a VR experience a background layer of birds cannot really fill the world sufficiently to function as environmental content. The issue here is that my perspective relative to the world can change, where in film and television it is locked. If I hear birds in the trees around me I can chose to walk up to a tree at which point the birds in that specific tree should get louder (or change in response to my proximity). I can also decide to walk around that tree at which point the spatialized position of the birds in that tree should alter relative to my position in relation to that tree. So should we just use a mono recording of birds that plays continually and place it into the tree so I can walk around it? This is closer to what we want but still not ideal for a few reasons.

If I use a mono recording that is 30 seconds long I get a reasonable loop of the bird in the tree. However, I have just populated a single tree with birds. If I want to populate every tree in the forest I am either going to have to use many different 30-second long recordings or I risk having the same ambience play in multiple trees which will likely become obvious fairly quickly. The other issue is if I position the 30 second loop into the top of the tree then all the sounds emanate from a single point, so it sounds like all our birds are stacked on top of each other within the tree. So our 30 second loop is a better solution in some ways, but still fails to provide the best result in others.

My solution for many years is as follows. I use individual bird calls, trimmed and cleaned so each is only a second or two long, maybe a few seconds for certain species. But in general, I trim my content down to individual bird "words" I then use the functionality within a game audio toolset such as Wwise to create a dynamic event that will sound far more like the behavior of real birds.

Using a selection of bird words, I provide Wwise with a pool of sounds—a bird vocabulary if you like. The object I create will randomly select a sound from the pool and trigger it. It will then wait a defined period of time and trigger another sound randomly from the pool. The period of time it waits can be defined as an exact value or usually I define it as a random range, so a bird tweet will trigger, the event will wait between 2 and 10 seconds, and then trigger again. In this way I can emulate the behavior of a small bird that chirps away fairly often or define a longer period of delay that you might hear from a large forest bird that only calls occasionally. It is also possible to automate this delay period so that the birds can dynamically increase or decrease their rate of calling so at dawn and dusk I can simulate the bird choir effect and in the middle of the day when it is hottest I can simulate a sparse environment with far fewer calls.

All of the above can be added into the game world as a spatial sound by placing a sound emitter into the tree model. So as you walk around the tree as we described earlier the birds are always in the correct location relative to the listener. In fact we can take it

A single "sound" made of multiple sound files that are randomly selected when triggered.
(Copyright Audiokinetic 2017. With permission.)

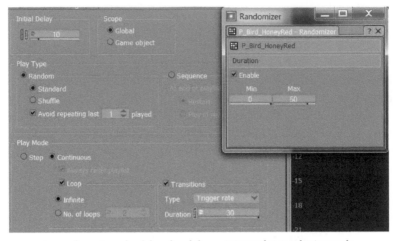

A sound event can be delayed and then retriggered at regular intervals.
Both these values can have random offsets applied.
(Copyright Audiokinetic 2017. With permission.)

one step further and apply some randomization to the positioning. So if a tree has a canopy of five meters we can place the emitter in the very center and then randomize the position of the individual bird calls within that 5-meter area. So now we actually have a type of volumetric effects with a tree canopy full of birds in different locations tweeting at varying intervals. The final aspect that makes this a very good approach is that the individual bird sounds we use in the pool of random material often take up less memory space than even a single 30-second recording. So this method is incredibly resource efficient. When we add a small amount of pitch randomization to the bird calls we can take this single group of bird calls and add them to every tree in the environment, and get a unique sound from each tree that will play dynamically for hours on end without repeating.

This technique uses fewer resources, sounds better, and spatializes far more effectively than our traditional methods of sound design. This technique also transfers directly across to new reality content as it is just as effective when experienced through a VR headset as when used in a screen-based game. So when I build a game environment and someone says "we want to create a VR version of this for people to experience" my response is usually "the audio is pretty much ready to go." This technique can also be extremely cost effective for any project that might exist as both a traditional game form and a VR experience.

Every tree in *Yonder: The Cloud Catcher Chronicles*
is a micro habitat of birds and insects.
(Copyright Prideful Sloth 2017. With permission.)

So a technique that is years old and has been used to create 3D game world environments transfers immediately and simply to VR experience creation. Game audio design has worked with object-based content for many years and so many of the approaches transfer directly to VR and AR. The exact tuning and mixing of the content into a new reality experience will likely require a different approach, but the basic design and implementation is appropriate.

Example: wind and water

A similar technique can be adopted for the creation of wind, rain, water, and other longer streaming types of assets. In the case of longer atmospheric sounds you still use the trigger delay method of implementation, but you set the lengths of the delay to match the lengths of the sound files being used, and you trim the sound files so they are all similar lengths. So for a stream you would use two or three sound files maybe 5 seconds long and dovetail them so that just as one was nearing its end the next would trigger. This avoids the obvious loops that exist in many environmental sounds and also allows you to position them to create interesting spatial effects. When the player walks under the waterfall it can surround them on all sides and create a far more effective immersive experience than a single mono sound file.

The fact that this system selects from a pool also allows you to include more interesting content that might otherwise expose a loop in a traditional looping sound. If you have an interesting splash

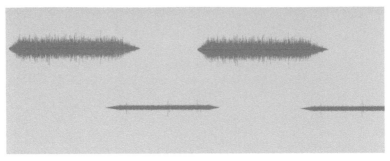

Instead of a single loop, multiple files can dovetail and provide more variety.

Any sounds that stand out within a loop will expose the loop and reduce
its effectiveness.

sound of water rushing over some rocks, if that is present in a normal looping sound it will be audible every time the sound file loops
and will expose that there is a loop in the file. So unless the sound
file is 30 seconds long (which will take up lots of memory) then you
usually need to choose something without any obvious features and
so your sounds tend to be a bit bland. Within the randomized pool
of sounds you could include one that does have an interesting splash
sound and then set the weighting of that sound so it only triggers
occasionally. Add some pitch randomization to this and you will get
an interesting sound feature that adds to the overall effect without
being repetitive and exposing a looping sound.

Ocean waves

The sound of the ocean is a welcome and relaxing sound for many
people. It brings forward thoughts of holidays and lazy days in the sun.
However, in many games and interactive experiences the sounds of the

ocean can be dull and flat. Often a single sound is added that represents the ocean sonically and this is inaccurate as in the real world how we hear the ocean changes significantly depending on our proximity.

From a distance, the ocean is usually just a low soft rumble of waves. We can hear very little detail, but we will usually recognize it as the ocean as very few other sounds are similar. But as we move closer we get more detail reaching our ears as the higher frequency content is now audible. We start to hear the shifting white noise of waves crashing and moving, but all the while the lower frequency rumble is still present.

This behavior is how I would implement waves into a game world. Multiple layers of sound that layer as you approach. The waves utilize the same random pool for selection as the previous world elements we have discussed. A series of sound files are randomly selected from and have pitch and volume randomization applied. The rate of triggering can be set to exactly match the visual effect of waves and this can even be controlled via a parameter so if a storm influences the waves and causes them to crash more frequently, the sound can immediately sync up to this change.

As we continue to move closer to the water's edge the low rumble and white noise of the waves is reduced and a new detail layer is added. The slosh and splash of water at your feet provides the final element of a convincing shoreline. For this particular project, the ocean was never particularly violent and the waves were usually fairly small, so the transition from distant to close splashing could be achieved once and then applied to the entire world environment.

The shoreline has multiple layers of audio to create a more familiar sound.
(Copyright Prideful Sloth 2017. With permission.)

But all of this could be mapped to include multiple states of ocean movement from mild splashes to violent storms.

The sound itself emanates from a single emitter in the world space. This emitter tracks the player's movement around the world. It is like a loudspeaker mounted on a railroad. As the audience moves along the coastline the speaker follows their movement. So the functionality reacts to their proximity to the emitter and alters the layers to suit how the waves should sound, but the entire ocean is only playing from a single location that moves along the coast in relation to the audience's position. This implementation technique is both effective and efficient. The exact same method can be applied to any moving water object such as a river, stream, or waterfall, or even for something like a lava flow.

Footsteps

I mentioned footsteps earlier and though they are the sound a character makes I think they are worth discussing as part of creating an environment especially for VR and AR experiences. Currently many VR experiences are avoiding allowing the audience to move around within the world space by walking as this can cause nausea with many people. However, I suspect there will still be VR and AR experiences that do utilize the traditional methods of having characters walk around within a virtual world space. If walking is going to be part of the process of movement then I think the implementation of footsteps is going to be critical and I do think it belongs under the category of environment, because it is the central key point where the audience interacts directly with the environment.

Apart from VR warehouse experiences and some Vive games, we are not yet at the point where we walk around in a room that simulates our environment. Until we create Star Trek style holodecks we have the very real issue of walking into walls and having a very small space in which to move. So generally we will be sitting down or standing still as we explore our virtual worlds. But I think we still need to pay attention to the context between the audience and the world, and how audio influences that.

Whether we are walking, sprinting, or creeping in our virtual space the footsteps are feedback to our brain that we are moving within the virtual space. In the real world the sound our feet make when they impact the ground depends on more than just the road surface under our shoes. Our body weight and the speed at which we are moving all influence the degree of impact on the ground. If we are carrying a heavy item this would further influence our footstep impacts. If we try to creep then we often roll our steps from heel to toe, on a gravel surface this would result in a slow grinding sound as our weight rolls over the tiny stones. The physics involved with walking is quite complex and the range of factors such as surface types, the shoes we wear, and how we are trying to move all affect the sound generated.

I think that for a virtual experience this could aid significantly in grounding the audience into the world. If the audience looks down, see a virtual representation of their legs and feet and then choses to very slowly step forward over fallen leaves and twigs, the sound is going to determine much of how realistic that experience is. If each leaf slowly crunches under their feet and a twig breaks or doesn't because of how carefully they place each step, this is direct feedback for the audience about how they are relating to the world they have been placed into. This is like striking a note on a piano or pressing a key on a computer. The audio feedback we hear tells us that we have interacted with that object and also tells us exactly how we have interacted with the object. Until we can create experiences with accurate haptic feedback, the role of sound is going to be important in providing that link between audience and the virtual world spaces.

There are many ways this concept can be utilized and like most things exploring the possibilities can lead to interesting results. It can even work for creating unusual musical content. Techniques like this are excellent for creating interesting and efficient dynamic content for the new realities and when combined with spatial audio techniques can result in more engagement for the audience.

Noise Reduction

Noise reduction is a common aspect of audio production for many audio folk. Unwanted noise can manifest in many ways from raw source recordings, through the signal chain of a project workflow and even into compression and delivery formats. As audio artists, we never want to leave unwanted noise in a project, but sometimes time and the difficulty in removing some sources of noise can result in a certain level of noise in a project being acceptable. I think that for AR and VR there are a few new problems that may be affected by noise issues and so should be discussed.

The key difference of VR and 360 content is the ability for the audience to turn their head and look around the experience. When we add spatial audio, the audience can now change their perspective in relation to the defined sonic world. It has been mentioned several times in this book that a "point of difference" is a key aspect of highlighting the audio environment to the listener. We want them to experience that change in perspective as they turn their heads. But importantly, we want them to notice that difference for the RIGHT reasons.

When I turn my heard with a VR headset on there are two possible scenarios which can draw my attention to the audio environment. The first is the spatial placement of a sound source. We have used the ticking clock in several examples to demonstrate that as the audience turns their head within a virtual experience, the spatial sound source of a ticking clock can highlight that the clock is fixed relative to the world space. The audience can move their head around and interact with the difference between their position and the clock's. This is generally a desirable outcome and one of the benefits of spatial audio.

The flip side of that is head movement that exposes issues with the audio and exposes the existence of unwanted noise. In the past when I have implemented bird ambiences that function in a generative manner, I have had to be very careful of the quality of the source material I use. As the process triggers and retriggers bird sounds the space in between should be filled with silence or at most, the other aspects of the environment I have deliberately added. So what we should hear is this: tweet tweet tweet tweet tweet tweet and so on.

If the sound files I have selected to use are not clean and clear of noise then what we can end up with is:

Tweetsssssss tweetsssstweetsssssssss tweetsstweetssstweets
sssssss

This sounds bad in any format, but if you add head tracking it is likely to be far worse. Each noisy tail of a tweet sound is not just an unclean bird sound it is a tag that continues to draw your attention to that spatial location. So if the birds are positioned all around you spatially then you get these constant bursts of noise from all the locations where the birds have been positioned. This will indeed highlight the spatial effect of your experience, but in a very undesirable way. It's not just the presence of the noise, it is the point where the sound file finishes and the noise stops. This is an example of a negative point of difference; something that will catch the audience's attention when we do not want their attention caught.

Another aspect is that frequency content is important for the localization of sounds. Noise often includes frequency content that is different to the sound we actually want. So a bad example of this would be distant road noise in a recording of birds. The birds are generally high-frequency content but the road noise may have lower frequency content in the form of a background hum. This low-frequency content, as part of the bird calls, will be positioned where the birds are positioned, so potentially high up in the branches of our tree objects. But now we also have a "distant" hum of traffic also positioned up in our trees. From the perspective of crafting a realistic and immersive environment for our audience, this hum is going to confuse the spatial mix and generally leave the audience wondering what they are hearing.

So while unwanted noise is often something we try to address when we create audio media, I think that for spatial content we need to be extra careful on how we approach this material. While the background traffic hum in the birds kind of blended in and was "covered up" in our 2D film mix, it may not be so easy to just brush over these issues in a spatial mix where all the frequency content contributes to how the audience processes the environment. There are some outstanding tools available today to help remove unwanted noise content from sound files, and making the cleaning process part of preparing audio content to work with should be considered carefully for all new reality experiences.

Near Field versus Far Field

HRTF is one of the primary tools we use for creating effective spatial audio for the new technologies. However, HRTF like many things has its strengths and weaknesses. During my research into various aspects of technology for the new realities I discovered that many tools are using existing HRTF data libraries to calculate how the sound will function. But many of the HRTF data sets were taken in situations where the data was collected from at least a meter away from the listener. The consequence of this is that many early HRTF solutions and those that don't develop their own data are relying on hearing simulations of no source closer than 1 meter. Essentially this means HRTF can be less effective at sounding like it is close to the listener. So a ghost whispering in your ear will probably lack a sense of proximity.

To further complicate this situation, it can be very hard to find any information on near field vs. far field, and technology developers who might be developing something more flexible will often not be prepared to speak about their technology. So, we are left often not knowing exactly what our tools are capable of, or what alternatives may exist. For many projects this may not be an issue, but when you do need to deal with close sounds, what options do you have?

There are some methods you can utilize to trick the listener and create a near field effect, but I would also recommend that if it is important to your project you speak with your technology provider. The more people who need and want near field HRTF capability the more someone is likely to develop a useful tool for it.

One technique is to use a combination of binaural recordings and also a limitation of how humans localize sounds. Binaural is very effective for presenting content that feels like it is right behind you. This is partially because of the recording technique and partially because humans will favor rear positioning if they cannot see a visual representation of a sound source. But this does mean our ghost whisper can indeed sound unsettlingly close, even "breath on the back of our neck" close. But binaural does not support head tracking and so it does have some limitations.

A short sound event could be triggered and finish before the audience is fully aware, so even if they turn their head the sound is not playing, and so the lack of head tracking support is not as relevant. So, very short words or a two-word phrase might work effectively. You could add code support so these sounds only trigger when the audience is not moving their head, to increase the effectiveness.

Another aspect of this is that humans generally use the initial sound heard to localize sounds in short bursts. So if I hear three short beeps, my brain targets the first and locks on to that location. So if the first beep was a binaural recording, followed by two HRTF spatialized sounds, then the binaural may have established enough of a sense of its position that my brain will associate the entire sequence with the original close proximity binaural sound. I have not tested this one myself, so it would be interesting to see how effective it would be.

The issue of course is if the brain does not instantly lock onto the position of the sound; we tend to turn our head back and forth to try and triangulate its location. So this technique would need to be tuned to work for the specific content you needed. But in general, binaural can be effective in presenting close proximity sound to fill the near field region that HRTF can otherwise struggle to deal with.

sound? what sound? gathering assets for your project

gathering, designing, and creating your raw assets

Like any other form of media, experiences for the new realities are created from raw source assets, the sound, music, and vocals content you use to produce a finished product. Also like any other form of media there is no single best source or method for gathering the assets you use. There are a range of factors that can influence how any production team goes about preparing to build a product and these factors will all influence the decisions made.

Cost, Time, and Quality

This is an often-discussed triad of elements that can be applied to practically any project or the creation of anything. It takes materials to create a thing and it takes time to create a thing; both of these will affect the cost of creation. The level of quality you want for production will also usually influence the cost of production. When applied to each of the possible ways of sourcing or creating assets we can map out how each approach can influence your end design.

The good thing is, of all the possible methods of sourcing assets, none of them need to be adopted in isolation. So recorded material can be combined with SFX libraries, procedural content can be layered with material from your personal collection, a single sound file from a library can be used as is with no editing or alteration. Any combination of source assets and workflows can be utilized to achieve the results you need.

In the next section, I will take a look at a range of potential options for sourcing your sound effects and compare their suitability for different kinds of projects.

Sound Libraries

Commercial sound effects libraries have been available for many years. A great many media companies rely on the use of SFX libraries every day and they provide a solid foundation for the creation of content. Like all things there are good SFX libraries and there are bad SFX libraries, but sometimes deciding which is which is entirely up to personal preference and the project you are working on.

Technology has advanced so significantly in the last ten years that it is now possible for almost anyone to record their own collection of sounds, and many audio professionals have their own personal collections. But the jump between a personal collection and a library suitable for commercial release is quite steep. Paying users have a real and justifiable expectation that when they purchase a library to use professionally their money is buying a quality product they can rely on.

Good quality SFX libraries should be recorded at a high level of quality and presented in a format that is easy to use. 96 kHz 24 bit is fairly standard for content these days, but it is possible to find even higher quality from some libraries. Clear and concise metadata and naming conventions make the sounds easy to search and work with for the user.

To be worth buying, a library should contain material that is either impossible or impractical for you to record yourself. It is hardly worth your money to purchase a library that is recordings of generic cutlery being moved in a kitchen drawer; you should be able to do that yourself. A library of rare animal sounds or of antique cars however is something that for the right project could make a massive impact on how you create your sounds.

No matter how big a library is though, you will often find you cannot find the exact sound that you were looking for. My combined collection of libraries is well over 150,000 SFX and yet I am surprised how often I find that the river sound is not quite what I wanted, or the wind sound groans rather than moans, or a page turning sound is just slightly too slow for my needs. But the reverse of that is, the times when I have had significant projects that have had very short timelines and I simply could not have achieved the level of work required in the time available without the use of a sound library.

For content produced for the new realities I think some care needs to be taken with sound libraries. Content that has noticeable reverb or echo captured in the sound file may make spatial implementation difficult. As the technology improves we will rely more and more on the software to define the room reflections for our virtual experiences to help humans localize the positions of sounds and also to help make an experience more convincing, to make us really feel like we are in the virtual space we can see.

Because of this we will often need to work with content that is very flat and has no reverberation within the sound file itself, so we can then add the correct type of reflections to match the experience. While the sound of a heavy object dropped in a cathedral has an awesome booming echo to it, it simply may not work at all within a new reality experience. If we need to spend time trying to clean sound files in an attempt to remove or reduce reverb behavior then the advantage of a sound library is significantly reduced. So be aware when you are scanning a library for content that it needs to work within the confines of the new technology and how we implement content.

Another aspect to be mindful of with SFX libraries is noise. The clean capture of recorded content has been the primary goal of every recordist since microphones were first invented. Wind noise, line noise, and unwanted background noise, are all undesirable artifacts when recording any sound source but often they are unavoidable or difficult to minimize. In some cases the value of the content can outweigh the presence of noise in the recording. Rare animal sounds or sounds specific to a one-off event are scenarios where noise may be unfortunate, but capturing the sound at all was a minor triumph.

There are software tools available these days that can be very useful in removing unwanted noise and some of them do an amazing job of converting near useless recordings into content that could be utilized for a variety of purposes.

The good

- Sound Libraries offer a quick solution to sourcing assets.
- You do not need to go out and record material so do not need expensive equipment.
- SFX libraries are very useful building blocks for creating original content.
- You can gain access to sounds you might otherwise find impossible to source.

The bad

- There is no guarantee that a sound library will have the exact sound you want.
- Good quality libraries can be expensive.
- Use of stock sounds risks sounding like other projects that use the same material.
- A lot of older content may not be suitable for use in new reality experiences.

Location Recording

I have spent many years doing location recording and I find it quite enjoyable, but I can also understand that for many studios it can be time-consuming, expensive, and a real hassle depending on what you wish to achieve. I will discuss microphones in a separate section, but needless to say there is a lot to discuss just on the subject of microphones alone.

Location recording gives you the opportunity to go out and capture unique and original content for your project; the downside is that you need to go out and capture unique content for your project. The issue is, while essentially location recording is the act of pointing a microphone at anything that is making a noise it is also much harder than that in reality. This short example provides some good context.

Many years ago I was speaking at a conference and as part of my presentation I spoke about one of the sound libraries I had spent time working on. I had created a library of classic and antique aircraft recordings. I had a large number of interesting aircraft that I had managed to get some great sounds from. For the sake of the conference I made a passing reference to the process of recording these sounds and commented that it had been an enjoyable experience for me. After my presentation, I was answering some questions when a young man came up to me.

He thought the idea of the aircraft library was a good idea and he said the following: "How do I go about getting access to the planes? I could do that, pointing a microphone at some planes is easy, I can do that." He was young and enthusiastic and it was obvious from the looks of the others there that many of them wanted to explain to him that it was not as simple as just "pointing a microphone" but I decided to focus specifically on the question he asked. How do you get access to the planes?

I explained to him that I had organized access with several groups to maximize the number of planes I had access to and the opportunities to get out and record sounds. One of these groups was the Australian Airforce museum and the other was a private aircraft museum. In both cases I had spent many months speaking with the people in charge, explaining to them my purpose for wanting access to the aircraft and how I would go about it. We discussed safety, both mine and everyone else's and after several months I would finally get limited access to some of the aircraft. And then slowly over an 18-month period as I proved myself, I gained greater access that allowed me to build up a series of more than 3,000 sounds which I then needed to carefully edit and format for the library. The young man lost interest almost immediately. As soon as he heard that he could not just walk up to an aircraft at an airport and do whatever he wanted, it all became too hard for him.

This is a bit of an extreme example in a couple of ways. First, aircraft are particularly hard to gain access to because of the safety concerns and regulations. In this case, the young man was unaware of what kinds of challenges might be involved. Aircraft are particularly hard to gain access to because of safety concerns and regulations. Although most recording targets are less complicated to access, this does demonstrate that location recording is not just as simple as walking out your door and pointing a microphone at something.

Anything that you might want to record has a list of considerations that need to be dealt with to maximize your chances of capturing the best sound material possible.

Weather: Is wind or rain going to prevent recording or add unwanted noise? Or damage equipment?

Temperature: Is the warm weather going to carry the sound from that distant freeway?

Location: Is the location you plan to record suitably quiet or next to a freeway?

Seasonal concerns: Are the birds you want to record elsewhere because of migration?

Societal concerns: Is the park you want to record birds in full of families because of a holiday?

Time of day: Is it peak hour? Great for recording traffic sounds, bad for recording nature sounds.

Deciding to go out recording birds in the forest on the day of the huge local sports ball competition could be great timing. If 80% of the population is at home watching the game they are not outside driving their noisy cars or visiting the area you want to record in. This might sound funny, but thoughts like this can really help you plan. Alternatively, it's the perfect day to go and record a sports ball crowd!

The benefit of location recording is that you can capture truly unique content and with some careful planning you can capture the best possible content for your project. There is a reason why AAA products will go out and record their own gun sounds, or car sounds, or whatever else. First, they can capture the exact perspective that works best for their project. So they don't have the issue we encountered with sound libraries of the wind moaning when we want groaning or the stream flowing a little too slowly. You can source exactly what you need. Unique content is also important. When you record your own raw source material it means that your project is no longer at risk of sounding like anyone else's product. There are way too many well-known sound effects that get used again and again in games, films, and animation. Obviously as a sound designer I am more likely to notice these, but I have had friends comment on certain sounds in films "oh, was that that camel sound again? This time they used at for a dragon, last film it was an elephant."

Location recording is not a quick fix though. It can provide exact and original content but you either have to set up a specific recording session or you have to scout and travel to specific locations to capture the material you need. Both examples require time and both examples require equipment.

Advances in recording technology have provided all of us with an incredible series of tools and equipment to use for location recording. Handheld devices are more powerful than ever and also less expensive than ever and this will likely to improve over years to come. I own a range of handheld devices and I usually always carry at least one on me at all times. Many of my favorite recordings were opportunistic recordings because I just happened to be in the right place at the right time. For new reality content mono, stereo, multichannel, binaural, and ambisonic recordings can all be useful and relevant depending on your approach so almost all types of microphones and equipment can be useful.

For point-source spatialized sounds to add to a project, standard mono sound files are often the best way to go. Recording clean mono recordings of birds, insects, water sources, vehicles, and many other things allow you to position those sounds into a spatial environment and then control their sound behavior using your authoring tools.

Ambisonic content can create interesting bed layers for 360 videos and is a quick way to create linear atmos and environmental content. Ambisonic recordings can be used in interactive content but there are some limitations on how they can be implemented. Ambisonic recordings of music could provide spectacular immersion for a 360 video.

Many people have said that binaural content is not suited for VR and 360 video because it doesn't support head tracking and cannot be placed spatially like mono sounds. I think binaural may have some very interesting applications for new reality content but it will be up to the individual to experiment with the exact best way to utilize this material. Binaural is excellent for providing a sense of proximity and this is still currently an area where HRTF content has some limitations, so clever design and use of binaural content could fill some gaps in our current audio palette.

Many tools such as the Facebook Spatial Workstation allow the inclusion of multichannel surround recordings. These are sometimes implemented as virtual channels and in some cases tools exist to help convert his content into a limited ambisonic domain. Regardless of how you use this content it is still something that can have value so don't disregard any old multichannel recordings you may have, they may find new life in a virtual experience.

The good

- You can capture exactly what you need if you invest the time and effort.
- It provides unique content that no one else will have.
- You get to travel.
- It will sometimes capture content you never would have dreamed of.

The bad

- Location recording equipment can be very expensive.
- Cheaper equipment can sometimes have quality issues.
- It can be very time-consuming.
- You need to be prepared to travel.

Foley

I have listed foley separately to location recording for a number of reasons. I consider foley to be the art of creating sound effects through performance rather than simply capturing a recording. In linear media foley is the process of recording sounds that are created by the foley artists in sync with the film content. So the foley artist watches the film and makes actions that will create sounds appropriate for what is being displayed on screen. The simplest example of this is footsteps being recorded as the foley artist walks on various surface materials in time with what they see on the screen. A more complex example of this is a foley artist that uses a series of tools and objects to represent an actor onscreen trying to pick a lock and then disarm a bomb. The actual objects used by the foley artist may be very different to what we see on screen. It is part of the craft of the foley artist to select and manipulate objects that have interesting sounds to produce good audio content to add to the film.

The second reason I list foley in its own category is because of the controlled nature of the recording environment. I personally extend the term "foley" to include the recording of sounds for any SFX work within a studio. So for games we seldom perform foley in time with a video, but we do create sounds just like the picking lock and disarming bomb to use in a game and we may well approach it in the same manner as a foley artist, mainly because they are awesome at what they do and we get super inspired by them. So when we "create" sounds that we are recording directly I like to refer to that as foley, but the controlled and silent environment of a recording studio or foley stage provides us with a far better work space than being out in the wild where we have to deal with uncontrollable elements and the randomness of nature.

Foley has its own challenges and workflow tricks, but it can be an excellent way of generating assets for a project and I think for VR especially foley has some very significant advantages. When we spoke about sound effects libraries, one issue was finding the content you really needed. I think the personal and private nature of VR experiences and 360 video will mean that foley recording will become very useful as a regular source for content.

In VR and 360 video we are placed into a virtual experience, but the key aspect is that we are there in that world space. So we see everything from the perspective of someone right there in the space. From a sound point of view that means the sound of any action we take in the virtual space needs to really feel like we performed it. Those personal sounds need to have a real sense of closeness and proximity. For this reason, I think foley work from a first-person perspective can provide assets with an excellent feel for virtual experiences. If we place a microphone directly in front of a foley artist right at chest level and then ask them to manipulate an item such as a clock or a locked container the microphone should pick up a good close-in and detailed recording of those actions, which is exactly how we would likely hear those sound ourselves. When played back to the audience, the quality of the sounds already has the quality of a user's perspective before we even apply spatial positioning.

I also think the exaggerated nature of some foley work might also apply nicely to certain new reality experiences. In the same way cartoon sounds are often overplayed, exaggerated, and larger than life I suspect that for certain virtual experiences this exaggeration might enhance the experience for the user. Remember the audience in VR and 360 is part of the experience and in many cases is the star of an experience, so including sound content that highlights this central experience and helps draw focus to keys aspects of the narrative may increase the immersion for the audience even though we are may be moving away from realistic audio to stylized audio.

I will talk about microphones more later, but the choice of microphone can make a significant difference to the material you capture.

It is more than just choosing a mic that records a clean sound with less noise or a mic that is capable of capturing sufficiently high SPLs for a loud bang. Recording engineers for music production will tell you that many microphones have very distinctive qualities to the sound they capture. Some are clean and clear with a crystal-like quality to their sound, while others can capture the warm dark tones of a double bass being played with a bow. These microphone characteristics can be utilized just as well for recording foley content as they can for capturing musical instruments. The exact same sound recorded with two different microphones might provide an excellent point of difference between the sound being generated by the audience's actions and when it is produced by other characters. A sense of proximity and warmth would help sell to the audience that it is their hands performing the action they see through their headsets. Then if another character or even another audience member took over the action from them a recording of the same sounds but brighter might highlight the room reflections and assist in localizing the sound away from the original user's perspective.

The good

- Foley is captured in a controlled environment.
- Foley can produce some excellent and original content very quickly.
- Working with a professional foley artist can create some inspiring results.
- Foley allows for rapid iteration where the artist can change and revise the content immediately.

The bad

- Building your own foley stage is expensive and requires a fair amount of space.
- Using a professional foley artist can be expensive.
- It can take time to develop your own foley skills. Do not underestimate how good the pros are.

Sound Creation

Sound creation can cover a huge range of processes. Mixing two sounds from a sound library can create a new and unique sound, using synthesis or generative processes. Recording unusual and unknown sounds and then using them to represent something very different to the object you recorded is essentially creating a new sound. The process or combination of processes is less important than the desire to create something new from scratch.

Crafting each sound to exactly fit a specific purpose in your project is the approach taken by most of the top-level studios and production companies. There is a reason why groups such as Skywalker Sound have such excellent reputations; I think this is largely because they take the extra effort to create new and unique content for so many of the sounds they need. This allows them to present fresh audio that is fit for purpose rather than just rolling out the same library sounds every few projects.

Crafting new sounds is a time-consuming process. An individual sound may not take very long, but the overall approach to creating new material for a whole project requires planning, sourcing of raw material, and then time spent designing, building, and then reviewing each sound. This is not an option for a fast turnaround project or something with a smaller budget, but for the right project it will almost always result in a better end result, as each element can be tailored more closely to what you need for your project rather than choosing the closest option from a library of available sounds.

The good

- You can craft your assets to fit your exact needs.
- Your product can achieve a truly unique sound environment.
- You should not be limited by the contents of an existing collection.
- It requires significant design input from the audio team.

The bad

- It requires significant design input from the audio team.
- It requires more time for production than using libraries.
- It is usually more expensive because of the time and effort required.

Generative or Procedural Audio

There are veracious tools, methods, and utilities for creating generative and procedural audio content. And again, like all things there are both good and bad methods of doing this. I have encountered some tools that claim to procedurally generate realistic weather sounds and when I tried them they just produced various forms of white noise, none of which really sounded like the weather types they claimed to represent. There are regular articles claiming that someone has produced a program that will put all sound recordists and sound designers out of work, but there still seem to be many of us employed, and so far none of these claims have achieved much.

I find generative and procedural sound design far more interesting to create sounds that we could never imagine, than to try and create sounds we know so well where we will instantly notice any discrepancies. So many games, movies, and television programs have a need to create interesting and surreal environments where unusual sound content is exactly the kind of content we want. For these projects a generative effect that manipulates other sound content, and builds, and layers, and alters the original material can be a very good approach to production.

Generative and procedural designs let us create content that is unique each time it is played and considering the immersive nature of the new reality experiences this could provide some excellent options for virtual spatialized audio. Many forms of generative audio are created by providing a system with some raw source sounds and then defining how you want them to be triggered. In this manner randomization or random selection between carefully defined guidelines allows the author to have a range of elements that are not finalized until the exact point of playback. Volume, pitch, playback rate, exactly which source material is triggered, and a range of DSP processes can be set within certain ranges and when playback occurs, the final "render" is created in real time. So in reality it is not possible for the exact same content to ever play more than once. These changes can be subtle or wildly variable depending on the wishes of the creator.

I have lately heard it mentioned that in the future some audiences will enjoy the idea of the music they listen to being authored fully spatialized, but also with many random elements built into the composition so the overall theme might be similar but each listening of the content is slightly different. With the way trends in art, fashion, and music change, it is entirely possible this might become a thing. Only time will tell.

microphones

Microphones are such a broad and important category for any discussion about audio and audio production that they could essentially become the topic for an entire book, and I am sure they have been. In this case they are a critical part of collecting the assets for the creation of your project, and because of the very wide range of formats that can be utilized they need to be discussed.

The exact choice of which microphone is best for which task is a very personal decision. There is a wide range of specifications, tonal colors, reliability issues, and just usability that means it is very difficult to state that microphone X is better than microphone Y for any specific task. All I can do is speak about my personal experiences and the things I have noticed about various microphones. Some of this information is quite general and could be applied to recording any content, but in all cases I will try and apply my knowledge and experience to how these microphones can be specifically useful for capturing material for the new realties.

I will speak about some of the microphones that I have used over the years and how they are relevant to capturing content for the new realities. In all cases I am not specifically recommending a particular brand or model, but by speaking about my experiences with a particular microphone, I can illustrate some of the issues I may have encountered using that equipment and what benefits or issues arose. In some cases, issues might have been because of user error, but it is important and valid to describe my experiences as they provide a useful context for people who may not have used a specific type of microphone.

Directional Microphones

By directional mics, I am generally referring to cardioid or hypercardioid microphones, which are usually referred to as shotgun mics. These have been the primary microphone used for capturing source sounds for over 50 years and are used by film and TV crews, location recordists, and even in studios for foley work—and of course dialogue capture on set.

The directional nature of a shotgun microphone makes them excellent for recording source material for spatial audio production.

Mono sounds usually work best for positioning spatially and shotgun microphones are designed specifically to capture a strong signal from the sound you point the microphone at, and to reduce the signal of other sound sources that are off-axis. So a good shotgun microphone allows the user to capture a cleaner signal than many other types of microphone. Also, generally shotgun mics are designed to not add any tonal coloration to the sound. As with all things there are different qualities you can find in different microphones so it is worth selecting the right tool for a specific task.

I have a variety of shotgun mics that I have used over the years and I how I use them depends on their qualities.

Sennheiser MKH60

This is probably my primary workhorse mic for 90% of the work I do. I have used this mic for over 15 years. It is rock solid, reliable, and seems to be practically indestructible. It has excellent side cancellation and good sensitivity so it can capture sounds at a good distance. This is a good general purpose microphone for capturing mono source material and a microphone like this one can be utilized across a range of purposes.

While I find its tone darker than some of the newer microphones I have tried, it continues to outperform others for side cancellation, so any time that is important this mic is the first choice to go into the field. Much of the mono content I use in designing spatial audio environments was recorded with this mic.

Sennheiser MKH60.

Rode NTG3

I purchased this as a backup shotgun mic and was pleasantly surprised by its crisp tone. The content it records is brighter than the MKH60 and as such it can be very good for recording bird and insect sounds as it records the frequency content well. However, the NTG3 does not have nearly as good side cancellation as the MKH60 and so this becomes a point of consideration. For the material I am gathering, which is more important? While bright clear recordings are nice, it becomes a hard choice if you need side cancellation to capture a signal clear of unwanted noises. The NTG3 is a more affordably priced microphone and so can provide a good low cost option as either a "my first shotgun" option or as a backup to a larger collection.

Audio Technica stereo BP4029

The Audio Technica is a balance between the directional capabilities of a shotgun microphone and the desire to capture a stereo field. It has three settings so that it can capture more directionally, an MS format or a wider stereo field. In this regard, the flexibility makes this microphone a useful versatile tool. It may not have the same level of side cancellation of the MKH60 or perform as well as a dedicated stereo mic but I have found it performs well enough within each of its settings to be a very useful mic and the combination of the three modes makes this an excellent piece of equipment.

Rode NTG3.

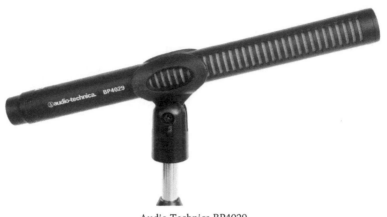

Audio Technica BP4029.

For capturing new reality content, it provides a very useful function. In directional mode it can record the material that you might want to use to build up a spatial environment. Once you have recorded the directional material you can then switch it to wide stereo mode and capture good reference material to use later when building your virtual environment. This can work well as a guide for how your directional material can be implemented into the virtual world so that it creates a suitable simulation of the real world that you can reference in the stereo files.

Sanken CS1e

This is unusual in that while technically classed as a shotgun mic, it is really not a mic that I would use outdoors. I found the description of this microphone quite inaccurate when Sanken described it as a mic suitable for external sound gathering and for use for onset dialogue recordings. When I tested it for these purposes I found it very inadequate for the task. It is not sensitive to capturing a sound at any real distance and so struggles when compared with other shotgun mics.

However, used inside or in a studio this mic is capable of capturing incredibly clean, clear, and detailed recordings of even very quiet sound sources. So this microphone is excellent for studio foley work of detailed sound sources or for capturing hard-to-hear content of small devices or other quiet sounds. Sometimes you will want to be capturing really good detail in your sound sources, so that you can

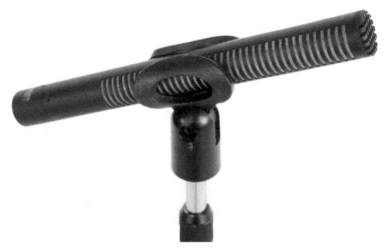

Sanken CS1e.

zoom right into the workings of a clock when our virtual self places it against our ear; this microphone is an excellent tool for capturing those details and providing you with content you might not otherwise have had access to. I find this an outstanding mic. I am just bewildered by the inaccurate marketing description from the people who made it. It is an excellent example of why you should test any microphone before you purchase it, and to not take the marketing spiel of the manufacturer as gospel. It really doesn't matter what a company claims their equipment can do, it's up to you to assess it and importantly listen to it and decide for yourself if it suits the purpose you intend to use it for.

Dynamic Microphones

The mic categories in this section are a little mixed up. Directional and omnidirectional categories refer to the response pattern of the mic, while dynamic describes the structural design. However, for the purposes of this book the categories are more designed to describe their purpose and how I utilize them, so my directional mics (which are all condenser mics) get used for similar purposes, my omnimics all get used for similar purposes and even though I have a range of dynamic mics I tend to use them in similar ways.

Shure SM7B

This mic was recommended to us because we needed a good consistent mic for dialogue recording and that is what it is used for most of the time. In fact, it sits on my desk as my main mic for online conversations. It has an excellent warm characteristic for capturing dialogue and I think this is perfect for the first-person perspective of VR experiences. The quality of voice captured with this mic is ideal for the standard "voice in your head" whenever you need to record the dialogue for the character the audience will be controlling.

The warmth of this mic can also be quite useful for capturing sounds on location sometimes. They may not have the sensitivity or directional nature of my shotgun mics, but when capturing loud sounds like firearms it can provide a good additional layer of sound that can be mixed in with the condenser recordings and combined to achieve nice results. Dynamic mics are also good and hardy, which can be a bonus.

Shure SM57

Speaking of good and hardy mics, the Shure SM57 and its sibling the SM58 are possibly the most rugged mics ever made. Both of these

Shure SM7B.

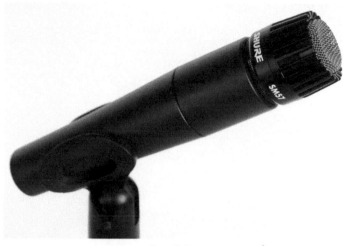

Shure SM57.

microphones have a history and reputation with live musicians simply because they can go to hell and back and survive the journey. For field recording the SM57 has the limitations of any dynamic mic, but as an extra option for tonal color or to capture content in a location that is likely to destroy any other microphone the SM57 is worth having around. I have dropped mine many times and it is always comforting to know you can rely on a tough piece of equipment. Even better, if they do get damaged they are inexpensive enough that you do not need to panic.

AKG D112

A purpose designed kick-drum microphone might seem like an odd choice for a location recording collection. Except when you look at the SPLs this mic can capture and then you realize that a mic that was designed to kiss a giant booming bass drum can be a super useful thing to have around. The D112 has the similar warm sound of many dynamic mics and the extreme amplitude capabilities means it can be used to capture loud machinery, weaponry of all kinds, and of course, loud musical instruments. This is certainly not a microphone that gets taken out on every gig, and its shape does mean you need to position it carefully and get used to working with it, but when it does come out it is another dynamic mic that is rugged, capable, and reliable to do what it was designed to do.

AKG D112.

Omnidirectional Microphones

Omnidirectional microphones capture a mono image of the entire 360 field around the microphone. They are very useful for capturing content without an on-axis, off-axis element. An omnimic is the core part of an MS recording format and also the core of any ambisonic setup. But as a standalone mic, are they useful for capturing new reality content?

Lapel mics

Lapel mics are designed to clip to the clothing of actors so you can record their dialogue and for that purpose they generally do a very good job. For production of new reality content lapel mics are excellent for capturing VO content when actors are also performing motion capture content. So an actor can be performing body movements that sync up to the script, essentially fully acting their parts and the team can be capturing both the motion capture data and the voice recordings at the same time.

Michael D. Csurics explained a technique of recording voice actors by placing a lapel microphone on top of the head of the actor.

The capsule sits on the forehead with the cable running over the top and to the back of the head of the actor. This positions the microphone centrally and also avoids interference from clothing, which is very useful if you are doing dual voice-over and motion capture sessions as the actor can move and speak without their movements being recorded. The main benefit of this position is the quality of the sound. A lapel mic clipped to a lapel or other position under the head has a real issue with interference from the body. The chin actually blocks a lot of the signal that travels to the mic and the resulting sound can be muddled or too nasal in quality. By comparison the mic up in the hairline can capture a much brighter and clearer sound for spoken voice recording. So for any vocal recording this is a much better result, but for any content designed for new reality content I think it will produce a more realistic and direct vocal result. So if the vocals are being spoken from the audience's perspective it is more likely to sound like the voice in our head, but if it is being spoken by a third party the clearer signal should make localization of the sound more natural for the audience.

Lapel microphones can also be excellent at capturing sound effect content. Because of their design many lapel mics have excellent SPL capabilities, that is, they can deal with really loud sounds. But lapel mics have a close-range sensitivity because they are designed to capture the voice of the person wearing them, but not all the other sound around them. This is why lapel mics are often used for recording musical instruments on stage and in ensembles. They record an excellent signal of the object they are near, but not much beyond that. They tend to be omnidirectional as well, so you don't need to worry about getting the exact angle correct. Because of these factors and also because they are small and lightweight, they are very good for recording vehicles.

DPA 4061

I have been using DPA 4061 microphones for quite some time and I have many times attached them to cars inside the engine bay, or right at the exhaust pipe or even on the wheel arches above a spinning wheel. They work equally well on motorbikes, trucks, and tanks. In all these examples, I have been able to record excellent quality isolated content from the vehicle I am working with, even to the point of capturing two or three perspectives under the bonnet in the engine bay where one mic captures the fans spinning, another the pistons working, and maybe a third near the manifold. The high

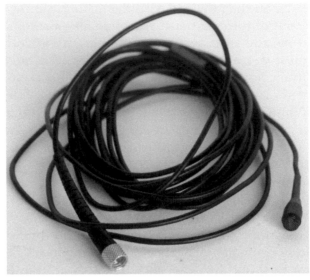

DPA 4061.

SPL capabilities mean the recordings do not distort and the small size and light weight mean they do not interfere with or damage the vehicle you are working with. This process is an excellent way to capture engines and devices in great detail to use in new reality projects.

The depth of detail discussed earlier is something that lapel microphones really help you achieve. The small size allows them to be positioned extremely close to many sound sources and the omnidirection pattern allows you to capture an accurate and detailed example of your target sound. If your choice of lapel microphone has a high SPL capability combined with a rapid response time then they can also be very suitable for recording firearms and detonations. The biggest risk with this type of microphone is that the cable is integral to the microphone and cable damage can result in the entire microphone being rendered unusable, so they need to be used with extreme care.

Binaural Microphones

Binaural miking has existed for quite some time, but is often mislabeled or misrepresented. Binaural recording is achieved by simulating the way in which human ears hear sound. This is usually done with a device that mimics a human head with the microphones positioned where the ears are. A model of a human ear around the microphones results in an approximation of ILD, IID, and IPD behavior of the sound as it reaches each microphone. The "head" provides the shadowing effect that a human head does. So while some devices position microphones at the correct distance and others even simulate the ear shapes, the more complex devices that include a full head model tend to get better results.

Binaural mics record on a flat plane. That is, they do not convey a sense of elevation in the recorded material in the way that ambisonic microphones can. Binaural recordings are also best heard through headphones as this removes any issue with speaker crosstalk that can reduce the effect of a binaural presentation. One of the most effective binaural experiences is the barbershop experience which has been created many times over the years.

The barbershop experience is a recording of someone having their hair cut. The barber walks around the binaural microphone, making small talk with their customer, while using scissors to "cut their hair." The combination of how the binaural microphone functions and the limitations of how humans hear makes this quite a convincing experience for most listeners. It is particularly good at making the audience feel as though someone is close behind them operating scissors. This is partially due to the design of the recording equipment but also partially due to human's tendency to position sounds to our rear when we cannot see the source of the sound in front of us.

Binaural recordings can work well for capturing music as it provides a good sense of spatial depth for the audience when listened to. The recorded material is essentially captured using the HRTF of the dummy head. The consequence of this is similar to using any HRTF data in that some listeners will find it more convincing than others, most likely due to the level of difference between their own personal HRTF and the dummy head data.

One key area where binaural content could be useful to new reality experiences is the effectiveness of close proximity sounds. Binaural recordings capture a far greater sense of "close in" sound content than most ambisonic microphones. For this reason, I think there are still several key areas where binaural material could be useful for new reality experiences. One of our primary goals is to convince the audience that we have placed them inside the experience and that they are really there. A life-threatening situation such as a battlefield takes on a different tone if it includes sound content at close proximity. A bullet whizzing past the audience's head is likely to raise the stakes of a virtual experience if the audience really feels like that bullet is a threat. Ambisonic implementation of a bullet whizz may be able to provide a sense of movement within the listener's area, but most ambisonic techniques at this stage do not deal well with content that is very close to the listener. A binaural recording of a bullet fired past a binaural microphone at very close proximity could provide a far more convincing sonic experience.

The key point with binaural is that we need to compensate for the fact that it does not support head tracking. So if I play a binaural recording of a piece of music to someone wearing a headset that binaural recording is head-locked and will follow them as they turn their head. For head-locked content this is suitable and desirable. But if you want to use binaural content as spatialized sounds it is not desirable. One workaround for this is to keep any binaural content extremely short. A single bullet whiz sound is both a very short sound and also one where the exact position of it can matter less than other sounds. It is an "effect," a sonic artifact designed to grab the listener's attention. The quick but close proximity of the sound is more important than where it is positioned. So that "zing" sound can happen in any position and it is still likely to startle the audience.

Another example is a short "ghost whisper" effect. A single word, or a couple of words spoken quickly could be presented in binaural format to create the effect of the speaker being right behind your ear. A short example will be finished before the audience reacts and turns their head. They turn to find nothing there, which highlights the discomfort of the experience. Again, this could be captured with an ambisonic recording, but a binaural recording can achieve the close proximity more convincingly.

Binaural recording as a new realities audio technique

Because of the way binaural recording simulates how the human ears capture sound the listener can feel like they are actually in the location that was recorded. This usually involves microphones that are mounted in a dummy head. The dummy head has accurately formed outer ear shells and a density similar to a real head. The microphones are placed inside the head approximately where the human eardrum is located.

A binaural recording works because the sound within an environment travels to the microphones in a similar way to how sound travels to our ears. The artificial ear shells result in a similar delay and frequency in processing the sound waves as we hear with our own ears. So a sound coming from behind is filtered by the shape of our outer ear, a sound to the left takes longer to travel to the right

Binaural dummy head with a few scratches and dents.

ear as it travels around the head. These factors create a convincing reproduction of real human hearing. Some of the more modern binaural recording devices remove the head model and provide just the ears positioned at the correct distance. Other devices allow the user to place microphones into their own ears like earbuds and these use the recordists' own ears and head to influence the captured material.

Binaural does provide an effective and interesting sound capture format, but for the new reality formats, it is quite limited. Binaural cannot capture material that can be implemented to support head tracking. Let's take a moment to explore why this matters.

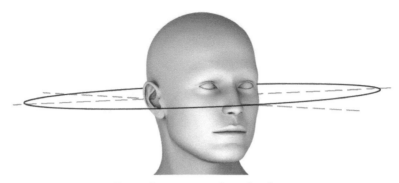

Binaural captures sound on a flat plane.

A binaural recording will capture a fairly convincing image of the space in which the recording device is placed. You can get a sense of depth and positioning of sound sources within that space. But it is a static image. You cannot take a binaural recording of a forest and use it in a VR project where the user can move their head. The binaural image would rotate with the player's head and as a result break the immersion of the experience.

Binaural also does not effectively capture a sense of elevation, that is, audio content above and below the listener. Much like more conventional recording techniques, binaural recording is more like a flat plane or slice of the world with no up or down variation.

DIY binaural dummy head

Many years ago, I had need for a binaural head for some test recordings. The equipment is rare and expensive, and at the time our team could not afford to purchase one, so I made one. There are two essential qualities for a binaural dummy head mic setup: the authenticity of the ear shape and the density of the head cavity. I bought an inexpensive mannequin head that had accurately shaped outer ears. Then I just needed to set it up so I could add microphones to it.

I cut the upper back off the head so I could access the inside. I then drilled two small holes inside the ears where the ear canal is positioned. I measured my own ear canal and selected a drill bit that was about the right size.

Next I glued two plastic tubes inside the ear holes. I made them long enough so I could slide lapel capsule microphones into the ear canal and still have room to adjust the mic back and forth. This meant I could adjust the sound by repositioning each of the microphones.

Mannequin head with ear canal holes.

Once all that was done I sprayed the head with black paint and then filled the inside with spray foam to add some density. The weight and density was not as much as a real head but it did significantly improve the sound captured while still allowing the head to be light enough to be convenient to use.

As the images indicate, my rig has been well used. The inconsistent height of the ear canals is actually a more accurate representation of how a real person's head is shaped. I already had some good quality lapel microphones, and I had measured the ear canal tubes so my DPA 4061 mics would fit in. Any type of lapel mic would technically work, but the better the quality of the mic the better the

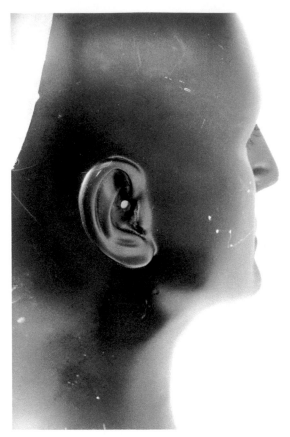

Binaural dummy head interior. Note the different
heights of the ear canals.

overall result is likely to be. This allowed me to utilize microphones I already owned and capture binaural content for about $100 worth of parts and some time in the workshop.

Ambisonic Microphones

Ambisonic microphones are currently "the new black." Many companies are producing different pieces of equipment in different price categories. The price range tends to align with the order of ambisonic field that the microphone can capture. Microphones such as the Sennheiser Ambeo and the Tetramic are first order ambisonic mics, while the Eigen mic is a fourth-order microphone with a price tag to match.

All true ambisonic microphones will capture a spherical 360 sound field. The difference between the orders is an increase in resolution. It is like adding more pixels to a camera. The additional microphones capture more points within the spherical field and so there is a higher resolution of spatial data designed to give a more accurate representation of real world audio behavior. The ambisonic format is also useful in that it can be transformed into any other audio panning format such as mono, stereo, or surround—great for source capture.

Ambisonic content however is not a simple fix or magic bullet for spatial audio. It has its limitations like anything else. Capturing a perfect ambisonic sound file that will just fit nicely into your project is no easier that trying to capture the perfect stereo image of an environment that will just fit nicely into your project. There are a huge range of challenges in capturing any recorded content and ambisonic mics sometimes just add more elements to the complexity. An ambisonic microphone is a tool and needs to be used well by the operator to capture good quality content which is then implemented well into a project.

Under ideal circumstances such as a remote forest environment with lots of spatial sound sources, an ambisonic microphone could capture an excellent spherical sound field that could work well as an atmospheric layer for a 360 video. In this example you would have a base layer that would support head tracking and could work to establish the sense of space for your environmental scene. From this point you could then add additional layers on top of the ambisonic content to build up your audio content.

Another place where ambisonic recordings can work extremely well is in capturing musical performances. A live orchestra or choir performance in a suitable performance venue could let you capture an excellent musical sound environment with all positional sources preserved. As a listening experience this would be a wonderful use for the ambisonic format. The audience could feel as though they were in among the singers or musicians. A musical performance also often requires little editing or the addition of extra content.

The issue for me with an ambisonic recording is that I cannot move through it.

Sennheiser Ambeo

I do not own an ambisonic microphone as yet. I have a Zoom H2N that can capture a basic flat plane kind of ambisonic recording, but a true ambisonic mic has the capsules set out in a specific formation.

Sennheiser very kindly gave me access to an Ambeo while I was writing this book to allow me to capture some content to evaluate its capabilities and get used to working with an ambisonic field. For this I would like to thank them sincerely.

Beyond the loan of the microphone itself I have done some research into the various ambisonic microphones and seen what others have to say about them. Interestingly I have seen various people on social media downplay the usefulness and performance of the Ambeo for various reasons, however what was interesting was few of those who criticized this equipment seemed to have ever used it. By contrast I have several colleagues who own and use the Ambeo and they all speak highly of it. Like all new technology we need to be careful about how we assess it and who we listen to.

One piece of interesting pretest research I found was a review and assessment of a selection of ambisonic-capable microphones. This review compared the Ambeo with other mics including the higher order and much more expensive Eigen mic. What was interesting was several comments that while the Eigen was very good for spatialization with its many capsules, its tonal quality was not as good as the less expensive microphones and the Ambeo was specifically mentioned. While the Eigen is certainly an impressive feat of engineering and the large number of capsules will allow for a deeper ambisonic field, Sennheiser has been producing microphones for decades, so it does not surprise me that the Ambeo would have good sound quality. So my expectations of the Ambeo were as high as they would be for any other piece of Sennheiser equipment.

After testing

In many ways, the Ambeo lived up to what I expected. The sound quality was extremely crisp and clear which I think is important for an ambisonic microphone. I found the overall tonal quality to be good and recordings made were precise. I conferred with some colleagues and we agree that the Ambeo is good for capturing general ambisonic content of environments with lots of point sources. Recording a crowd at a market, cars driving by, or a fireworks display, are all scenarios that allow the Ambeo to capture a good quality representation of spatial point sources. I can see myself adding an Ambeo to my collection in the near future.

For something like recording quiet, constant sound environments such as a gentle breeze in a forest or room tones, the Ambeo is less well suited. This is not because of the limitations of the mic as an

Sennheiser Ambeo ambisonic microphone.

ambisonic capture device, but more the general limitations of capturing that kind of content at all.

There are two aspects here that are important to understand for the recording of spatial sound content. The first is that localizing constant noise sources is really difficult for humans at the best of times. Even with the best recording and playback equipment available, a human will always find it easier to track the regular repeating pulse of a ticking clock than the constant, unchanging noise of a wind or ambient drone. That is simply how we process sound information, so this is a limitation of our hearing as much as it may be a limitation of any piece of equipment.

Second, and specific to the Ambeo, it is a microphone that is constructed to include the four capsules necessary to record an ambisonic field plus the circuitry, housing, and complex cabling for such a system and all this for a bit over $1,000. Within my entire range of microphones, I have many that are both more and less expensive than the Ambeo with only one or two capsules and most of those would be ill suited to record very quiet ambiences. For comparison's sake, I created a sound library of room tones and atmos recordings a few years back and I knew I would need a specific microphone to be able to capture what was essentially a bunch of silent rooms. To do this I borrowed a set of microphones from a colleague. These were high-end microphones that could deal with extremely quiet environments. Each microphone had a single capsule and the set of four allowed me to record a spatial representation of the empty spaces. This set of four microphones was worth closer to ten times the cost of the Ambeo mic. They performed brilliantly, but they were designed for that specific purpose and had a price tag to match.

The point I am making here is that often, people have expectations of equipment that are way beyond what is reasonable. I am very careful about the equipment I purchase and where I invest my money. Our microphones, and recorders and DAWs are the tools of our trade and it is critical to us that we get good value out of the money we spend. But we also need to be careful not to expect any one piece of equipment to be a silver bullet, and also to compare its capabilities with other equipment of similar design and price. I have no problem

Array of microphones to capture quiet spaces.

with criticizing equipment that does not perform to the standards I expect, but equally I will call out people who seem to expect miracles.

Specific Purpose Microphones

There are many microphones designed and built for specific purposes. These mics may only get used on very rare occasions, but when they are needed they can allow you to capture some interesting and unique content.

Aquarian H2a

From the moment I first heard about hydrophones I wanted one. The ability to record sound underwater was always appealing to me. At one point, I did go swimming with a small handheld digital recorder in a zip lock bag and I got some interesting material from that, but it only confirmed that a real hydrophone was something I would enjoy working with. The Aquarian hydrophones, I think are designed more for scientific purposes than to gather raw content for creative projects, but they work well for either purpose.

These microphones come options on one aspect, and that is the length of cable provided. When I purchased mine, I selected a 30 meter length of cable, but I believe they can have up to 300 meters of cable as an option. I have used the H2a to record boats of all different shapes and sizes, and a range of water sounds from waves

Aquarian H2a.

to splashes and bubbles. It is a mono microphone, but because of how I usually create my spatial environments a series of mono wave sounds recorded underwater is ideal for creating an underwater virtual environment.

I am sure this microphone could be used for a range of unusual purposes such as recording any kind of liquid. So if you have a need to record inside your oatmeal or what a can of soda sounds like from the inside, this is the type of microphone you might consider. Hydrophones are rare and often expensive. One of the primary benefits of this model is that it was quite a reasonable price for a specialist mic.

Portable Digital Recorders

I once had someone reprimand me for using a portable digital recorder to capture some sounds I intended to include in a commercial sound effects library. "What? You can't possibly use those sounds. They will not be nearly good enough quality!" This statement was made without the person having listened to either the original source material or the recordings made. Their assumption was, that it is a cheap device therefore it should never be used for professional sound capture. I suspect there might even be some people reading this now how might agree with those thoughts. But context is relevant to all things.

The specific recordings from the above conversation were captured as part of developing The Aviation Collection, a SFX library made up of over 3,000 recordings of a wide range of classic and military aircraft. This library took over 18 months to record and compile. During that time aircraft were recorded at various locations and many different types of aircraft were recorded. One of the significant aspects of many of the aircraft was that I captured recordings from inside the cockpit during flight and this would have been impossible without a "cheap" digital recorder.

At the time I had been recording the aircraft from the ground. I was often able to get very close to them during start up and then as they would taxi away, take off and fly around I would need to position myself in the best place I could to record them flying back and forth.

At one stage I decided I wanted to capture some recordings inside one of the planes, mainly to hear it for myself. I had developed quite a good relationship with some of the pilots and I asked how this might be possible. We looked at the aircraft and decided the quickest and most importantly safest way to do this was for the pilot to put a

Gaining access does not mean you are free to do anything you want.

recorder into the leg pocket of their flight suit. I thought it might get a little muffled, but at least my curiosity would be served and I would get to hear the inside of the plane.

What I got was an excellent capture of how the plane sounded from inside the cockpit during operation. In fact, the recording was so good I then made it standard procedure to capture all planes in this manner. I believe I am still one of the few people to record the inside of planes such as a Spitfire and Korean Sabre jet during flight.

There are several important aspects to this story. Those vehicles generate a huge amount of sound when they operate and generally that sound is massive mechanical noise. You do not need much to capture those sounds and more importantly the idea that a cheap device might introduce unwanted noise is simply absurd because the aircraft engine is one huge noise machine pumping out 100 dB of sound, so quality preamps become less critical.

The second aspect is one of safety and practicality. A WW2 Spitfire is a craft made out of thin wood over a metal frame. They are designed to be lightweight and maneuverable. The cockpit has nothing inside it that is not critical to the plane's operation. So no matter how much time or budget I might have, the reality of mounting any kind of high-end recording device into the cockpit would be impractical if not illegal. Air safety rules are strict about altering or adding objects that might be a danger to the pilot or aircraft. So the equation was really simple.

A selection of professional recording devices.

Capture a recording with a handheld device in a pocket, or ... capture nothing at all.

If stories have morals, then the moral of this story is this: "The best tool for the job is the one that gets the job done." I have since attached portable recorders to the underside of skateboards, the outsides of tank turrets, swam with them underwater, and placed them so close to fires they have almost melted. I will defend to anyone their usefulness and suitability in capturing content for professional projects. They have their place like any other piece of equipment. As with most equipment, it is not what you have, it is how you use it. Remember—the SFX for *Star Wars* were recorded on tape.

music: how and why music in the new realties forces a shift in perspective

How we design and implement music for film, television, or inter-active experiences has always been a complex discussion. There is never one correct or "best" way to approach this topic. The technical possibilities and depth of immersion for the new technologies means that this conversation has just gotten even more complex.

blurring the line between diegetic and nondiegetic "musical" content

I have purposefully placed the word musical in inverted commas in the above heading. For many years now the line between sound design and musical content has been blurring and there are still many who find this lack of clarity challenging. Recently, the Academy of Motion Picture Art made a decision that the score for the 2016 film *Arrival* was not suitable to be nominated for best score. One of their stated reasons was that it was difficult to distinguish between what was music and what was sound design. I personally find this explanation absurd as an awards committee should be seeking and encouraging new and innovative approaches to the creative arts, not dismissing work simply because it is challenging to categorize neatly.

In general, the blending and blurring of the line between sound design and music has allowed for the creation of some unique and fascinating content. Overall I think it benefits us all as creative individuals. When we move into the realm of the new realities, the technology provides new possibilities, but the delivery format also allows the presentation of material never before experienced. The new realities allow an audience to access visual and audio content that cannot be presented on traditional devices. Head rotation, surround audio, interaction through gestures, and even haptic feedback are all methods of communication that are still being explored and I think we will be discovering new experiences that can be created that we have never dreamed of.

Some of the most enjoyable experiences I have had with games and other interactive media have been specifically when those lines are at their blurriest. *Portal 2* presented its musical score in various ways within the game. In some areas, the player's actions were accompanied by a typical underscoring of the game with nondiegetic music. In most cases this music was completely linear and served to enhance the emotional state of the environment in which the player was exploring. It was a form of "mood music." In other areas, the music was produced by objects within the environment and this music would adapt and evolve depending on the player's actions. Unlike an interactive score that might adapt to match the narrative, the dynamic music in *Portal 2* was directly affected by the player's actions. It was as though the music-making devices existed within the game space and the character was activating and tuning them as they moved them and operated various devices. For example, if the player picked up a companion cube, the music would change from being underscored to sound as if it were coming from the cube itself, with more layers of music and an increase in volume. Blurring the boundaries between diegetic and nondiegetic music added a significant level of enjoyment as the player progressed through the level but also served to underscore the narrative progression at the same time.

Playdead's *INSIDE* was a game that had no underscored music in the traditional sense. The initial audio for the game played at a bare whisper and yet it did not feel empty or lacking for the want of music. The general ambience of the forest worked so well to establish the emotional language of the game that it could be argued it served the same purpose as a musical score. As the game progressed musical sounds

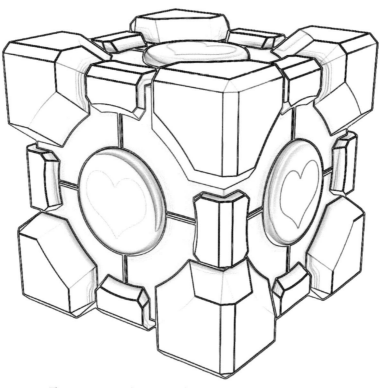

The companion cubes in Portal 2 are a source of diegetic music.

and sound-designed music highlighted and underscored actions, environments, and events. The resulting experience was a powerful narrative where there is not a single word, or spoken, or written text.

Where Is Our Music?

When we use HRTF technology to create a virtual world it provides a much larger canvas on which to position our audio content. Music editors and mixers often are challenged to combine the many elements of a project into a coherent single narrative by spreading the audio content across the dynamic and frequency ranges within the available spatial area. The more spatial area available, the more the mix can be separated. This can add clarity if done well but if implemented poorly it can create an overall sense of confusion. I would like to say that the rules that apply to any multichannel format also apply to spherical surround, but I am no longer sure if this is the case. While researching this book, I have been constantly surprised at how many rules may not apply to the new realities, or at may apply only in a modified form. My instincts tell me that we should apply many of the lessons we have learned from traditional media. We should present a coherent and logical mix for our audience. But think of how our current technology evolved. Stereo recordings changed from the early days of *The Beatles* where it was two instruments on each side, to complex blended mixes of instruments across the stereo spectrum. What may seem odd or even wrong now, might become the standard in 10 years' time. Do we position a 60-piece

Playdead's Inside.
(Copyright Playdead 2017. With permission.)

orchestra all around the listener in a spherical manner? It seems unthinkable right now, but the only reason someone has not tried it previously is because we didn't have the technology to achieve it. I am often left doubting what the "best" approach is, because this new era of technology allows so many possibilities that perhaps there are no longer the same limits that led to the "rules" we currently follow.

Spherical HRTF provides a sonic canvas that, in some ways, is beyond even what we experience in real life. When we go to a concert or band gig the experience is mostly static. We either sit in a single location to experience the event or the performance is presented through amplified loudspeakers. This means we hear two sound sources, a left and a right speaker. So a live orchestra may consist of 70 musicians arrayed over a 50-meter stage, but the audience is static. If it's a band gig, the audience may be able to move around or dance to the music, but the output speakers are static. There are certainly the indirect soundwave elements that will respond differently as we turn our heads or move around a performance space, but our physical relationship to the musicians mostly doesn't change.

In a surround format we have the opportunity to change our physical relationship to the performers. The audience can mingle among the orchestra, position themselves in, on, or behind the instrumental sound sources. For the first time ever, an audience can hear a performance from the perspective of the conductor or from the perspective of the musicians in the ensemble such as the second clarinet. As a former orchestral horn player, I can assure you there is a very different energy to be had being in and among a performing ensemble. Also, being part of a marching band during a parade has a real energy and excitement that is quite different to the audience's perspective.

We are yet to fully realize the possibilities of using a spherical spatial environment to deliver music mainly because we are still discovering them. Not all possibilities can or should be used. Will it sound amazing to be able to wander around a performing orchestra, or will it simply be a gimmicky distraction?

musical possibilities

Using HRTF we can position our musical sources anywhere around the audience. So a full orchestra with a section of fanfare trumpets singing out from up in the balcony can be experienced through headphones with a sense of elevation very much like the live performance.

It is a unique sound to be in among the orchestra.

But it is not just the addition of extra positional information that spherical audio provides.

Rotation and elevation are the obvious additional benefits of spherical audio. We can place a sound source anywhere around us in a 360-degree flat plane, so our ensemble can surround us completely.

This provides us with the perfect central listener position for a string quartet. This arrangement could be a fairly easily replicated on any speaker system with four or more speakers if the audience is static, but the advantage of the new technologies is that they let the listener move. Head tracking in HRTF would be similar to turning your head if each of the instruments was routed through one of four fixed speakers in a room, with one significant difference.

In the real world if the instruments are routed out of loudspeakers, then each channel plays back a representation of the recorded instrument in the environment it was recorded in. The rear right speaker would play the cello with a captured ambience from the room in which the cello was recorded and those ambiences would only be from the perspective of the microphone that recorded the cello. If you turn your head in relation to the speaker outputting the cello you will hear a change in how you hear that output as your relationship to the speaker and the playback room changes. But what you are hearing is the coloration of the speaker signal in the playback room you are in, not the space in which the cello was performed. If the cello was recorded with no reflections at all then the only reverb will come from the playback space.

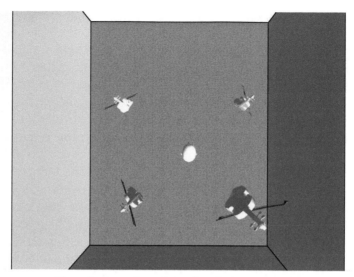

The audience can be positioned inside the string quartet.

This experience in VR with HRTF audio can be created to emit the cello audio from a point within the virtual performance space. If you turn your head the HRTF will alter what you are hearing in relation to that virtual space. So if the virtual space is a beautiful cathedral with wonderful acoustics you will hear the changes in the acoustics relative to your listening position within the virtual cathedral, so there should be no coloration of the sound from whatever room you may be in in the real world. In this regard, we can experience performances with a far more accurate representation of the original performance space. Whether this is a desirable or useful format for music is still to be investigated. There is a gap in our knowledge between imagining what could be possible in the new realities and knowing what works and what doesn't from experience.

Before we investigate some of the other possibilities of HRTF musical performance it is worth discussing some of the potential dangers of working with new technology.

musical risk: just because you have a thing does not mean you should use it

Many people are unaware of how basic the stereo panning in *the early Beatles* music actually was. In general, the music was produced with two instruments on each side—drums and guitar on one side, and bass and vocals on the other. The early pieces were not designed to be stereo. Consumers did not own stereo equipment so it was seen as a bit of a gimmick; the technology was limited to either hard panning to the left or right channel or being positioned in the center. Often the recordings were done in stereo simply to allow more options for mixing afterward. For one album, one of their producers wanted a record to be released in stereo and so we have the result of hard panning with two instruments on each side. It is easy with hindsight to criticize decisions made at the time, but the technology was new, there were few rules or guidelines, and the novelty of stereo was enough to make it interesting to experiment with. The same thing occurred with the early projects created in surround format, whether that be 4-channel, or 5.1, and likely occurred again with the introduction of Dolby Atmos. Introducing any new technology will likely result in some unusual creative choices. Whether they are seen as being boring or ground breaking will only be determined as people listen and decide what they do and don't like.

So the choices we make of how to use the 360 degrees of spherical space that we have available may define how successful our audio content is. Do you need to be "careful" to avoid making poor choices? That depends entirely on the project you are working on. If you are producing a mass-market experience that is supposed to be safe and conservative in its content, drastic experimentation may not be the best approach. But if you have the freedom to work on a purely artistic independent project where the only driving force is to create something truly unique, then shoot for the stars. The reality is that most projects will fall somewhere in the middle and as such there will be room to innovate while still providing entertaining content that does not confront the audience too much.

Don't Deafen Your Audience

The other real issue is safety. Many of us enjoy listening to loud music, for me soundtracks from my favorite film or game will often be turned up to high volume levels that are probably not great for my ears. The energy of many music pieces and the emotional weight of those pieces is much more impactful when played back at high volume levels. But if we are going to allow for spatial positioning of sound sources and for the audience to move within the environment then we introduce an element of risk.

In the same way that a 3D game is mixed in real time as it is played, spatial audio in a VR experience or 360 video has a dynamic element where the final mix output depends much on the actions of the audience. If the listener moves closer to the trumpet section just as they are playing the final fanfare and turns their head toward the bell of the instrument then the output volume is going to be far higher than if they were positioned further back.

Spatial audio doesn't just allow you to ramp the volume up to 11, it allows the audience to position themselves in such a way that from their perspective it is volume 13 and that can be a risk to the health of the listener. Deafening your audience is not the best way to produce your content, unless you have a reputation within the heavy metal community.

Many tools being developed for spatial audio do account for the unpredictable nature of the performance in VR and 360 video and the tools will measure and indicate the loudest possible output during monitoring. This should allow for producers to compensate for any major issues with hearing safety. But a mix is more than just avoiding the redline so you don't blow up your speakers. A good mix should maintain the quality of sound of all of the elements and often excessive volume is not just dangerous to listen to, it can distort to the point that it makes the music basically just crap to listen to. So regardless of any tools that might exist to limit dangerous content, your ears will always be the best and most important reference guide for the content as you produce it.

how to utilize your space

There are no right answers to how you should use your spherical audio space. With creative content, there is seldom a correct way to create something, but there are many options, and some will potentially work a little better than others. So let's discuss some possibilities.

Depth and Parallax

The following image of a string quartet is a basic example of utilizing surround positioning on a flat plane to place instruments all around a listener. Using HRTF can also provide depth of field, which allows parallax movement within the environment. From an audio point

The two additional instruments add additional depth to the sound field.

of view this provides significant functionality beyond what conventional loudspeaker panning can achieve.

In the above figure, we introduce two more violins: violin A and violin B. These are deliberately placed in irregular positions in relation to the rest of the ensemble. This arrangement adds more objects into the overall spatial array of instruments on the same planar level, but importantly we have added two different depth values. Violin A is further back from the ensemble than violin B and both are well outside the circle created by the original quartet.

Audio attenuation over distance has a variety of factors that can influence how we hear sounds as they travel from further away. Both amplitude and frequency content is affected when we move sounds closer or further away from the listener. But in the case of our ensemble we also have two instruments that are closer to the top wall. This means the reflections from that source will be significantly different than the original quartet arrangement. This layout would change the sound of any recording made in such a space, but when the listener is able to rotate their head and move around the performance space it further adds to the complexity of the audio environment. It is quite possible that production and recording for new reality experiences will develop methodologies that we would never have previously considered practical or desirable for live performances or conventional recording formats.

The other factor that is introduced when we position sound sources to utilize depth is sonic parallax. The two rear violins are offset both rotationally and by distance. This means as you turn your head while listening to the ensemble you will hear not only the positional source of the original first and second violins, but also violins A and B filling the gap between the original two. But both violin A and B are further back and as such will have a subtle variance due to distance attenuation. Also, A and B are at different distances to each other, so even if they are playing the exact same music, there will be a separation of the two sources much like if they were panned as individual objects in a stereo mix. The rotational panning and distance attenuation provides a much larger panning space where movement can have a more significant effect.

As we turn our heads back and forth, violins A and B fill a gap in the original ensemble position, but if we move our location within the virtual space then their depth and position will create a parallax effect where we sense their movement relative to our position as listener as different to the closer sound sources. This further expands the possibilities of 360 spatial panning well beyond the more traditional media formats. I think the most important uses of many of these new techniques will be to establish subtle points of difference between creative styles. Exaggeration or overuse of these techniques will likely result in gimmicky results, but careful implementation and tuning may have interesting results.

Conventional Linear Stereo Music

There will certainly be projects where conventional stereo mixed, linear music will be the best option for music to accompany a new reality experience. There is no reason at all why linear stereo music cannot provide exactly what an experience needs if that experience is also basically linear. The question is, do we place it as a static element within the virtual space or do we attach it to the player's perspective? What we need to decide is, does the music shift when our audience turn their head or not? The conventional approach would fix the music to the user's perspective as though it was fixed to the headphone channels and irrelevant to the 3D spatial area. Alternatively, there might be some instances where fixing it to the world provides an interesting result.

If we do fix the music to the headphone channels, we are still able to utilize the HRTF spatial area in a way that can allow more room within our mix. Instead of positioning the music in the conventional space of the flat line between left and right, if we push it slightly to the rear of the 3D space it opens up the sides for more sound effect content. We can utilize the peripheral vision zone of our listening space for sound content that might be interesting from a narrative perspective. More importantly for an interactive experience, it permits clearer directional localization to the sides because there is no musical content occupying that region.

Attention Focus and Music

The more I work with attention focus functionality the more I think it is an important aspect of spatial audio production, especially in these early days of the technology. Much of this book speaks about the limitations of both the current technology and the weaknesses in how humans hear sound. The attention focus function can enhance spatial audio significantly and I think it might have useful application in the design of musical works.

As I write this I am halfway through producing a piece of music specifically to test out some theories of attention focus. The basic concept works like this. A variety of tools provide a function where the producer can define an attention focus area, usually a cone. This area is defined in degrees and essentially tracks the central position that the user is looking at either through a VR headset or even a flat representation of a 360 video. Basically the center of where you look is the center of the focus area. The focus area then expands into a cone to the extent defined, so maybe a 45-degree cone around the central point you look at.

All audio within the focus cone plays at its defined volume level. This content is essentially "normal volume." Anything outside the focus cone is attenuated by a value defined by the producer. In many ways this works like a flashlight in a dark room. You can see some general shapes and objects around the room in the dim light, but the place where you point the torch is lit up brightly and can be seen clearly. For audio you reduce the volume level of all sounds outside the focus cone to reduce the importance to the overall mix at that time, but sounds within the focus cone play normally. The exact size of the cone and the degree to which you reduce volume outside of the cone depends on the needs of your project.

For something like a full orchestra mix spatialized around the audience, the overall reduction outside the cone might only be very subtle. You can always hear all elements of the music and it is wrapped around you spherically. But anything you look at has just a slightly stronger signal so you can more clearly hear the second flute part in among all the other instruments, or you can high-light the cello solo so you can catch every note. Perhaps the level of attenuation could be adjustable by the user. As a study tool this would be invaluable. To be able to focus on any one instrument within an ensemble as a student and isolate the third horn as the entire section plays a four-part harmony phrase, would provide significant benefit for the listener.

This level of functionality moves beyond real-world simulation and more toward enhanced sensory abilities. To know how these ideas would work for an audience we would likely need to test it out. A general audience who wants to listen to a piece of music for pure enjoyment may need no attention focus at all, or perhaps only the subtlest of effects to enhance the sense of spatialization as they turn their heads or move within the ensemble space. But when utilized more as an app for study purposes the functionality would likely be used in a more significant manner. The benefit of this technology currently is that the ability to do both is possible from the one set of original source material if it is setup correctly in the first place, so a single recording of an ensemble could function as a performance for an audience and a study resource for educators.

let's go to extremes

I heard a quote at some stage while writing this book in reference to a potential future for music. Sadly, I cannot remember where I heard it or who originally said it. It is not my quote, but I will pass it on as I think it provides an interesting basis for discussion.

Future music listener: *"Wow mum, I can't believe that in your day the music you listened to was always in the same location and always played the exact same notes!"*

The quote referred to the fact that current music has a fixed, head-locked format and that a piece of music is always the exact same recording each time it is played back. The idea being that in the future, music is both spatial and generative, or procedural, or in some other way alters each time it is played. Now both spatial music and procedural music have existed in some form or other for many years, and I am not sure that currently either is going to hit the charts and dominate in any real way, but the world is constantly looking for new, fresh, and interesting forms of creative content so maybe one day your music player will be capable of presenting a full spherical 360 performance that also adapts and evolves when played back.

I suggest this because we really cannot predict what will succeed and what will be popular. An "audience" can be a fickle thing and what is popular today can be very uncool a week later. It also falls somewhat into the category of "should we do a thing just because we can?"

For some projects, it really is worth pushing the boundaries and trying crazy ideas to see just what might work. At other times, we just need to complete a piece of music, fit a standard or genre, and keep the client happy.

generative music

I have been experimenting with elements of generative music for many years. There is no single definition or format for generative music and this in some ways is its strength. Generative music is also not something specifically designed for new reality content, but it is another useful tool in our arsenal for creating new reality content.

When I use the term "generative music" I use it to describe musical content that has a series of definitions or guidelines established by the composer that allow the music to generate in real time during an experience. The exact nature of the musical content can vary widely and it can be used to fit almost any genre or style with a bit of effort. I have advocated elements of generative music for use in open world and exploring style games for a while and there are some examples where it works very well. The issue is that many people seem to think their project has to be all one format of musical content. They want a giant orchestral score during the action and narrative stages of the game and so believe that orchestral music needs to be the format for everything. It would be very easy to combine several formats. Giant orchestral music for combat and scripted scenes, generative music for open world exploring, and a small band or ensemble for specific locations like home base or settlement areas.

For 360 video, VR, AR, and MR content generative music could be combined with other formats to create unique and interesting emotional textures. We just need to be slightly less conservative in our approach to creating content.

Basic Approach

Initially my work with generative music was simple and the pieces quite sparse. A mobile game project I worked on about 10 years ago had a limited memory budget and I had used almost all the memory I had available just getting all the sounds in. I asked the developer if they wanted any musical content and they replied that, yes that would be great, but they could not see how that would be possible as we had reached our hard limit for memory. I asked him to let me think about it and I went away to see what I could achieve.

I had designed much of the game SFX using a generative method, this meant that most of the sounds would render in real time during gameplay from a series of sound files I added to the project. This meant I had access to all the raw content within the project because many of the sound layers did not combine until playback. After playing with some of the raw sounds within the project I realized I could probably create some musical content out of them. I was using quite a few percussive sounds and I also had quite a few long ambient layer types of sounds.

I set up a couple of pieces that would select an appropriate sound file, trigger it to play and then play it back for a random period of time and pitch the sounds randomly from a selection of predefined pitches. This meant I could create some sparse, etheric types of tracks that ebbed and flowed over time, but that would never loop or repeat. These were perfect for the menu and exploration stages of the game.

Then I went through all the percussive sounds and did a similar thing, but this time I set the trigger times to be exact from a rhythmic point of view. So layer one might play a pattern of crotchets, layer two with a different sound might layer on semiquavers and layer three would add a low bass beat. In this manner, I could create high energy drum tracks out of individual sound files. Effectively I was using my sound engine tool as a sampler to create drum tracks. All of this was achieved without adding a single extra sound file to the project, so when I presented this to the developer he was impressed with the musical tracks, but amazed that I had managed to create them using only the existing sound files within the game.

For new reality content designed for mobile platforms this technique is useful as it allows you to create dynamic content that is resource efficient. Using your sound engine as a sampler also means your music can shift and change on a beat so it is incredibly interactive and responsive to the audience's actions, as well as being cost effective on resources.

Taking Generative Music to Extremes

Over time I have played with my ideas around generative and pushed the concept to see what was possible. In 2015 some friends showed me their latest project. I had worked with these guys many years before at a studio and I had also created the audio for their first Indy game, so when they showed me the concept for their latest venture I jumped on the idea immediately. I told them I would love to create a really complex dynamic music system for their game. Initially the programmer was worried that my design would require significant time for him to implement, but once I told them it would all me created in the sound engine tool they were happy to let me go crazy.

Learning from Defect: Spaceship Destruction Kit

The concept behind Defect was that the player would design their own ship from a large library of components. This would allow players to design the aesthetic they wanted as well as control the functionality and combat effectiveness of their ship. The list of components was designed to mirror many of the famous ship designs from modern media, so when combined the right way you could create a ship that looked close to your favorite film and game designs.

My approach to the music was to design a dynamic music system that would push me and the toolset as far as possible. Initially I was not even sure my concept was possible, but I was determined to give it a try. I spent several months designing the concept on paper. Much of this was scribbled diagrams, brief descriptions, and lots of flow charts to try and work out the mechanics. Once I started to design the project in the sound tool I discovered various issues and roadblocks I needed to overcome.

One thing I did realize as I worked through this project was, it is very possible to get too carried away and be too clever for your own good. I go so caught up in trying to create a complex dynamic system that often I didn't realize I had made something complex for no reason other than to make it complex. Often, I would sit back, look at a system that used 10 layers to achieve something, and then realize I could do it with two. So while our technology and tools are capable of really amazing combinations of functionality there is no point in

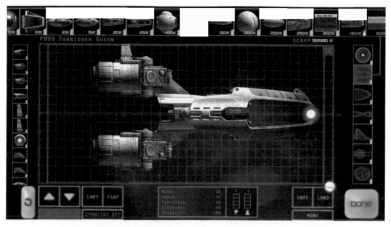

Every component in defect had its own unique musical theme.
(Copyright Phase 3 2017. With permission.)

adding extra steps just for the sake of it. Once this sunk in I was able to design a better overall system.

Defect included over 250 components allocated into six ship systems. Hull, crew compartments, wings, engines, weapons, and miscellaneous. I designed the music to utilize four of these to create the track layers for music.

- Hull – percussion
- Engines – bass line
- Crew – harmonic layer
- Wings – melodic layer

All ships also had a single core that provided the energy and defined how big the ship could be. The cores all produced a base drone sound. As a player built up the components for their ship design a unique musical track would be created for that specific design. From a design point of view, I needed to create a unique theme for every component what would layer and lock in with all other possible components to create a theme that would trigger during gameplay. Each component "theme" was actually a series of themes, one for the construction yard, one for basic mission flying, one for combat flying, and one for level victory. All the themes were created around the same chord structure to ensure they all locked together and there were no harmonic clashes when playing.

During combat the music would change as you did damage and took damage.
(Copyright Phase 3 2017. With permission.)

This system essentially turned the game sound engine into a sample player. The themes were built from individual notes with a level of variation built in to improve the playback. This did initially cause some issues with CPU usage as the multiple layers and many instrument notes required a lot of CPU, but as I progressed I redesigned aspects of the functionality to reduce CPU drain. During gameplay the music would build and change depending on the design of the player's ship and the state of the mission as they progressed. There were a range of similar melodic passages that gave the game its main "theme" but the exact playback was varied and no two players were ever likely to experience the exact same music while playing.

Defect was an extreme example of just how far you could go with dynamic music. I have continued to utilize dynamic and interactive music in my projects, but never to the same extent as Defect. Did the dynamic, generative music system for Defect work? Mostly yes. Did it significantly improve the experience for the player? That I cannot answer. It did not interfere or lessen the player's experience, but it did take a significant amount of time to design, build, and implement this system so for a project such as this it was probably overkill, but I do think it demonstrated some useful and valid techniques for creating musical content that reacts to the experience over time and successfully underscores the ever-changing content of a video game.

The new realities open the door to create experiences vastly different to all our current forms of media. Dynamic musical content in a virtual environment could be designed to carefully and accurately underscore all elements of the experience for the audience. In the same way film music underscores the linear events within a film narrative, dynamic, and generative music could allow us to underscore the unpredictable and dynamic actions of the player as they experience the narrative of a new reality project. This does not mean a dynamic music system needs to be overly complex, it just means it needs to respond at key moments to highlight the actions of the audience and the narrative events of the experience.

working together: navigating the team project minefield

The production of creative content is seldom a solo effort. Even a solo artist writing an album of songs needs the assistance of dozens of people to create the finished work. Artists, designers, engineers, marketing, and business support, the teams for media production, can range from a handful of people up to thousands for large movies and TV projects. The new realities will likely be no different. There will be smaller projects created by small intimate teams and eventually I suspect there will be massive complex experiences that take many years to produce and employ hundreds of creative individuals to realize. So is this new technology any different in how we approach production? Are there any considerations for team structure and workflow that we should consider before we dive on in?

Time will provide the real answer to those questions and as we as an industry undertake larger and more ambitious projects we will discover exactly which elements of production are key to new reality projects. My instincts and a bit of logic have me feeling that there are at least some areas where a different approach might serve us better in establishing efficient production methods.

consistency of environment

I mentioned earlier that I have heard of at least one engineer who has a cupboard full of headphones that he sends out each time he produces a VR or 360 experience. His motivation is to ensure that his clients get to hear his work in the exact same way that it was produced, so he has copies of the headphones he mixes VR content on that he ships to the client with instructions for them to listen to the content on those specific headphones before they listen on any other device. This means he provides a baseline and a consistency to the work he is presenting to his client. While this might seem a little extravagant I think there are quite a few benefits to taking this approach.

I know that in the past when I have worked in more traditional game studios, that at any time when artists required an update for computer monitors it was considered important enough for continuity and consistency to make sure all artists were using the same brand and model of computer monitor. This was designed to reduce instances where one artist may have a different representation of the color palette to other artists because their monitor presented the colors differently. Interestingly this was not always the approach with sound departments. Quite often individual members would use their own personal preference of headphones, or monitor speakers might differ from user to user. Audio often has a final mix stage where all the elements are brought together and perhaps for this reason the consistency of ongoing monitoring was not considered as important.

For a VR or AR experience we have a unique situation from a visual point of view that all our audience will be experiencing the content through a limited range of devices. For the primary consoles this means Vive, Oculus, or PSVR. Often a project is authored for only one of those platforms, so a team can optimize all visual content to be presented in the absolute best manner for the specific headset. They know that they don't need to compensate for a range of different monitors of different brands and models, positioned at different distances to the audience, in different lighting. In many ways, this is a huge boon to the creative team. Sadly, this is not the case for audio for all these devices.

While we know that our experiences will almost certainly be heard with headphones on, the massive range of headphones available these days means that we have a significant level of variability that we might need to compensate for. There is a very real difference between listening to a new reality experience on a set of earbuds, no matter how good they are, and listening on high-end closed backed full ear covering headphones. Worse is the fact that today we have headphones available that are not cheap to purchase and yet still provide imbalanced and generally poor quality audio. There is a trend of fashionable, but overpriced and underperforming equipment that consumers have been convinced is their best option.

Within a production team I think there may be real value in establishing which type, make, and model of headphones is the best to work with for a particular project and to make sure the team is using this equipment. It might not be necessary for the entire production studio to use the same model of headphones, but I do believe that the audio team, QA department, and other key staff such as the producer and director should all be in sync with the equipment they are using to craft and evaluate the audio. I would even go as far as to suggest it might not be inappropriate to provide that information to your customers as well. It is unlikely that many customers will go out and purchase a new set of headphones to experience a single product, although it can happen, but by telling your audience, "Our team used model X headphones in the production of this product," you are providing your customers with a choice. They can research that equipment and find something that is similar from a sound quality point of view, or, if your studio is one they consistently follow and purchase content from then they may decide they want to enjoy the experience as closely to how it was crafted as possible and buy the same brand that the studio uses.

We all hear slightly differently and we all have our own preferences for things like speakers and headphones. But audio is so critical for new reality experiences, so there is a good argument for this consistency. It certainly makes QA and mixing issues easier to track as you do not need to account for variation in presentation devices. Consistency removes a fairly large variable for most issues. Importantly it also allows a team to craft and tune to a specific benchmark. If you know that your chosen devices have areas of weakness and strength in their sound reproduction you can compensate for those specific issues and potentially achieve a far better end result. It also streamlines communication between team members because everyone should be hearing exactly the same content in the same way.

As a brief aside, this is may also create unique business opportunities between studios and headphone manufacturers. Video card companies have been doing this for decades, where developers and card makers agree to certain partnerships that benefit both hardware and software companies. There is no reason why the same could not be done with headphone manufacturers. Cross-marketing of products and promotional agreements can be beneficial to both sides and if it raises awareness among the general public and steers people toward using headphones that are actually good quality, then everyone wins.

The concept of unifying headphones is related to the overall approach of calibrating your tools within your team. Larger studios may adopt this approach with studio setup, and equipment purchase and setup, but it is often seen as a critical aspect because there is a final mix process to catch inconsistencies. My feeling is that for new reality content creation there is merit in a calibration process that could extend beyond just the hardware equipment being used.

If you are working on a large budget VR experience with an audio team, there are a range of factors that could influence how the content being created fits within the final product. The first of these is the HRTF data being used and more importantly how each member of a team interprets this data. A blind test of potential HRTF solutions or spatialized plug-in tools is likely to be adopted by many teams as they decide on which tool set serves them best for any particular project. This is no different in most ways to deciding which DAW to use, or which suite of reverb plug-ins, or which sample libraries the team prefers. But I think it is important to make sure each team member provide accurate feedback on how they respond to different HRTF and spatialization plug-ins.

Some of the research I have done followed this process and team members would all run through a test program and listen to different types of audio content, and provide their feedback on which they preferred with an explanation of why. What was common was that people's experiences could be vastly different. Some would find plug-in A sounded best and some might find plug-in C was their favorite. This is not that unusual as human preferences to anything are subjective. But often it was the reasoning that was interesting. In some cases, an individual would state that plug-in A sounded best for spatialization and that plug-in B sounded best for music. But then another team member would actively counter this by saying that out of all the plug-ins they found, B was the worst for music playback.

The issue was not that opinions differed, it was that in some cases they diametrically opposed each other's viewpoint. It is unusual among a group of individuals all working on the same project to have this level of contrast, but I think our interpretations of HRTF experiences is so unique and unpredictable that anything is possible. The important consequence of this result is that a decision needs to be made for the sake of a project and that it is possible a team member may find the team adopting a solution that, to them, was the worst of the available options. This has real consequences for the team and for the overall production.

If a team overall finds that solution A is the best option then they will likely adopt that solution. But if one team member happened to find that specific solution unconvincing for spatial localization and in general did not feel that solution A provided a convincing experience for spatial audio—what consequences are there for adopting that solution within the team? At best the team member who struggles with the solution may find working with a spatial mix difficult as they do not feel the same level of immersion. But in the worst case scenario this individual may find is difficult to produce content for a project where the HRTF data does not give them a good sense of a spatialized environment. If this is the case, that individual may suffer confidence issues as they are less able to contribute to the spatial content.

This may seem like a psychological issue or something more suited to a book dealing with human resource issues, but I think it is relevant because a large part of how spatial audio functions is based on psychoacoustics and so we should not overlook the impact of individuals not responding to a specific HRTF system. It is also very likely that if this individual does not respond well to the plug-in tools then so will a reasonable chunk of your audience. So instead of this individual being less valuable to the production team, they could be utilized as an excellent test case.

Not all work that is created for a spatial audio project is dealt with within the spatial environment. Most sounds designed to be implemented into a spatial environment will need to be created in mono to be suitable for implementation. So the production of mono assets, location recording work, music composition, processing, and editing of dialogue are all areas of production where the sense of spatialization will not negatively impact a team member's ability to function. But our individual who does not respond as well to the plug-in solution provides excellent feedback for our mixing and mastering process.

From a diversity and accessibility point of view we should be ensuring that our projects can be experienced and enjoyed by as many people as possible. This includes people who have hearing issues or who are potentially even partially deaf, either in a single ear, or across both ears for certain frequency content. Our team member who did not respond well to the chosen HRTF data is a sonic equivalent of someone who is color blind. By involving them into the mixing and mastering process they can help us to ensure our project is as accessible as possible. Is our experience completely unplayable to someone that does not respond well to our specific choice of HRTF data? Are there cues and scenarios within our experience that means someone who is deaf in one ear or who has limited hearing across certain frequencies will not be able to navigate the experience and as a result is essentially blocked from completing it?

The more I investigate sound and its role in new reality content, the more I am convinced it is a vital part of immersion, communication, navigation, and emotional narrative. As a result, we need to be mindful of how our content is experienced by the wider audience and if possible tailor our content accordingly.

It may even be worth considering running the calibration and comparison process each time a new version of the plug-in or an update is provided. Software is constantly updated and we have all experienced the frustration of syncing up new versions into our existing projects. A simple program designed for A/B comparison of possible plug-in solutions was what we would use in the initial instance of selecting our HRTF tool of choice. The exact same program could be used for updates. Each time an update for an HRTF plug-in is added to the project, add it to your simple evaluation tool as a new option. Then allow the team to compare the new version of the plug-in with the current and past versions. This makes sure that nothing has changed too dramatically that it significantly alters the spatialization of your project, because even an update that is designed to "improve" the overall spatialization may not work well with however your current project has been designed. A comparison tool outside of a project may expose issues like this much faster than just hoping team members notice potential issues that have snuck in.

Communication with non-audio Team Members and Clients

This topic is not strictly limited to new reality content—it can be just as relevant to any project—but for developing in this space, clear communication within teams is going to be vital for various reasons. Firstly, the brand new nature of these formats means we are all struggling a bit to understand what we are doing, how best to do it, and how we can draw all the elements together in the best way to produce excellent content. We are also getting used to new terminology and information we need to convey within a team to people who may not have the same background as we do. Communication between the different departments within media production has always been a challenge so any improvement to that process is worth investigating.

The job of anyone within the creative industries is to serve our customers. As asset creators, we serve the designers and writers in building the assets to support the narrative. Programmers often serve us by creating tools we can utilize and we serve them by creating our content in the correct format to suit the code they have created. Ultimately, we all serve our customers, audience, and fans by producing content they will love and want to experience. Within a team there are a variety of ways in which we can improve communication.

I once had a producer comment on the sound that I had created for a trailer video. He told me that overall it was good but there were a couple of key points he wanted to address, so we went into the studio and ran through the trailer. When we got to a certain point he wanted some changes made. I asked him what he wanted. He replied by apologizing that he did not know the correct terminology and descriptions for audio content to be able to tell me what was needed. I suggested that this was not needed and asked him to just throw descriptive words at me. I wanted him to provide adjectives that were relevant to him for this particular element of the video. He started with terms like dangerous and threatening and as we discussed the trailer, eventually came out with the words buzzing and grinding. Over the time it had taken him to speak a handful of words he had quickly developed from general terms of threat to more specific words that provided a feel for the event. This allowed me to pin down a few key terms and based on the word buzzing I mixed in the sound of a sawmill saw operating. It was only part of the overall sound, but the result was a sound that was more threatening and provided the producer with the feeling he was looking for.

We often seem to struggle to communicate with people even though we are all working on the same project. Our interpretation of certain elements or how the overall feeling of the narrative affects us personally can influence how we would communicate about it. But the issue is that sometimes we get too caught up trying to describe how a thing works rather than how a thing makes us feel. Ultimately, most stories are about how we feel when we experience them and so as often as possible providing feedback and speaking about a project from an emotional point of view can be useful. When working in an anime studio in Tokyo I had a fellow worker who was translating most of the instructions from the boss. He spoke no English and my Japanese was basic. One day the feedback about a piece of music was "it needs more notes but less" My colleague thought that this feedback was completely useless, but I assured him that I understood completely what our boss was after. I placed the comment into the perspective of what was the boss feeling when he heard the music and so his statement provided me with useful information.

Emotional Mapping

This is a term I heard many years ago in relation to game design and how to plan a game project, but the term could be applied just was well to film, television, or any of the new realities. It is also a term I have heard surprisingly seldom since I first heard it. It may be that studios use a different word to describe a similar process, but I have not seen this process adopted as much as I thought I would considering it seems to be quite a useful tool.

Emotional mapping is the process of plotting out the narrative of your experience without including story beats or climactic events, but rather highlighting the emotional journey of the audience. What does our audience feel at each point of the narrative, what direction does each branch of the story lead us down from an emotional point of view? This process could be applied to something as complex as a large story-driven interactive game with many character interactions and decision points, or it could be used to track how a single piece of music guides the listener through various emotional states as they listen to the song's narrative.

Regardless of the size of the project, emotional mapping is an excellent way of communicating to your team the emotional changes within the story. It means that ambiguous dialogue or challenging narrative choices that may appear in the experience are not misinterpreted by the production team. It is also incredibly useful for the music production side of things as music, as a language, deals mostly in emotional content so we can more clearly communicate between composer, audio team, writers, and producers to ensure consistency through production.

Let's apply a simple example of how this could work.

Little Red Riding Hood (LRRH)

LRRH sets out on her way to grandmother's house carrying a selection of food for her grandmother.

Happy–innocent–loving–reminiscent–expectant

LRRH knows she must travel through the forest to reach her grandmother's house.

Reminiscent–uncomfortable–cautious–determined

Even though she has traveled through the woods before it always troubles her to do so.

Reminiscent–cautious–concerned–worried

The reality of the forest is always worse than she remembers.

Reminiscent–concerned–scared

The wolf appears for the first time.

Startled–scared

The wolf is polite and asks LRRH her intentions.

Uncomfortable–wary–relieved

The wolf allows LRRH to go on her way.

Relieved–uncomfortable–cautious

LRRH continues on her way as she must get to grandmother's house.

Uncomfortable–cautious–determined

Each entry in our emotion map indicates the primary emotional state of the character and also guides us on what we are portraying to the audience. In some cases, the emotional state of the character may not be the prime consideration of what should be mapped through the overall narrative and this could be indicated when relevant. The other aspect of this list of emotional states is that there can be many and varying states.

The wolf is polite and asks LRRH her intentions.

Uncomfortable–wary–relieved

The emotional information reads as a priority list. In this example LRRH is mostly uncomfortable as she has been confronted by the wolf, who has just previously startled her. But the wolf's actions are not immediately threatening, yet it is still a wolf, so LRRH is wary of the situation. However, there is still an element of relief as the initial arrival of the wolf could have signaled an attack and yet it did not, so LRRH, while still uncomfortable with her general situation in the forest and specifically cautious of the wolf's presence, has some level of relief that the wolf is there to speak with her rather than attack her on sight.

If this line were being used as a guide for the music production then there is information here to indicate tension and intensity, but that there is the promise it might release. In the next line the primary emotion is relief and so the promised ease of tension could be resolved in the music. From a sound design point of view this could also be highlighted by the birds in the forest being scared away by the wolf's initial arrival, but as the conversation between LRRH and the wolf progresses, things around them start to return to normal. So in this way the guidelines of the emotional map allows both the sound team and the music team to even work independently and still arrive at the same general feel for the scene's progression because they have useful information on the emotional tension and release as the narrative progresses.

This process would apply across an entire production team, so even if each department worked in isolation there should be a far greater chance of the overall product having a far more consistent emotional result at the end. The emotional map also becomes a good tool for facilitating communication. Discussions of various states of the creative process can use the emotional states as points of reference.

"When we say cautious, do we mean timid caution, or the caution of a trained professional wary of imminent danger?" "When it says startled, does it mean scared startled or the feeling of wonder and surprise when you are startled by an old friend making an unexpected visit?" We know the story of Little Red Riding Hood and so we understand that the wolf's arrival is likely a scary event, but if it was a story we didn't know the wolf may be a dear old friend and represent the arrival of someone to guide and protect LRRH while she ventures through the forest. She may still be startled, but the entire emotional weight of that statement shifts dramatically. We might use the other emotions in a series to indicate intent, but for all we know someone may go from excitement, to surprise that is negative, or excitement to surprise that is positive, depending on the situation of the narrative.

So the emotional mapping may need additional notes for clarity, but overall it is a useful guide to keep a team on the same track when building an experience.

Team Workflow

Because we are still in the early days of creating content for the new realities there are many opportunities for communication to break down and fail us. This, more than anything, highlights the important of good communication and planning. But also because of the early nature of this form of media we have not yet discovered the best ways of working.

Over the years of working on game audio, I found that in most cases an event, or object, or model, or creature would be placed into the game world and I would respond by creating a sound for that thing. Film and TV almost always work in the same way. The visuals are defined, captured, and edited, and then the audio is dropped in at the end. The primary exception to this is music videos where the video content is designed and created to suit the music. But is this the best way to develop content for the new realities?

One artist that I worked with many years ago used to make little animations in his spare time and I would add sound to them. This was just something we both enjoyed doing and it was good practice for both of us. On a few occasions though he would create little animations, I would craft a sound that was appropriate and sounded good and then he would go back and tweak the animations to make them work even better. Once or twice he showed me an unfinished animation that was like a design concept of a creature and ask me to do the sound. He wanted me to craft something I felt was appropriate without constraining me too much with the animations; once I created an interesting sound he would go away and build the animation to suit the sound rather than the other way around.

This was an interesting approach and it produced good results as often as the more traditional process did. So do we create our VR visuals first and then build the sound for them, or do we craft an amazing spatial audio environment and then build up the visuals? Any method could work, or equally both sound and visuals could be developed simultaneously and then each revised to achieve the result that works best. The point of this little thought exercise is that with a brand new form of art, we can explore brand new methods of production.

platform considerations: how different platforms affect what you can, can't, or shouldn't do

---

tools that enhance our workflow

I want to start this chapter with another contribution from an industry veteran. It is the pioneers in our industry who help us all to create the content we love and engage our audience in new and better ways. The platforms that we deliver on are a constant challenge as we navigate their capabilities and limitations, but they are how we present our content to our audience. It was important for me to reach out to a team who create tools for our craft, to hear their approach to this new technology and perhaps gain some insight into what the future may offer for us as creative producers. Martin Dufour is the CTO at Audiokinetic and has spent many years creating tools to allow audio producers to craft dynamic audio worlds.

The Interactive Audio Workstation

The Interactive Audio Renaissance: Bringing Sound Back to Life After a Century of Baking it on Film

Martin Dufour

Production quality in video games has been steadily evolving over the past few decades, and this is true of the audio portion as well. This, in no small part, is due to advancements in tools and techniques. In this section, we'll look at what sets game audio apart from more traditional mediums, what the current state of the art is in terms of workflow, and how this relates to audio in the new realities, interactive or otherwise.

The Linear Audio Production Workflow

First, let's look at how audio content is produced in the case of linear experiences, such as film and television. Artists work based on a video reference and produce a corresponding audio track. Several crafts are involved in this: music composition, music editing, foley editing, sound editing, dialogue editing, and mixing. Artists, experts in these respective fields, have the luxury to be able to do this using a tool called the digital audio workstation (DAW). Layers upon layers of the finest ingredients, crafted, tuned, and mixed by expert hands, are arranged to match video perfectly, supporting and enhancing the overall experience.

In the ideal case, we can say that artists can create the audio content based on a perfect reference—the visual component of the experience exactly as shown to the audience—and have complete control over the final experience: what they export from the DAW is exactly what will be played back.

The Interactive Audio Production Workflow

Moving on to interactive audio production, a fundamental change happens: there is no complete, linear piece of video to use as a reference. Games are interactive, and interactivity means that the timeline of events is not predetermined, emerging instead from the player's actions. So, instead of a linear reference, there will

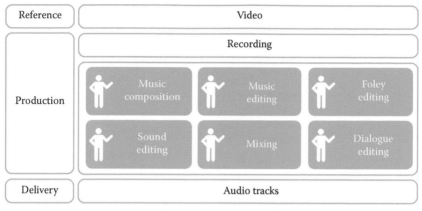

Linear audio production. (Copyright AudioKinetic 2017. With permission.)

be ideas, concepts, bits of animation: fragments of the experience which will be combined together when the game is played.

What the audio department needs to produce is individual audio assets: individual WAV files exported from a DAW.

The game team integrates the audio assets in the game, the game's engine drives playback according to spatial audio rules and parameters defined in code or in the game editor.

Too often, this is where audio artists' involvement in the process gets reduced or even eliminated. They will have created assets out of context from the final experience. All of the aspects of the soundscape suffer; most obviously, the mix can be completely unbalanced, and music relegated to being just "background music" instead of a real storytelling element.

The Game Audio Production Workflow—with Dedicated Tools

"Implementation is half of the creative process."

– Mark Kilborn *(Call of Duty)*

The need for artists to be involved in the implementation phase, so they are able to define how audio should react based on the playback context, emerged with game audio, creating the demand for dedicated interactive audio production tools. Game audio pioneers found little in terms of available software tools that could be used for this purpose. Audio programming environments, such as Max/MSP and Supercollider, offer the necessary programmability, but are unfamiliar territory when coming from DAWs and are not oriented for productivity at the scale of game asset production.

This is how game audio middleware was born. From the early days of direct programmer involvement in the sound design, best practices were extracted and artist-friendly toolsets were built around them.

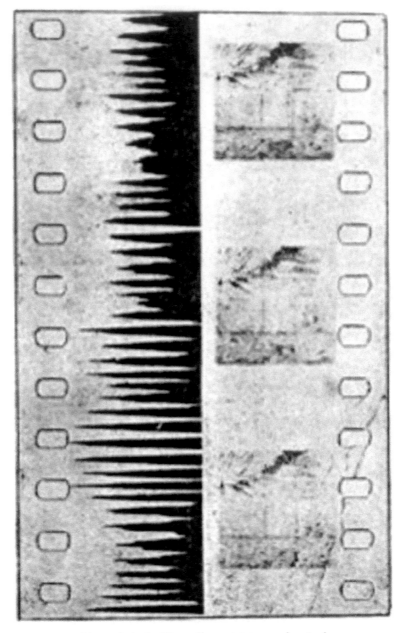

Linear playback—35 mm film containing synchronized
sound and pictures. Lauste system circa 1912.
(Copyright AudioKinetic 2017. With permission.)

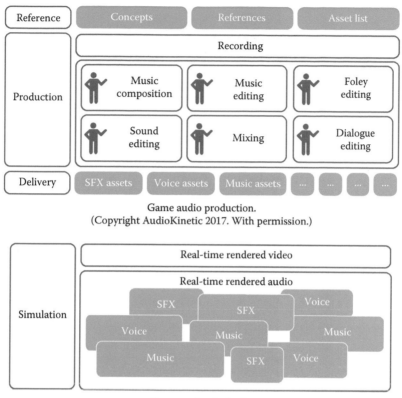

Game audio production.
(Copyright AudioKinetic 2017. With permission.)

Game audio playback.
(Copyright AudioKinetic 2017. With permission.)

Game audio middleware is an additional step in audio production, between the DAW and the game editor. The idea is to use the DAW to handle the purely linear aspects of audio, and then move to another authoring environment where an artist can produce complete, intelligent audio structures: the combination of assets and behaviors.

Explaining all the features that it contains is beyond the scope of this article, so let us focus on the interactive music toolset to get a glimpse at what building an interactive audio structure entails.

Interactive Music Toolset

Individual segments from tracks are exported from the DAW and imported as clips on tracks in the Wwise interactive music hierarchy.

Game states can be bound to music segment selection as part of a music switch container, and specific gameplay elements can trigger musical overlays called stingers. Finer segmentation allows for a more interactive structure and a more accurate response to the behavior of the game simulation.

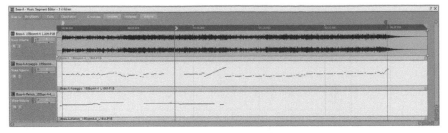

Wwise music segment editor.
(Copyright AudioKinetic 2017. With permission.)

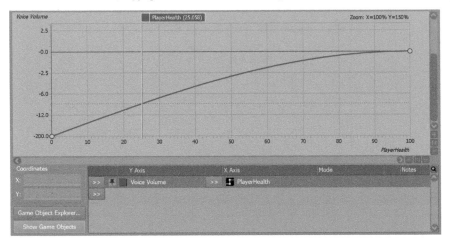

Wwise game parameter graph view.
(Copyright AudioKinetic 2017. With permission.)

Iteration is the key to achieving perfection. In the same way that a DAW allows a composer to quickly make adjustments to his musical composition and instantly hear the result, an interactive music composer needs to be able to adjust the game bindings until the desired behavior is achieved. Wwise offers both the ability to manually simulate game stimuli, and the ability to connect to an actual running game, inspecting how the structures react and making changes on the fly.

Application to VR Storytelling

There is no question in our minds that all of this directly applies to VR games, but what about the more linear, storytelling-like experiences? Of course! To illustrate this, let's explore the most linear category of experiences: 360 videos.

The shift from regular video to 360 introduces one degree of freedom for the viewer: viewpoint rotation. As the viewer's head rotates, the view in the display shifts to correspond to the new perspective and, at the very least, it is completely natural for the audio to react in the same way. This has become the baseline standard for 360 AV content, with ambisonic soundfields being the audio sphere complementing the video.

Wwise music switch association editor.
(Copyright AudioKinetic 2017. With permission.)

We can go one step further and acknowledge that some part of the audio is not actually part of the world (nondiegetic) and, therefore, should not be spatialized but simply played back as a stereo stream straight to the headphones. Additionally, it is possible to implement a sort of "listener cone" so that what is currently in front of the viewer stands out in the mix. An example of this is the focus effects in the FB360 spatial audio workstation.

Such a pure binding between rotation and spatialization is the realistic and accurate thing to have (although the introduction of focus is not), but it does not leave much room for artistic direction! In traditional video, the sound department will often steer well clear of realism in order to convey the right impression and extract the right emotions from the audience. As with games, artist-defined, playback-time behavior needs to be introduced.

So what is our suggested approach to building the soundscape for a 360 video? It consists of creating the same kind of interactive audio structures as illustrated previously, and using the combination of viewpoints and parameters from the video to inform the audio playback (instead of the simulation data from the game engine). Music is the first element of the soundscape to benefit from this approach. As an example, the effectiveness of leitmotivs is closely tied to their timing in relation to the appearance of key characters in the field of view. This simply cannot be achieved unless music is controlled interactively.

Another element is the audio mix itself. As an example, you can picture standing on a beach looking at the waves, then away from the ocean to look at the city on the other side. A film director would almost certainly request greatly

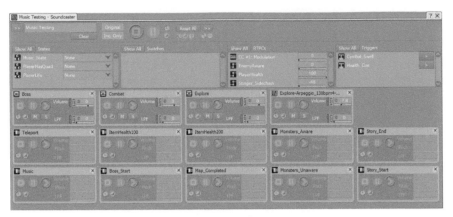

Wwise soundcaster.
(Copyright AudioKinetic 2017. With permission.)

Wwise interactive music profiler.
(Copyright AudioKinetic 2017. With permission.)

contrasting mixes depending on what the focus of the camera is, while a purely spatial rendition would simply influence the positioning of elements.

In the end, it is fairly easy to see that this single degree of freedom is enough to warrant a serious look at sophisticated interactive audio methods. This is the natural thing to do when a game engine is used to render the experience, but I expect that at least some of these techniques will become available to 360 video content distributed through on-demand channels; they are necessary to deliver the level of experience that the audience expects. It's an interesting return to having a live improvised performance accompany picture in film, as was the case in the years of silent cinema.

user experience: the device conundrum

Video and audio used to be just played back on mobile devices, but as mobile hardware becomes better, video and audio are increasingly processed, rendered, and transformed on the mobile device.

There is another important concept that can be used to more clearly define one of the blurry lines between interactive media and linear media. Many modern media products are experienced by the audience on mobile devices. Whether this is watching a streaming movie service or playing a game, the convenience of mobile devices has made them an excellent platform for consuming a wide variety of media.

As a general rule, linear media is produced, exported, or rendered and then presented in whatever format works for a specific product. This could be a television or radio program broadcast over the airwaves, a movie played directly from a file located on your device's storage or a video streamed over the Internet. In all these examples the product is completed, rendered, and delivered to the audience. The audience experiences the product that the production team has created and the editing team has defined as the final version.

An interactive experience, by contrast has its design and behavior defined by the development team, but the final product is created in real time as the audience views it. So each aspect of the product is essentially being rendered and exported as the audience interacts with it. Our mobile devices use their memory and CPU resources to produce the final version that we experience right then and there. This means there is no one definitive version of any interactive experience. A thousand people could play through an interactive game and have a thousand unique experiences.

So the power of a device can impact directly on the experience the audience is having. Slow load times, poor frame rate, jittery animation, would all lessen an interactive experience played on a device with insufficient power to run it optimally. A linear experience may be lessened by being viewed on the tiny screen of a mobile device and heard through tiny speakers, but an interactive experience can suffer from both of those issues in addition to the processing resource issues.

This comparison may become a useful one in clarifying to which category a particular piece of media should be assigned.

delivery platforms

At the point of writing this book there are already numerous delivery platforms for new reality and 360 video content. The popularity of the new technology has created a rush of new devices, new formats, and new tools all competing for attention and retention. The likely reality is that in five years' time many of these platforms and processes will have faded and died. Hopefully we will be left with those that provide the best experiences and have the most potential.

One of the issues with the current wealth of platforms is that it is hard to generalize and provide accurate information on exactly how best to utilize each one. For one reason, right now many of the available platforms can have short life-spans as they do not live up to user expectations or are not promoted successfully.

In general, there are two broad categories of platform: the mobile market and the console/PC market. These two categories do share some aspects of functionality and performance, but they also have some significant differences as well.

Mobile

The mobile category includes any mobile phone that utilizes headsets like Google Cardboard or other generic headset adaptors, the Samsung Gear VR as well as the AR devices such as the Microsoft HoloLens and the as yet unreleased Magic Leap Sensoryware. One primary characteristic is shared across all of these devices and that is their hardware limitations.

Mobile devices have become extremely powerful in recent years, but they simply cannot compare to larger consoles or desktop computers. The needs of building a small form factor device means it can only hold so much memory, storage space, and is limited with the methods that can be utilized for cooling. So it is not just that a mobile device may have a smaller processor and less memory, but the very real issue of overheating.

The processing required for new reality visual content is considerably more than an average utility application or 2D game. When combined with the processing for 3D audio as well, then we get into the well-documented problems with overheating. There are already numerous articles and discussions about coping with overheating. Most mobile phones and tablets have built-in regulators and so if the device gets too hot it will regulate the CPU (i.e., slow it down) or even shut down the device entirely. Nobody wants a device that is too hot to use or at risk of exploding.

Developing on mobile platforms has always been a challenge for audio content as they often have limitations on memory and CPU, but the new realities can make these issues even more of a challenge.

I will focus on the CPU issue as it really has become key to how we develop on mobile platforms. Back in the days of the Playstation 2 console, the primary issue was always memory. The PS2 had 2 Mb of memory and all sound content had to fit into that 2 Mb. The PS2 also had a limited number of simultaneous voices for playback and other limitations, but that 2 Mb was the key challenge for many developers.

For mobile devices active memory is usually the same as storage, as the devices use flash memory for storage. So if it's on the device, it is in memory. But everything else comes down to the CPU.

Managing lots of channels can be accomplished these days with the use of the various middleware tools. Wwise, Fabric, FMOD will all administer the channel allocation for audio once you define the priority of certain sounds and exactly how you want overrun to be dealt with. The most common process is to assign a sound event to a virtual channel. That means your audio engine will keep track of your sound event

Smartphones are one of the most common devices in the world.

without actually playing it, so it makes it "virtual" to free up an output channel. But this administration of the channels uses CPU power.

The adding of any effects to an audio environment also requires CPU power. So mapping reverb for a virtual space or controlling frequency filtering will all utilize the CPU on the device. For accurate occlusion and obstruction, and the general processing of accurate room reflections, the load on CPU can be extreme.

I have worked on regular mobile projects where I have used too much CPU and been told by the programmers to alter my project to minimize how often I access it. When trying to create accurate virtual environments using HRTF the potential load on a CPU could make most mobile devices hot enough to fry an egg on.

So the question becomes, how do we address this challenge? Is it possible to create engaging content on a mobile device for new reality experiences without cooking the device? The answer is … sort of.

Mobile devices are limited in many ways. No one expects to pick up a smartphone and have an experience the equivalent of a latest generation game console machine. We understand that the screen is smaller, the input methods are cruder, and the sound is likely to need to be simpler.

The issue with VR is that because it replaces our access to the real world, we might get used to a certain level of immersion. "Once the headset goes on I expect an awesome new reality." So our audience might hope that their mobile VR experience is always as cool as their home console VR experience. It is also important for us to get mobile VR experiences as good as possible because for many people, mobile VR will be their introduction to VR in the same way mobile gaming was their introduction to gaming.

Let's look at some techniques that may assist with mobile development for spatial audio.

Probably the most useful to start with is limiting the output channels. If multiple spatial audio sources are a potential for resource consumption, then starting by limiting those may provide a good foundation for efficient implementation. We can do this by creating a virtual speaker array. This technically undermines the major strength of HRTF spatial audio, but it's a useful way to control efficiency.

This method works by creating fixed points around the audience that emit sound just as if we had created loudspeakers in the virtual world space. So we define emitters positioned around the head much like we would a home theater sound system. Front left and right, and rear left and right. All audio content is routed out of these in a pair-wise mixing style. So we are emulating a room with fixed speakers in it, but the support for head tracking broadens the experience to be more suitable for the VR format.

This is specifically choosing to limit the benefits of the HRTF functionality to compensate for CPU consumption. The exact number of "speaker" emitters that you use can be controlled as part of development. More speaker locations will result in a smoother, more enveloping effect from the audio environment, but it will also utilize more CPU. This approach can be tailored to suit the needs of a project.

It is somewhat ironic that this method specifically creates an output format that functions in the same way as our "limited" linear surround box format discussed in earlier chapters. But in the same way that the linear formats of film and television have been suitable and successful for decades we can use a similar format to provide a surround experience while being more resource efficient for our mobile platforms. With all things, we must work with what we have available.

HoloLens

HoloLens is currently one of the main AR headsets on the market. It is certainly not the only AR headset available, but many of the others have been created for specific purposes, often industrial, and do not present in the same manner as most of our modern media devices. Our consoles of Xbox, Playstation, and Nintendo provide known formats for developers to create content. Similarly, Apple iOS and Android provide mobile platforms for the development of games and apps. These platforms along with PC have marketplaces and known feature sets that make it easier for developers to create content for customers.

AR is still a very new and somewhat uncertain format. There is the promise of great things to come from many directions, but right now the uptake of the tech is slow and as a result the creation of content is also slow. In general, AR seems to be used for more serious content while VR leans toward games and entertainment media.

Having used the HoloLens, I can immediately see some of its strengths and some of its weaknesses. In general, all the challenges and techniques we apply to spatial audio will be mostly relevant. AR has the potential to really create some interesting and engaging content. But the differences in the hardware will define how much of the content will need to be presented. Much of what I write about HoloLens could be applicable to any AR device. The basics are often similar and the specifics will define which device achieves any particular task in

Microsoft HoloLens.

the best way and also which of the devices achieves a market position through sales to customers. So even though I have experienced other AR devices such as ODG and the Magic Leap technology I will not refer to them because either I am not allowed to, or there is little point in speculation. But in the same way using a Vive may give you a pretty good idea what an Oculus is capable of, a discussion around HoloLens works as a good general platform for AR device workflows.

Headphones, except not

The Microsoft HoloLens does not utilize headphones (it does have a 3.5 mm headphone jack if needed). Instead it has a speaker system built into the framework of the glasses. This is good from the point of view that there is a single form factor device, but it does have some consequences. Any audio played from the device can be heard to some extent by people other than the user. This is a little like holding a mobile phone—depending on the angle you hold it and the volume for playback, others can hear your conversation.

The HoloLens speaker system is cleverly designed so that the speaker is mounted higher up in the device with a reasonable sized driver and the sound itself is directed down so that it is guided into the ears more directly. This does help significantly in reducing sound escaping so that other people can hear it and also improves the clarity of the audio signal for the user.

When I first heard the HoloLens in action my friend was wearing it and I could hear some sound, but far less than I was expecting. It is a little like an open backed set of headphones except the focus into the user's ear seems to be better controlled.

Both good and bad

The position of the speakers away from the user's head has both advantages and disadvantages for content creation. Low-frequency content is hard to convey when the speaker is at a distance from the audience's ears. In general, the small speakers for headphones and earbuds are not capable of producing low-frequency content and there are a series of tricks we use to create the sense of low-frequency content, but proximity to the ear is critical for these to be effective. This is why earbuds that fit into the ear canal often sound like they have more base than small headphones that sit in the outer ear. So it is unlikely that anyone will be creating earthquake sounds for a HoloLens experience as they are limited in the frequency and power of the sounds they can produce.

At the other extreme, creating ambience sounds such as wind, rain, and bird ambiences can be super effective on this device. The distance of the speaker to the ear in this case actually enhances the effect. Instead of having wind sounding like it is inside your head, the sound actually exists exactly where it should in the real world, just beyond your ear. Combine this with the excellent spatialization capabilities of the HoloLens and you can get some really lovely and immersive results. So while low-frequency content is weak, spatialization is excellent, and high-frequency content can be produced with a good sense of depth. Dialogue playback also sounds generally pretty clear, although the lack of low-frequency support makes it difficult to present that nice warm proximity effect of someone being close to you as they speak because this is often reliant on some lower frequency content.

Cut your coat to suit your cloth

If we are developing content for devices that we know have limitations to the range of playback frequencies, but we still want to create effective spatial content and an immersive experience, do we then design our content specifically to suit our limitations? For instance an experience with birds, wind, rain, and high-frequency source material could potentially sound as real as it might be if we were in a forest hearing it ourselves. But giant crashing waves at the beach will lack the low-frequency rumble and roar. Equally, if we want a vocal narration, we could utilize a female voice actor as females usually have higher pitched voices and so the lack of low content reproduction might not be noticeable. It does depend on exactly what we want to achieve, but consider this. In the early days of television where only black and white transmissions were possible, I doubt many shows would focus on a romantic sunset and describe its wonderful colors. All that would do is expose and highlight the limitations of the experience for the audience. So, designing content to suit the capabilities of your device is not an unreasonable approach.

Designing content for AR platforms is going to be interesting. If you are designing a project to launch on Xbox and Playstation consoles, there are some technical formats you need to follow and a few differences in capabilities between the two devices. But on a broader level they are both essentially the same. They both output to a monitor screen and they both output to surround format audio, and in both cases they can receive input from cameras, microphones, and hand controllers. So if you produce content for one it is feasible to be able to transfer it or simply design the original content so that it will work on both platforms.

The nature of AR devices is that they are so new and the technology still under development that this is not likely to be possible for these new devices just yet. Creating content for one AR device may require significantly different steps compared to making it work on other devices for some time yet. If you plan to develop for a specific platform such as HoloLens then it is probably worth fully investing in that project and utilizing as much of the capabilities of the platform as possible. The goal of bleeding edge technology is to show what it is capable of and engage both potential audience and content developers by capturing their imagination. Early generation technology seldom achieves widespread market uptake, but it is a significant time for demonstrating the need for such devices and also a time when creative teams can establish their skills in a new medium.

Ossic Headphones

I am including Ossic headphones under platforms as I think they exist as a legitimate format for creation as well as a tool for presentation. Ossics are a new format of headphone, referred to by the company as a "smart headphone." They are designed to support the presentation of spatial audio content by utilizing a series of technological designs

Ossics 3D audio headphones.

that increase the functionality of headphones beyond the currently available devices. I think the interesting thing about the Ossic concept is that their primary strength may also be a big weakness.

Ossics have the ability to reproduce spatial content in an effective and immersive manner. I have heard them myself and I found the experience really quite engaging. The issue is content designed for Ossics, needs to be heard on Ossics. So, there is a catch 22 situation there where the company needs to encourage content creation to support adoption of the headphones, but the headphones need to be out there to support the creation of the content. This can be a common challenge for new technologies, so time will tell how this technology goes.

The device itself utilizes multiple speaker drivers to enhance the delivery of HRTF content. This means the perception of spatial audio is supported by the fact that we can hear audio from different angles because it really is coming from different angles. I ave heard a few people describe this as cheating but I consider it to be clever design. For the presentation of spatial content with elevation I have not heard anything that comes close to the Ossic playback. The example I heard was quite exaggerated in the content it presented above my head, but for a demo this was good—it showed me clearly what was possible, so knowing that, it gave me a fair idea of what I might be able to create myself.

The Ossic headphones are still under development at the time of writing and the full workflow for creating content has not yet been revealed. This means they really are bleeding edge technology. I suspect their most effective deployment will be for location-based VR experiences where the audience is provided with headsets and headphones for a set experience. Knowing that your audience has equipment under controlled conditions allows developers to design content specifically for that equipment. This is the ideal scenario for this type of gear. You can present an optimized experience for your audience because you know exactly what equipment they will be using.

For individual content creators and for smaller projects it might be viable to create an Ossic version of your content as long as it is possible to easily create a version that works well for normal headphones. This provides the best of both worlds. Ossic owners can listen to an enhanced version while people using normal headphones can still enjoy your work in spatial audio with regular HRTF.

Different Platforms, Different Solutions

As the new era of VR launched and a variety of platforms became available, they were matched with a variety of software tools and solutions. One of the main competitive aspects of the new technology was spatial audio plug-in solutions. All of a sudden, dozens of these sprang up from nowhere offering varieties of different approaches for workflow and delivery solutions for audiences. But that landscape changed quickly.

Two Big Ears was a spatial plug-in solution started by two gentlemen in Edinburgh, Scotland, and was available for a range of different platforms and provided a solid spatial audio solution. They were purchased by Facebook and their software became the toolset for the Facebook Audio 360 Spatial Workstation.

Phono was another competent contender for spatial audio solutions, and then they were bought out by Valve and are now the core of the Valve spatial audio solution. Sony developed its own solution for spatial audio for the Playstation VR and it can produce excellent results. I am yet to work with it so I do not know how easy it is as a toolset.

What is fairly obvious is that any of the software developers who created content that was useful and effective, quickly found themselves gathered up by larger companies. I know of at least two other situations like this that are not publicly known about. So in the race to create solid spatial audio technology those who are creating good quality software are being sought out and are quickly gaining unicorn status.

It is not quite a situation of specific tools only available for specific platforms, but it is getting close. At GDC 2017 Microsoft announced their spatial audio solution which integrates the Dolby VR audio system. Windows Sonic approaches the problem with a broader-based solution that allows content creators to mix and match between channel-based mixes (with extensions to existing in-plane channel sets—up to 8.1.4.4) as well as object-based mixes. Windows Sonic draws on the lessons learned by the HoloLens development team and so I will be interested to hear what develops in that direction.

There are still middleware solutions such as Wwise and FMOD Studio and they continue to support various spatial audio plug-ins, but even Wwise has now moved toward a recommended solution for their toolset in the Auro 3D spatial plug-in.

So where does that leave us as creative content producers? It certainly means that for the foreseeable future it is going to be quite difficult to produce multiplatform content from an audio point of view. Developing for Sony PlaystationVR it would be silly not to utilize their excellent toolset. But does that mean you need to use three different tools if you want to release a cross-platform game? Middleware such as Wwise and FMOD were designed to remove that old problem. It is possible that in the short term there is a period where cross-platform games become more difficult again, which in itself is less than desirable as we are already having to learn entirely new procedures and concepts for the new technology. While writing this book I have looked at a variety of tools and plug-ins and they each have different terminologies, workflows, and strengths and weaknesses, so it is certainly a challenge to absorb them all and gain any level of competency. Don't feel you need to understand how all of them work all of the time.

Over time it is likely that some unification of tools occurs as we refine the processes and some platforms will likely fail along the way. It is important though to communicate carefully with any development team you may be working with. Creating assets for cross-platform, especially in engines such as Unity and Unreal is quite straightforward and in many cases, may not need any additional work at all to deliver across two or three devices. But if the audio needs to be created for multiple platforms, flag that as early as possible and clarify exactly what the challenge is so the team can plan accordingly and support you in creating engaging content.

remember the audience, our customers

Technology and technological development is usually an aspect of business development. We invent, develop, and sell devices, services, and content to make money, so we can then go and invent, develop, and sell more and better devices, services, and content. This is not a bad thing. Human society is based on people doing things that are useful to other people so they can earn a living to survive. Sometimes we, as a society, consider it bad to speak of business and making money as though it lessens the value of our work; this can often be the case for creative content. For some reason making money from our work lessens the creative integrity of a product.

The reality is that almost everything we do that is not a hobby or relaxation activity is focused on our careers and earning an income that allows us to survive. Hopefully if we do a good job we will earn more money which will allow us to live better. But also, a good income can allow us to develop and create better products and content. It takes a significant investment of mental energy and time to create something of good quality and having sufficient money provides us with more freedom to focus wholly on those tasks. There is a paradox here in that it can take money to make a good product, but you need a good product to make money. For this reason, most of us build up our careers slowly and increment each product or creative piece to improve on our last project.

It is not inappropriate in a book such as this to talk about our customers, their expectations, and how we can better serve them with the content that we are creating. We do hope that people will pay us for what we create, so that we can continue to create, but as creative people it is also important to us that our customers or audience also like what we create. Creating is hard; it takes time and significant effort. Artistic creations also have the added challenge that they involve a significant aspect of ego.

The more invested you are in a creative project the more you are likely to commit your time and effort as well as both your mental and emotional energy. It is far easier to be enthusiastic and go above and beyond for a project you truly believe in and enjoy working on. The more significant a project is to you the more prepared you are to invest your passion into its creation. This can often lead to amazing creative results and when multiple passionate individuals collaborate the results can be something special.

In this chapter I want to steer the discussion toward understanding how we approach creative projects and allow our passion to create something wonderful, but also to keep in mind that our end goal is to service an audience that we hope will pay for the right to experience our work. This is never an easy challenge, but my instincts tell me that the new realities will certainly not make this challenge any easier and will likely make it more complicated.

Being aware of our customers, their potential likes and dislikes, and what they are prepared to spend money on is a critical aspect of developing content. Unless your motivation is a pure artistic focus on a specific message or medium, most projects need to produce an income to remain viable and I am sure even those who dedicate their passion to a specific artistic content would still like for them to generate income, even if that is not the primary purpose for their creation.

Humans are generally pretty good at knowing what they do and do not like. Obviously marketing and PR can influence certain decisions that we all make and how we perceive certain things. But generally, a person knows that if they purchase phone X over phone Y, or gaming console A over console B, that they are doing it because one device suits their needs over the other. And if a person purchases a device and finds it doesn't live up to their expectations of requirements they will be less likely to purchase that product again in the future. When it comes to creative content such as films, TV, and games it is even more important that the audience likes what they are experiencing. Media is generally provided as an entertainment service. It does not provide a utility service or everyday need. So, if the audience doesn't enjoy an event they can simply stop experiencing it, turn it off, or walk out halfway through.

I think the new realities are going to be even more susceptible to the attitudes of the audience than traditional media have been, and for this reason I think it is even more important that we are sensitive to some of the potential issues with presenting this new content.

Already there are issues that create a barrier to entry for potential audience members.

Comfort and Control

The new realities generally all require new devices to present the experience to our audience. VR or AR headsets, headphones, peripheral controllers, and motion trackers or cameras are all common aspects of the new technology experiences. If you read through various reviews it is already apparent that some people vastly prefer VR headset A to headset B for ease of use and comfort. AR goggles or glasses are still in their early stages and while the experiences can be engaging the devices can be heavy, unwieldy, unflattering, and a range of other descriptive terms that are mostly negative. As someone who wears optical glasses I can personally attest to the fact that any headset I have worked with can be an awkward experience to get on and off my face without pulling my glasses off or crushing my nose. Even something simple as getting used to the order in which you should put on the headphones and headsets can add to the overall challenge of the experience of new reality experiences.

Why is all this relevant in a book about audio creation? How can a content creator influence this aspect of the overall experience when the hardware is what it is and works the way it does? As content creators, we cannot alter the physical makeup of hardware devices or the awkwardness that may be involved in putting the equipment on, but I think we can do various things within our work that can improve an experience if we do them right and more importantly we can avoid making the experiences worse if we were unaware of the impact our content can have. Right from the start, how we present to our audience really matters.

A welcoming environment

I have been quite happy to see that many of the virtual interfaces created for the new devices have taken quite a good approach to creating a welcoming environment in which to first place our audience. The Oculus home menu is an excellent example of this. The somewhat Zen-looking space provides a nice isolated and safe space in which our audience first finds themselves. It is soft on the eye and also a peaceful location where the audience can take their time, explore, and feel unrushed. The environment lets the user spend time just acclimatizing to the whole concept of being inside a virtual space.

They can ignore the menu and just look around and feel their space. Importantly, as I write this, even though I have used this interface several times recently I cannot honestly say if there is any audio in that space or not. Either there is no audio at all or it is so subtle that I didn't notice it. Either way I think this is the perfect environment to welcome our audience.

I think this evolution of our console interfaces is a welcome and important one. I still own many older consoles and they generally liked to announce their activated presence to the world with a giant blast of sound or fanfare. I think the developers felt that as game machines it was a fun and appropriate identity for those devices. For experiences that enclose the user into the device and surround them with a virtual world I am glad we no longer blast the audience with a welcome and I think the subtle approach should always be the first point of contact for our users. The common use of headphones should make this almost mandatory as we must give the user time to acclimatize and adjust to feel safe before we present more intense content, and allow them to select the level of intensity they are comfortable with. In fact, the Oculus menu when used on GearVR even warns you every time you adjust the volume upward and its default level is approximately 60% of maximum. This acknowledgment of the importance of output levels is an excellent approach to user comfort and safety.

Even when a user enters into an experience or game we can make that transition less harsh. The *Star Wars Battlefront* VR experience starts with a giant ATAT walker, but it is positioned well off to the left-hand side and slowly walks toward the audience's position. This means there is a large and obvious object that is moving toward you, but it starts far enough away that it is unlikely to be too loud initially. As the walker makes its way toward the user's position and gets louder it allows the user to adjust volume down if needed. This simple approach creates an excellent initial impact for the experience as the size and impact of the walker hits you, but it also cleverly eases you into the sonic environment of the experiences and maximizes your control over your own comfort levels.

The initial menu for any game works best if it provides an interface that is useful and accurate for the user, but also has the function of being a safe staging ground. While the front-end menu for an experience may need to be resource-light for optimization purposes it is important not to cut back so much that there are obvious looping sounds or musical tracks that are too short, or too intense and prevent the user from feeling comfortable to spend some time in that environment. Initially the user may spend time adjusting settings for video, audio, and controls; they are establishing a baseline for the experience they are about to enter. The visuals should be typical of the lighting they will see in-game and the audio can also work to establish some context of things to come.

Setup

Because of the immersive nature of VR experiences and 360 video I would consider a brief calibration test not an unreasonable feature to include if your overall product is more than a few minutes long. While many games and experiences provide audio levels that the user can adjust, they seldom provide any context for those levels, instead leaving it up to the user to guess, or to wait until something is either too loud or soft.

For a new reality experience, we could consider adding a simple additional message. When the user enters the audio settings for many games, it is common for the interface to play a sound effect from the game continuously so that the user can hear something relevant as they adjust the levels. But we provide no context for those sounds. If instead we added three playback button choices then the player has additional information and additional choices.

X Quietest experience sound

X Average experience sound

X Loudest experience sound

The player can toggle each of the buttons and find an output level that is most suitable for them based on the loudest and softest sounds in the experience. Many games have a video display option that instructs the player to adjust the contrast slider until they can only just see a certain object. This creates a baseline for the visuals relevant to the user's specific display. The above example is a similar sonic equivalent that sets up the audio to a good default value.

It is also probably a good idea to test the basic left-right orientation of the user's headphones as well. We are all capable of putting our headphones on backward and some sound systems can occasionally have crossed wires, so something as simple as a head check that plays back a voice that says left and right through the appropriate speakers for first-time playback is a simple process that allows the user to adjust. This might seem like a redundant step; "the audience will discover pretty quickly if their headphones are not aligned properly and then they can fix it." And yes, they might, but why would we allow their experience to be anything less than as good as possible? It is a simple solution to ensure that they do not miss any of the content as they adjust their headphones and are not distracted from the initial narrative as they wonder "is that sound coming from the wrong direction?" Once an experience starts the audience should be free to engage and be immersed, not to have to work through technical issues for a technology that is already complex and demanding of its users and that can seriously undermine an experience if not calibrated correctly.

I have found that setting up VR equipment on a first-time user can be a tricky scenario. The user is really not sure exactly how a thing should be worn. There is a balance of comfort and usability. For most VR headsets, there is a very real sweet spot in relation to your eyes and any deviation from that sweet spot results in blurry visuals. Similarly, with headphones, they need to sit comfortably but equally they also need to block out the real world, so both VR headset and headphones need to "seal" against the user's face to block out the real world. Trying to explain this to a new user can be a challenge and you are unable to see and hear if things are working for them. I found for myself, I was adjusting my various headset and headphone combinations quite a bit to get them really comfortable for extended use and to get the best experience. As this is a barrier to easy entry for new users, anything we can do to streamline the process and make the experience more as the creators intended it I think will improve the overall perceptions of this new technology.

Communication

UI sounds provide feedback; that is their primary purpose. When you press a button some form of audio feedback lets you know if the button press occurred and if it was a positive or negative result. There are numerous examples of games and experiences designing thematically appropriate UI audio for a specific project, but above all else the clear communication of information must be maintained for UI sounds to work correctly. A good example of this is entering your PIN number at an automatic teller machine when the volume is too low. There is a moment of uncertainty when you press the flat button and you hear no sound. Teller machine buttons do not depress, so there is no haptic feedback for the action. They also do not light up when you press them so there is no visual feedback. Because of these two limitations the audio beep is far more important to confirm for the user that the button press actually occurred. UI feedback is one of those functions that can often be underestimated; until it is not there we do not realize how important it is.

I do not think UI sounds should be an avenue for highlighting the nature of your game. What I mean by this is, if your game is a giant action-packed highly intensive experience, that is fine, but the purpose of UI sounds do not alter, and designing gigantic loud metallic crash sounds each time a user presses a button mostly misses the point of the UI functionality. Moreover, you might want to wait for the explosive action in-game to deafen your users and not try and achieve it before they even load the game up. I say this because I have played games where the front-end sound effects were so over the top, loud, piercing, and uncomfortable that it made the game barely playable. Loud is not an issue. Many excellent films and games have super intense audio tracks with tons of content crammed into every possible gap of headroom. But poorly designed repetitive crash sounds that you need to listen to over and over as part of designing a character before you enter the game are seldom going to improve the player's experience.

Within the functional requirements of UI sounds there needs to be clear communication of feedback for the audience and occurring actions within the UI environment, but apart from that I believe that UI sounds should border on being inaudible. They are feedback, so they need to be heard, but only just need to be heard. So nice quiet UI sounds allow the user to navigate a menu system and hopefully enjoy the excellent music or ambience that accompanies those menus. This may seem contradictory to the teller machine example. A teller machine is usually outside in a real-world environment. As a piece of equipment, it must serve its function in an unpredictable environment. So loud clear beeps are critical as entering your PIN number and the correct amount of money you wish to deposit or withdraw are critical to its overall primary purpose. Within a game or interactive experience, the UI sounds are part of the overall audio mix, and as such should be balanced appropriately within that mix. In fact the UI aspects of a project's audio are just as critical in the final mix as the main musical theme and all the SFX content. When it comes to spatial audio we now have new possibilities for how we present these UI sounds. But should that change how we create a UI menu and its audio?

Use it wisely

The new realities have added additional functionality to many of the existing media formats. I would suggest that it will still be many years until the full potential of possibilities has been discovered and there will be many and varied clever uses of this technology to create interesting and engaging content. But equally I think there are going to be many and varied terrible examples of things we should avoid using. Just because stereo audio allows you to rapidly pan a signal back and forth repeatedly does not mean it is something that an audience will enjoy. In fact in that example I suspect it would make people feel pretty sick, pretty quickly. This rule applies to almost any creative medium or format. Just because a thing is possible doesn't mean it should automatically be used.

The spatial nature of audio for the new realities is one of its major strengths, but this can also mean creators are tempted to utilize the spatial positioning just because they can. UI is certainly an interesting area where spatialization may be appropriate, but I think it will likely only be appropriate in very specific circumstances. Even with years of 3D audio being available for game development, most games implement their UI sounds in 2D rather than 3D. In this example I would suggest the reason is because there is often no real benefit to implementing 3D UI sounds. This reinforces the general rule for production and sound design:

- Can I do a thing?
- Is there a reason to do that thing?
- Is there a benefit, either functionally or creatively, in doing that thing?
- Should I do that thing?

I am not at all suggesting that we should not experiment with the idea of spatializing something like UI sounds. If your project gains a benefit, no matter how small, from utilizing spatialization for your UI then absolutely go for it! But I think we may risk trivializing and lessening the impact of some of our functionality if we just apply it everywhere and all the time.

One of my favorite examples of an early use of surround sound was in Studio Ghibli's Mononoke Hime (*Princess Mononoke*); I did not notice any surround panning for any of the first half of the film and then at one significant point a scene broke into full surround. The impact was incredible because the filmmakers held off on the use of that functionality until they felt it would really impact on the story. Restraint is often one of our strongest tools.

While I have continued to use UI sounds to explain this concept, the idea can be applied to anything. We have a series of tools available to us in our arsenal of audio trickery. How and why we choose to utilize each and every tool will often make the difference between a clever, tight, and engaging audio mix, or a messy cacophony of cluttered noises.

Ask yourself these questions:

- Should we spatialize our music?
- Should we spatialize UI sounds?
- Should we implement the music so it is head-locked?
- Should we combine spatial content with head-locked content and how do we mix a combination of the two?
- Should we utilize speaker-based playback for our spatial audio?
- Should we utilize a low-frequency speaker for added impact?
- Do we spatialize the narrative dialogue?

These and many other questions are all part of the design phase of our project. How we approach each question is essentially defining the overall outcome of our project's audio and will influence how our audience and our peers perceive our work. There is no right or wrong answer to any of these questions, but it is important that you know the answer to each question for yourself as those answers are a guide to your workflow and design.

Fatigue

Listener fatigue is a very real thing, but it might be something that many people are unaware of. I became even more aware of the impact of listener fatigue when I moved away from a major city. We are currently lucky enough to live in a quiet country area. This is obviously pleasant and may be beneficial for mental health, but one of the most significant changes I have noticed is how it affected how I hear. The noise level where we live is usually around 30db when it is not windy or raining. We can hear almost no traffic or industrial noises, there are no railroad tracks or flight paths within our area and even the bird and insects are fairly quiet. I mention this because my hearing has adjusted to this new environment so now if I travel into the city the effects are obvious and extreme.

If I travel into the nearest capital city I find myself uncomfortable from the general level of noise, but on top of that I find the overall sound levels leave me exhausted within a brief period of time. Within two hours I feel like I have run a marathon or sat a major physics exam. I am mentally drained and find it hard to focus. This is an extreme example, but it demonstrates that sustained noise levels above the levels that we are used to can directly affect the listener. So a film, game, or experience needs to provide periods of lower sound levels to allow the audience to recover and have breathing space between the high-intensity content. I think this aspect is going to be even more critical for new reality content.

A VR setup as we have described previously is somewhat like a sensory deprivation experience. We isolate the audience from the real world and block their access to real-world vision and audio. When we replace the real world we are subjecting our audience to content that completely surrounds them and replaces almost all sense of audible and visual reference to the real world. This in itself is an intense experience to immerse someone into, even if it is a gentle and calm experience it could still be somewhat confronting to an audience. If we chose to then hammer at them with high-intensity audio and video content the likely result is to fatigue the audience relatively quickly. If the experience is supposed to be a short and intense one, such as riding a rollercoaster or some other extreme experience then the fatigued effect might be a desirable outcome from the experience. In the same way we step off a real rollercoaster with elevated heartrate and breathing, and both adrenaline and endorphins pumping, we might want to trigger the same result from a virtual experience. But few people would choose to ride a rollercoaster endlessly for hours, so we need to account for that and allow for some downtime for our audiences.

This is important to account for fatigue, but also to maximize the impact of the experience. Eventually even the most fearful participant would get used to endless rollercoaster rides. They would either acclimatize or simply fall into shock, neither of which is a desirable outcome. There is a reason why many Hollywood films preface a major audio event with a brief moment of silence. Before the Deathstar goes boom, there is a moment of silence that allows our hearing to reset and enhances that final climactic sound effect. Most music will ebb and flow in its dynamics and even the heaviest of heavy metal albums is likely to have a ballad or two thrown in as a contrast.

Fatigue for the new realities in regard to audio might result from various things. Obviously the overall volume level and sustaining high output levels can not only be fatiguing to the listener but is also a risk for hearing as we know these experiences are commonly going to be listened to via headphones. But my instincts tell me that spatialization may also be something of a potential issue for listener fatigue.

If I place you in a room full of people and I instruct you to try and listen to as many conversations as possible there is the likelihood that fairly quickly you are going to find it hard to focus and will possibly even end up with a headache. Humans have become fairly good at blocking out unwanted sounds, so at a partly you can focus on one person speaking to you and block out everyone else, but trying to focus on multiple speakers all at once becomes a far more difficult task.

When we design a spatial audio environment it is tempting to make use of all the new functionality and "wow" the listener with rich complex audio environments. However, we should be mindful that what we might be doing is creating noise that needs mental effort to block out so the audience can focus on the important audio cues, or worse, we might be providing multiple important audio cues that will lead to fatigue for anyone trying to focus on all of them simultaneously.

Just as it is useful to have silence to contrast periods of intense sound levels, it is also wise to use our full range of spatialization carefully and not require the listener to spread their focus too thinly. A design that varies from dense to sparse spatialization will also more likely provide a more engaging experience. When I say dense and sparse localization, I do not mean that you cannot have a lush, heavily populated rainforest with dozens of birds around. Even though this example uses many voices spatialized all around the listener, the choice of content is what is important. Ambiences created as backdrops, whether they are a busy rainforest or a noisy streetscape, can provide an engaging and immersive backdrop to your virtual environment. So long as the content can be placed into the background for the listener, this can work to provide environmental context without assaulting the ears. This can be achieved through a combination of techniques.

Overall volume level is the obvious first method of reducing the impact of an environmental ambience. Even a noisy forest or streetscape can be established without having the volume levels set to how they would be in the real world. As entertainment media, our primary goal is the narrative, so as long as we convey that the location is busy and noisy then the sound levels can then be dropped back to accommodate more important sounds. The audience understands the cinematic language to indicate we are in a noisy location, but now we will make it quieter so you can hear the important stuff. The choice of both content and how it is implemented is also important to achieving a balanced environment. The city can certainly have sirens in the background to add to the overall feel and indicate events occurring in a living city. But there is no need for a wailing siren to scream right past the audience unless it is part of the narrative. The same applies to the rest of your sounds, city or forest. There are many ways we can depict a busy city or a lush forest without having to have car horns next to the audience's ear or noisy parrots screeching a foot away.

When we craft an environment that needs to depict busy, complex, alive, and noisy environments, we can do so without the noises being painful or frustrating for the listener; instead, we can use more low-energy content that just creates an overall bustle and rumble in the background. This approach combines with, and enhances the careful setting of volume levels.

How we chose to spatialize may also impact the listener's experience if we do not approach it carefully. Head tracking might compensate for this, but I think time will be needed to investigate this further. An annoying repetitive sound in any media is going to quickly reduce the enjoyment of the listener: a poorly designed UI sound that beeps too often, a bad environmental loop that is short and noticeable, or insufficient variation of footstep sounds that makes the listener feel like they are listening to a ticking clock. We know from experience that repetition can be beneficial in musical passages when done well, but really annoying in all forms of media when done badly. I wonder if limited spatialization resulting in locational repetition would be noticeable and annoying.

If we created a spatial environment where a sound was positioned from only a limited number of locations, would this be obvious to the average listener, and would it become frustrating or annoying?—always hearing the sounds coming from the exact same position just above your left shoulder, for example. It would certainly reduce the sense of realism from a spatial perspective, but would positional repetition be as negative to an audience as the repetition of the same sound over and over? In this example it may cause confusion rather than fatigue, but either way it is likely to be an undesirable effect.

I use the term "fatigue" to represent undesirable audio content that will not just lower the audience's enjoyment of an experience, but actively drive them away from the experience through constant or repetitive annoying elements. Crappy audio may well have the same result, but it is less about fatigue and more just that the listener will not want to continue to experience a poorly crafted product.

Reality versus fun

We use and rely on technology to be able to produce most of our modern forms of media. Production tools, plug-ins, various hardware devices, all enable us to create content that we hope will engage and delight our audiences. The improvements in technology over the last generation have allowed us all as artists to create things beyond the imagination of our parent's generation. Technology is a tool that aids us in creating. Technology is a tool and it is important to always keep that in perspective.

When we choose to build an experience that we hope will allow the audience to experience an alien world we rely on certain aspects of technology to simulate the world to a sufficient level that the audience can suspend disbelief and feel like they really are in that alien environment. But most forms of media are also designed to entertain and so there is a balance between reality simulation and fun. Fun is an important word.

An action game where we play the hero and save the world allows us to escape reality in a fun experience.

A rollercoaster ride can be fun, even though many who experience a rollercoaster will spend the entire journey screaming.

A horror film can be fun, even though we spend much of the time overwhelmed with adrenaline and may sleep poorly for several nights.

A film that depicts the tragic events of a family that will leave us in tears and make us want to hug our loved ones can also be classed as fun under the definition I am currently using.

The key and common element across all these examples is emotion. As a species, we tell stories and we live experiences because they provide an emotional connection for us and the chance to safely feel certain emotions that we know we can turn off and tuck away till later if they become too much. At the age of 5, I found a Doctor Who monster in a rubber mask terrifying; as I grew older they seemed fairly silly, but the memory of the experience is part of why I became a long-term fan of the series.

In fact, *Doctor Who* is an excellent example where, for many years, the sets, costumes, and special effects were really quite basic and obviously not "real." Spaceships with cardboard walls and monsters with rubber masks however did not prevent the series from being immensely popular and successful, and that is because the stories were engaging and it was able to provide interesting emotional experience for the viewers. This is why I really believe that the equation of fun vs. realism benefits us more if it is weighted more toward the fun component than worrying about creating a hyperreal simulation.

For example, we know that as humans we are not great at localizing sounds to our rear. Our own ability is not great in that regard, but combine that with current HRTF solutions not being 100% perfect in convincing the listener exactly where sounds are, and we are left with a technical challenge. If we want to create an eerie experience that is designed to unsettle the audience we could position a sound source behind the listener in an empty room they have just turned their back on. Maybe the uncertainty of the localization will not affect the impact of this creepy audio event, but if it is successfully spooky that is less up to the technology and more up to the content. However, knowing the limitations of our technology and that HRTF is not 100% convincing for localization as well as HRTF not being as convincing for close proximity sounds allows us to realize another approach could be more effective.

If the eerie sound we want to utilize is short, such as a short ghostly whisper of a single word, a moan, or other short sound, then we could implement the sound using a binaural recording captured directly behind the listener. So, a "voice in your ear" type of effect, which binaural can create really well. If the sound is short enough then it can be executed before the audience can turn their head and so the need to support head tracking is not important. In this example, the super close proximity effect and realistic sensation of "just behind you" that binaural can achieve makes it an excellent solution for this little challenge. We arrived at this solution by understanding the various different technology solutions we have at hand, their strengths and weaknesses, and how they can work together to complement each other. So an HRTF room environment could be combined with a binaural ghost whisper to create an unsettling spatial audio experience. The ultimate goal of creating a scary experience for the audience to enjoy is what is important.

User Control: How Much Control Do We Give Our Players?

I have not personally looked into this aspect of design too deeply and I suspect as an industry it might be a little while before we work out the best balance. But games have always provided an unusual level of control that no other medium does, and it might be time to stop doing this.

Many games that I have played have the standard music, sound effects and general audio level controls. We provide them to allow the user to have more control over their experience. But why do we do this? You cannot go into a movie, or watch a television program and alter the balance between music and SFX. And these days some more complex games will even provide separate controls for voice-over and background ambiences as well. So we are essentially providing the user with all the controls they need to completely screw up the audio mix for a game. That's like having controls on your MP3 player to crank up the drums and mute the guitar. It would never happen.

Regardless of whether this legacy from games is a good or a bad thing, the idea of this level of user control being adopted for the new realities could have really significant consequences.

One consideration is that functions to allow the user to rebalance certain aspects of the audio can allow people with hearing difficulties to raise the voice volume independently, or for users to compensate for the limitations of the headphones they may own. This is certainly a logical argument for the desire to include the ability to tune your audio balance as a user. However, it could also be suggested that in many circumstances those functions risk creating an imbalanced mixed that would significantly affect the end experience. Our industry pays experienced professionals a lot of money in some cases to create a high-quality end mix of the media we produce. There is plenty of evidence to indicate that often consumers are unaware of how audio is best presented. There are numerous stories of users purchasing home theater systems and then lining all the speakers up in front of the television, or placing them at differing heights or hiding them behind books and other furniture. We should not expect a consumer to understand how audio functions—that is our job—so are the perceived benefits of user audio control significant enough to outweigh the potential for the user to alter the playback so significantly that any effort put into creating a good mix is essentially wasted?

How we spatialize and mix for the new realities is going to be an ongoing lesson for all of us. HTRF and spatial audio is extremely complex and trying to create well balanced and high-quality experiences is going to take significant amounts of work as we get used to working in a full 360 domain with room reflections and many other aspects of audio behavior. Turning control of any aspect of that process over to the user seems like a really bad idea and I cannot see any way in which this could improve the end experience for the users.

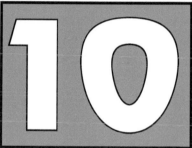

roadmap for the future: what do we do next?

---

we don't know what we don't know

It is hard enough to predict the future of any industry or craft, but as soon as technology is involved then all bets are off. I have often spoken to people about new technology advances and how they may affect society and culture, and almost always the people I speak with reply with statements such as "oh yes, but it won't happen that quickly." The best response to this is a presentation I saw many years ago at a tech conference. There was the regional CEO of a global tech company that gave a presentation and his talk was about the short-term and long-term future of mobile technology at the time.

He started his presentation by explaining he was going to shift his topic slightly. The reason why is that he had spent the last three months planning for this talk and assessing the state of the technology. When he started writing his presentation his plan was to assess where technology would be in about three years' time. He then explained that the very technology he was assessing had advanced so much in the three months that he was planning his talk, it had reached the point he originally predicted it would be in three years' time.

This will not always happen with all branches of technology all the time, but currently we live in a world where it is often completely impossible to predict where technology may leap forward and how the consumer market may respond to a thing. No one would have predicted just how total the uptake of smartphones would be and how this technology would affect the entire world. Companies such as Google, Amazon, Facebook, and Apple have all had such a massive impact on how everyday people communicate, educate, and consume that we now live in a very different world from the one we lived in before these companies existed.

A significant number of people are already predicting that AR is going to be bigger than VR. I think this might be an accurate prediction. If AR and AR headsets become part of the information infrastructure of mobile devices and for everyday uses then this prediction is almost certain to come true. I still believe that AR will be mostly for serious uses such as communication, navigation, checking your bus timetable, and other routine uses, while VR will continue to grow in the area of entertainment such as film, TV, and game experiences.

I suggested earlier in this book that we also cannot yet predict the types of experiences that will exist 10 years from now and this I sincerely believe this is true. Consider any movie created in the 1950s. Color cinema was possible, and sound was monophonic. The technology allowed for general filming on set or on location and the ability to record the dialogue at the same time. No one then could possibly have imagined or believed that the state of cinema now was even remotely possible. Giant Imax screen, Dolby Atmos soundscapes, incredible visual effects that can make us believe a giant robot is striding through a futuristic city. The craft of filmmaking has evolved so incredibly far in that time.

I would suggest that 50–60 years of advancement in cinema technology is probably equivalent to maybe 10 years' advancement in current technology. The rate at which we develop and evolve both our technology and work practices is so much faster these days.

Learning a Whole New Vocabulary

While writing this book I have researched and investigated aspects of VR and AR creation and production, concepts of how to film 360 video content, and of course how we approach audio design for all these new formats. I have realized that we use a specific vocabulary when we tell stories and this vocabulary is something that has been built up from decades of cinematography, television writing, and game design. If you consider how artificial some of these techniques are it is easier to understand how the new generation of media will also need to develop a new language for narrative.

Consider an often used and well understood cinematography technique. A scene opens and we can see an individual in the distance. They may be standing on a hill, or on a busy street, or pretty much anywhere. We hear their spoken voice and then the camera cuts to a close-up of their face. If we pull this technique apart it can seem somewhat absurd. The camera shows us a person so far away we can make out little detail. They are essentially distant and anonymous. Then we start to hear their voice as they speak. How can we hear them? They are miles away, we can barely see them and yet we can hear their voice. Then we cut to being right in front of them, looking them right in the eyes. How did we get here so quickly? Did we just teleport or magically leap the great distance to stand next to them?

We accept all of these storytelling techniques because we have gotten used to them over years of seeing them used in film, TV, and games. We accept that the single frame cut from distant to extreme close-up is a mechanic for telling the story we are viewing. The same applies to being able to hear a conversation from miles away. But originally someone made the decision to use these techniques and at the time they probably seemed strange and even an unnatural way of filming action.

The same is already happening with VR, AR, and 360 video. The fact that the audience can look in any direction nullifies many of our traditional cinematic language and process. We can no longer do a single frame camera cut from distant to close because if the audience is looking the wrong way they will be seriously disorientated. I spoke with an industry colleague recently who was describing a location-based VR experience. At one point, we were discussing a location where the audience moved as a group across the tops of buildings. I asked what happened if someone chose to step off the building. I was told that from everyone else's perspective that individual would instantly fall to their death and everyone would see the person's body tumble down to the ground. When I asked what the person who stepped off would experience I was told, they would see themselves walking across the sky.

I asked why the person would not see themselves fall down to the ground in the same way we would in any traditional game experience where your character fell. Apparently in a location-based VR experience the immersion is so effective that if you visually simulate someone falling off a building the individual is likely to fall to their knees and throw up everywhere. The stimulation to their senses is such that they lose control of their body. This has quickly been established as a limitation we need to accept when creating immersive VR experiences. We could just as easily intentionally highlight and utilize this behavior, but it might result in a messy experience for the audience. The point is that the new format has some very real differences in how we go about communicating ideas to our audience.

Research, Development, and Evolution

This book has been mostly about concepts and our approach to designing and building creative content for the new realities. The hard science and math involved is significant and critical, but it is also a very real challenge to assess each aspect of the science and evaluate how and where it may be useful to apply to our craft. There are many smart people who are constantly performing research into many aspects of this and other forms of technology and it is this research that allows us to evolve how a media format works. There are businesses who aim their development directly at producing a product that can be marketed commercially as a tool or user format. These businesses provide us with tools, but they also have a specific desire to generate income from their work, so those tools do not always speak to each other in the most direct and beneficial manner. Each business wants their solution to be the one that everyone adopts.

Sometimes the best tech is adopted, but sometimes the best marketed tech is adopted.

Academic institutions are another area where we can gain valuable knowledge and ideas to take our technology forward, but sometimes academic workers will move toward achieving outcomes that work brilliantly for answering specific questions, but have no consideration for how the information could ever be applied in a real-world industry application. It is usually a balance somewhere between purely academic research and commercial development that allows us to adopt the most effective and creative techniques for our work. Both academic research and business development are critical in evolving our craft, but sometimes they do not sync up as quickly as we would like, and sometimes they can be a bit ahead of their time.

It can be frustrating as a creative developer to understand certain aspects of the technology and not know exactly how to utilize that information. Maybe the information has real value, but the technology is not yet powerful enough to fully utilize it. Maybe the technology has made some significant advances, but as an industry we need to spend more time working with it to really understand it and get the best possible results from it. This situation may, I think, have possibly been the case throughout human history. We do not always know the exact best way to utilize a piece of information at the time we discover it. We then must spend more time learning what we can do with that information.

A good example of this is some research undertaken by a colleague, Sally-anne Kellaway. Sally has been working and studying various aspects of audio for the new realities for many years and in fact completed a master degree with research in this area. One of her research topics was on the topic of source spectra. This is an interesting topic of discussion, but like many research papers it is not something that is immediately applicable to all things and will unlikely have an instant earth-shattering impact on how we work. I think sometimes people expect all new research or developments to have immediate and massive effects and as a result can undervalue work that is being done.

So it is research such as Sally's that will allow us to evolve and develop our approach to the new realities, but it is up to us to work out how best to adopt and adapt the work of the academics and tech development teams.

Spotlight on the Impact of Source Spectra

Sally-anne Kellaway

As complex as our auditory perception systems are, they are also deeply susceptible to manipulation. Particularly in the realm of the monaural spectral cues, these cues are deeply susceptible to distortions. Distortions of our spectral cues compromise our ability to localize sound. While this is troublesome enough in the real world (perhaps more so considering the peril of not being able to detect the location of actual threats), capacity for localization is part of what makes audio incredibly important in the new realities.

Content in these nascent days of the new realities is still working through iterations in design practice, where all mediums must be as effective as possible to ensure the viewer has the optimum experience. Sound bears a greater role in this "effective presentation" because it is our only 360-degree sense, making it immensely important for cueing the viewer to turn around, or interact with specific objects that may or may not be in the viewer's field of vision.

When designing sound for the new realities, taking this into consideration is critical, and understanding the elements that impact on localization and how localization can be manipulated and skewed is critical to executing on effective design. Every element of the process of sensory replacement or augmentation in the new realities introduces new layers of potential coloration of source content. This can include (but is not limited to) source spectra, spatialization solution, software processing steps, and hardware such as headphones. We might take this for granted as the way audio has always been, but at least it's better now compared to those wax cylinders from way back when. The challenge now is to parse the effects of these sources of spectral manipulation against our academic understanding of the impact of spectra on localization and use the comparison to inform our creative and technical practice to benefit the experience of the end user.

To understand the impact that our listening systems have on audio in the new realities, it's important to understand some of the research describing the innate directionality of spectra. The relationship between spectra and direction has been the topic of research for many decades—with seminal pieces of research from Blauert (1969), Martens (1987), and Rogers & Butler (1992) creating the cornerstones for deeper research.

Blauert's 1969 research focuses on three major directional zones (forward, rearward and elevated) and found that the dominant frequency of a source sound does impact on the listener's ability to accurately localize sound in these key directional zones. This was tested with narrow-band noise panned on the median plane, revealing that the 1 kHz band was critical for rearward localization, and the 4 kHz band for the frontward.

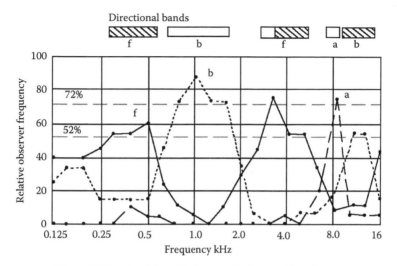

Blauert's "Directional Bands"—b = rear, f = front, and a = above.
This chart shows the relative observer identification of a direction
when narrow-band noise of various center frequencies (x-axis) is played.

Martens further explores this concept in his 1987 study, plotting spectral energy from HRTF measurements against azimuth angle to reveal the directional quality of 24 key spectral bands. In further detail, Martens confirms the bias spectra can have on localization by demonstrating the bias of 1 kHz in the rearward region and 4 Hz in the frontward on the transverse plane.

A similar concept was presented by Rogers and Butler in a series of studies on covert peak areas—areas in space where when narrow-band sound is played to the listener, that frequency band is elevated in volume above any other band. This indicates that the ear imparts a resonance on these bands at specific locations. Butler applied the CPA theory to studies on azimuth and elevation over several years, further corroborating the research linking source spectra to directional bias in localization.

The correlation of narrow-band noise to vibrant, time-variant sounds that are generated by the breadth of industries involved in the new realities might seem weak, but simplified tests are actually a critical example of how highly resonant sounds will impact our localization capabilities. In an example of this, studies by Kellaway and Martens (2014) assess the degree to which highly resonant vocal vowel sounds impact on the listener ability to correctly identify frontward and rearward sources. Findings pointed to further correlation with the studies from Blauert, Martens, and Butler, confirming that even for more spectrally complex sounds, the dominant frequencies in the sounds can create directional bias which impacts on the listener ability to correctly localize sounds.

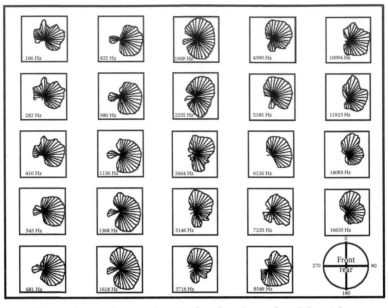

Martens' spectral energy plots. Reading the columns from left to right,
you can see how the spectral energy shifts in direction based on the band.
You can see the correlation between Blauert's identified front and rear
directional bands and these plots.

This theory could easily be applied to any content that sound designers of the new realities develop for their projects. Resonant sounds can include sound design elements such as explosions, musical instruments, and especially voice. Professional practitioners understand the concept of spectral masking, and this spectral directional coloring is merely an extension of that.

This problem becomes more complex when we acknowledge that any source of additional spectral coloration will contribute a similar effect. When it comes to reproduction systems such as headphones, we also face the reality of sound coloration from the frequency response of the wide array of headphones available to users currently. Bass-heavy headphones may make hip-hop beats sound compelling, but will surely let down the careful preparations of the sound designers operating in the new realities.

Resonant source sounds are inescapable in the "real world," even when creating for virtual, augmented or mixed realities (and perhaps even more so). Understanding that highly resonant sounds can impact on localization allows a sound designer working in the new realities to be mindful of how to achieve accuracy in the critical localization moment of their projects. Suggesting that simple EQ filters will successfully allow for increased localization ability is naive and inaccurate, but maintaining vigilant mixing practice and ensuring that critical sounds have "space" and "priority" in relevant spectral directional zones is one of the first steps to creating a wider practice of sound design and implementation for the new realities.

using the knowledge

Speaking with Sally, the results of her research are something she has already applied to her work process. Content with higher timbral qualities can be effective when placed to the front of an audience's space and lower timbral qualities behind. So in general you can position instruments spatially based on their timbral qualities. Or alternatively if you want to draw the audience's attention to their rear, making the rear sounds crisper and the front sounds duller can influence the audience of the importance of the sound to the rear.

The study, experimentation, and application of research topics into our daily workflow is something we can all adopt as time permits. This also allows all of us as industry colleagues to test different approaches and then compare notes. Experience each other's works and review how we perceive that content, and what we can learn from it.

Research and Practice

The more I am exposed to academics and academic research, the more I believe that there may be a place for closely linked collaborations. Many academics seem to work in a bubble and may not research topics that are useful to industry, but equally many industry folk do not have the time to perform research and advance their work practices. By linking academics and industry professionals directly I think there could be a significant advantage to both sides. A specific research project could be guided and influenced by the needs of an industry professional and in turn that industry professional could utilize aspects of the research immediately in a production environment, and stress test the finding under real-world conditions.

This process is not always going to suit all types of research and all types of industry work, but it seems to me that the isolation of academics and professionals into their own bubble worlds reduces the opportunities and advancements for both sides.

Endless Opportunities

I am already aware of colleagues creating AR applications for things such as sports training, education and training, and even simulation training, and this is just among people I know personally. Across the world the list of possible applications for AR and VR could fill an entire book. Considering how these new technologies function forces your brain to consider the possibilities and it is almost impossible not to come up with a huge list of possible applications.

AR – Driver. Navigating via route being superimposed over the real road you are looking at.

AR – Musical training. The app listens to what you are playing and highlights incorrect notes on the score.

AR – Jogging training. Device superimposes a virtual pace setter to run next to you that you have to keep up with.

AR – Weight training or martial arts. A virtual trainer demonstrates the moves and you must copy them.

AR – Medical procedure. The application superimposes X-ray or MRI info as surgeon performs procedure.

AR – Military training. Application creates virtual adversaries as part of live training.

AR – Live chat. A full-sized virtual friend walks next to you as you speak with them on the phone.

AR – Emergency evacuation. Safest path is displayed and updated in real time as people evacuate from a building.

VR – Friends gather together virtually from around the world to play role-playing games or board games together at the same virtual table.

VR – Counter travel sickness by wearing a VR device synced to the vehicle so it simulates the movement of the vehicle in a virtual space. Relieves boredom of long journey and counters travel sickness from inner ear confusion.

VR – Virtual classroom. Allows for users globally to gather in a virtual classroom where practical demonstrations can be more effective than simply watching a video.

MR – Performance experienced through stadium speakers with AR visual content.

MR – Art installations where visitors view physical artworks enhanced with spatial audio content.

MR – Stage plays enhanced with virtual characters and VFX as well as spatial audio.

MR – Location-based art exhibits. Desert drive is enhanced with virtual sculptures along the route.

I could add to this list endlessly and while many of these concepts came to me as I researched this book, quite a few simply popped into my head as I wrote the list. The point of this is that the combination of VR, AR, and MR as new technology, new mediums, and new forms of communication present us with practically limitless possibilities for not just creating new artworks, but for creating entirely new genres of creative expression. On the practical side, we are on the cusp of a whole new range of communication and education possibilities. Not all the new applications are going to be ground breaking or incredibly useful. Like anything, there will be poorly crafted experiences and badly designed applications. This is the nature of all things humans create; we get both the good and the bad.

Of course, not all applications of the new technology will require complex, creative audio content. Many will require basic UI functional alert sounds and little more. Some will require basic audio feedback and maybe some creative audio content. Serious applications still require careful design so even the most basic user-feedback audio should be designed and implemented carefully. How we utilize audio will be an important part of how these new technologies will be received. The better the job we all do the more people will enjoy working with series apps or enjoy the creative content we share.

Dreamers and Doers

I consider myself fortunate to work in a creative industry and I love creating worlds, crafting music, and building sonic playgrounds. I honestly have no idea exactly where the new realities will take us and this both excites and terrifies me. But most of the creative people I am inspired by say that living outside of your comfort zone is where you will find the most interesting and amazing work, and also where you will become the best you can be.

I am looking forward to trying and failing at a great many things with this new technology as I stumble my way forward. I started a creative career because I believed this was where humans really could wield magic and make it real. The new realities have such wonderful potential that I spend many days feeling like a child in a toy shop, full of wonder.

Be Fearless, Be Reckless, Be a Little Crazy

Do not be afraid to try and fail because failure is when we learn the most. Most importantly, enjoy working in this new reality because more than ever we can craft worlds and take our audience to experiences that humans have not even considered possible in the past.

I once said to my dear friend and colleague George Sanger that I felt that working with this new technology was like trying to send a person to Mars. George looked at me as said, "No Stephan, this is like we are trying to send the entirety of Disneyland to Mars!" I embrace everything about that and invite you all to join me as we make magic happen.

references

Blauert, J. 1969. Sound Localization on the Median Plane. *Acustica* 22: 205–213.

Furness, R.K. 1990. *Ambisonics—An Overview*. Minim Electronics Limited, Burnham, UK.

Hartley, R.V.L. and Fry, T.C. 1922. The Binaural Location of Complex Sounds. *Bell System Technical Journal* 1: 33–42.

Huopaniemi, J. and Riederer, K.A.J. 1998. Measuring and Modeling the Effect of Source Distance in Head-Related Transfer Functions. *The Journal of the Acoustical Society of America* 103: 2988.

Kellaway, S.-A. and Martens, W.L. 2014. *Further Investigation of the Effects of Source Coloration of Vocal Vowels on Discrimination of Forward and Rearward Motion in Virtual Auditory Images*. University of Sydney.

Martens, W.L. 1987. Principal Components Analysis and Resynthesis of Spectral Cues to Perceived Direction. *ICM Proceedings*, pp. 274–281.

Rogers, M.E. and Butler, R.A. 1992. The Linkage between Stimulus Frequency and Covert Peak Areas as It Is Related to Monauaral Localization. *Perception & Psychophysics* 52(2): 10.

Whiting, J. 1996. *Ambisonics Is Dead: Long Live Ambisonics*. Minim Electronics Limited, Burnham, Slough, UK. http://www.ambisonic.net/

index

a

Agency for the audience, 7
AKG D112 microphone, 225
Alternate reality (AR), 27, 56
  opportunities, 320
  prediction about, 312
Alternate reality challenges, 89–93
  audibility, 90–91
  choosing wisely, 91
  frequency range, 92–93
Ambisonic microphones, 234–239
  after testing, 236–239
  Sennheiser Ambeo, 235–236
Ambisonics, 37–49
  decoding, 48
  efficiency, 47–48
  encoding, 46–47
  explanation, 40–49
  field axis, 38
  higher-order, 44
  history and fundamental concepts,
    48–49
  microphone with multiple capsules, 39
Amplitude drop-off, 159–164
Android, 287
Apple iOS, 287
Aquarian H2A microphone, 239–240
AR, *see* Alternate reality
AR, James Bond adventure in, 176–190
  attention focus, 187–190
  audio format, 185–187
  bitrate, 185
  codec, 184–185
  "focus cone" function, 188
  frame rate, 185
  microphones, 182
  project encoding and delivery
    method, 184
  360 video, working with, 181–182
  360 video format, 182–184
  video file container, 184
Assets, 207–242
  ambisonic microphones, 234–239
  binaural microphones, 228–234
  cost, time, and quality, 208
  directional microphones, 219–223
  dynamic microphones, 223–225
  foley, 214–216
  gathering, designing, and creating
    raw assets, 207–218
  generative or procedural audio,
    217–218
  location recording, 210–214
  microphones, 219–242
  omnidirectional microphones, 226–228
  portable digital recorders, 240–242
  sound creation, 216–217
  sound libraries, 208–210
  specific purpose microphones,
    239–240
Audience (customers), 294–309
  comfort and control, 296
  communication, 299–300
  fatigue, 302–306
  reality versus fun, 306–307
  setup, 298–299
  user control, 308–309
  welcoming environment, 296–298
  wise use of technology, 300–302
Audience, agency for, 7
Audio Technica stereo BP4029
    microphone, 221–222
Augmented reality, 58

b

Barking Irons, 123–124
BBC special binaural audio broadcast,
    100–102
Binaural microphones, 228–234
    binaural recording as new realities
        audio technique, 230–232
    DIY binaural dummy head, 232–234
Binaural recording, 36
Bluetooth headphones, 128, 130

c

Challenges, 51–97
    adapting to new formats, 56
    aiding the visual experience, 86–87
    alternate reality challenges, 89–93
    balancing information and
        entertainment, 71–73
    battle between order and chaos,
        65–67
    challenges common to all new reality
        formats, 70–71
    choosing your reality, 68–73
    head tracking, 85
    hearing versus listening, 64
    how and why we hear, 56–64
    human problem, 74–77
    hyperreality, 96–97
    illusions, 61
    importance of getting audio right,
        86–89
    mixed reality challenges, 93–96
    mixing, 81–82
    physics, expensiveness of, 79–81
    ray tracing, 80
    speaker output, 95
    3D audio, 51
    360 video, 87–89
    triangulation challenge, 73–81
    uncanny valley, 57–58
    unique format challenges, 83–85
    virtual reality challenges, 83–84
    VR audio, development of, 52–55
    wavefront curvature, 69–70
    why what we hear matters, 60–64
Channel-based audio, 35–36
Clock, *see* VR clock, creation of
Cocktail party effect, 188
Cone of confusion, 32
Content creation, 190–206
    building a weather system, 191–194
    footsteps, 202
    forest creation, 196

    immersive audio, 194
    near field versus far field, 205–206
    new creation approaches, 190–191
    noise reduction, 203–205
    ocean waves, 200
    virtual environment, creation of,
        195–203
    wind and water, 199
    world building with audio, 191–195
Core concepts, 29–40
    Ambisonics, 37–40
    binaural recording, 36
    channel-based audio, 35–36
    cone of confusion, 32
    diegetic sound, 34
    flat plane or zero plane, 33–34
    formats, 34
    haptics, 29
    head-related transfer function, 29
    IID or ILD, 30
    interaural phase difference, 30–31
    interaural time difference, 29–30
    localization, 35
    mid-side recording format, 36–40
    transcoding, 33
    transfer function, 29
Creation and implementation, 143–206
    amplitude drop-off, 159–164
    audio diagnosis, 174
    breaking our sounds for better
        implementation, 151–153
    cocktail party effect, 188
    content creation, 190–206
    flight simulation, 175–176
    "focus cone" function, 188
    footsteps, 202
    forest creation, 196
    immersive audio, 194
    implementation, 145
    James Bond adventure in AR, 176–190
    microphones, 182
    min and max distance functions and
        attenuation curves, 145–149
    near field versus far field, 205–206
    new creation approaches, 190–191
    noise reduction, 203–205
    "observation" of audio, 153–158
    ocean waves, 200
    placement, 144–145
    project encoding and delivery
        method, 184
    reverb, 149–151
    serious audio design for serious
        purposes, 173–176
    360 video, working with, 181–182

video file container, 184
virtual environment, creation of,
    195–203
VR clock, creation of, 164–172
weather system, building of, 191–194
wind and water, 199
working analysis, 158–164
working with the new realities, 143–158
world building with audio, 191–195
Customers, *see* Audience (customers)

d

Dark Days, 105–109
DAW, *see* Digital audio workstation
Defect, learning from, 258–261
Definitions and core concepts, 15–49
    Ambisonics, 37–40
    AR (alternate reality), 27
    binaural recording, 36
    channel-based audio, 35–36
    cone of confusion, 32
    core concepts, 29–40
    diegetic sound, 34
    flat plane or zero plane, 33–34
    formats, 34
    haptics, 29
    head-related transfer function, 29
    IID or ILD, 30
    interaural phase difference, 30–31
    interaural time difference, 29–30
    localization, 35
    mid-side recording format, 36–40
    MR (mixed reality), 28
    new realities, spatialization in, 20–23
    spatial audio, thinking differently
        about, 15–24
    stereo, spatialization in, 17–19
    surround sound, spatialization in,
        19–20
    terminology, defining of, 24
    transcoding, 33
    transfer function, 29
    VR (virtual reality), 25–26
    VR and 360 video, spatial audio in,
        23–24
Device conundrum, 283
Diegetic sound, 34
Digital audio workstation (DAW), 276
Directional microphones, 219–223
    Audio Technica stereo BP4029,
        221–222
    Rode NTG3, 221
    Sanken CS1e, 222–223
    Sennheiser MKH60, 220

DPA 4061 microphone, 227–228
Dynamic microphones, 223–225
    AKG D112, 225
    Shure SM 57, 224–225
    Shure SM7B, 224

e

Earthlight, 102–105
Emotional mapping, 270–273
Existing projects, analysis of, 99–141
    Barking Irons, 123–124
    broadcast, 100–102
    Dark Days, 105–109
    Earthlight, 102–105
    GearVR, 105–109
    Knott's Berry Farm *VR Showdown in
        Ghost Town*, 130–131
    location-based experiences, 120–141
    planktOs: Crystal Guardians,
        128–129
    Playstation VR, *How We Soar*,
        109–113
    Playstation VR, *Star Wars Battlefront:
        Episode One X-Wing Mission*,
        113–116
    Vive, 102–105
    VR project analysis, 99–100

f

Field of view (FOV), 137
Flat plane, 33–34
Flight simulation program, 175
FMOD, 81, 293
Foley, 6, 7, 214–216
Footsteps, creation of, 202–203
Forest creation, 196–199
Formats, 34
Future of new realities, 311–322
    being fearless, 322
    dreamers and doers, 321–322
    opportunities, 320–321
    research, development, and
        evolution, 314–319
    research and practice, 319
    source spectra, impact of, 316–319
    using the knowledge, 319–322
    vocabulary, 313–314
    what we don't know, 311–319

g

GearVR, 105–109
Generative audio, 217–218

h

Haptics, 29
Headphones
    bass-heavy, 318
    Bluetooth, 128, 130
    close-backed, 94
    frequency response, 78
    limitations of, 308
    open-backed, 84
    Ossic, 290–292
Head-related transfer function (HRTF),
    29, 101
    binaural microphones and, 229
    near field versus far field and,
      205–206
    spatial audio tools, 4
    system, human problem and, 77
    teamwork and, 266, 267
Head tracking, 85
Hearing, listening versus, 64
Higher-order Ambisonics, 44
HoloLens, 287–290
How We Soar, 109–113
HRTF, *see* Head-related transfer
    function
HTC Vive VR headset, 2
Human problem, 74–77
Hyperreality (HR), 96–97

i

Immersive audio, 194
Implementation, *see* Creation and
    implementation
Interactive audio workstation, 276–282
    application to VR storytelling, 280–282
    game audio production workflow,
      277–279
    interactive audio production
      workflow, 276–277
    interactive music toolset, 279–280
    linear audio production workflow, 276
Interaural intensity difference (IID), 30, 76
Interaural loudness difference (ILD), 30
Interaural phase difference (IPD), 30–31,
    64, 76
Interaural time difference (ITD), 29–30, 76

j

James Bond adventure in AR, 176–190
    attention focus, 187–190
    audio format, 185–187
    bitrate, 185

    codec, 184–185
    "focus cone" function, 188
    frame rate, 185
    microphones, 182
    project encoding and delivery
      method, 184
    360 video, working with, 181–182
    360 video format, 182–184
    video file container, 184
Jump scares, 105

k

Knott's Berry Farm *VR Showdown in
    Ghost Town*, 130–131

l

Lapel mics, 226–227
Listening, hearing versus, 64
Localization, 35
Location-based experiences, 120–141
    audio and VR environment, 121–122
    authenticity, 133–134
    balancing audio for the environment
      and gameplay, 124–125
    Barking Irons, 123–124
    challenges overcome, 136–138
    cinematic moments, 135–136
    game environment and environmental
      audio design, 124
    headphones, 128
    iterative design and testing, 125–127
    Knott's Berry Farm *VR Showdown in
      Ghost Town*, 130–131
    "less is more" approach, 130
    music, 127–128, 130, 138
    nondiegetic music and VO in VR,
      122–123
    planktOs: Crystal Guardians,
      128–129
    underscore, 122
    VR system description, 120–121
Location recording, 210–214

m

Melee robots, 136, 137
Microphones, 219–242
    ambisonic microphones, 234–239
    binaural microphones, 228–234
    directional microphones, 219–223
    dynamic microphones, 223–225
    omnidirectional microphones, 226–228
    portable digital recorders, 240–242

shotgun, 219
specific purpose microphones, 239–240
Microsoft HoloLens, 3
Mid-side (MS) recording format, 36–40
Mixed reality (MR), 28, 58
    challenges, 93–96
    opportunities, 320, 321
Mixing, challenge of, 81–82
Mobile devices, 284–287
Music, 243–261
    attention focus and music, 254–255
    audio attenuation over distance, 252
    basic approach, 257–258
    conventional linear stereo music,
        253–254
    depth and parallax, 251–253
    diegetic and nondiegetic "musical"
        content, blurring the line
        between, 244–247
    extremes, 255–256, 258
    generative music, 256–261
    how to utilize your space, 251–255
    learning from Defect (spaceship
        destruction kit), 258–261
    musical possibilities, 247–249
    musical risk, 249–251
    sonic parallax, 252

n

New realities, introduction to, 1–14
    agency for the audience, 7
    art of Foley, 6, 7
    conflict, 4
    future sound of entertainment, 11–12
    head-related transfer function spatial
        audio tools, 4
    interactive 3D audio, 10–11
    perspective, 9
    prerendering, 10
    quality of audio, importance of, 5
    real-time rendering, 10
    "Wild West of technology," 3
New realities, spatialization in, 20–23
Nintendo, 287
Noise reduction, 203–205

o

Observation activity, 153–158
Ocean waves, creation of, 200–202
Omnidirectional microphones, 226–228
    DPA 4061, 227–228
    lapel mics, 226–227
Ossic headphones, 290–292

p

PlanktOs: Crystal Guardians, 128–129
Platform considerations, 275–309
    audience (customers), 294–309
    delivery platforms, 284–294
    different platforms, different
        solutions, 292–294
    digital audio workstation, 276
    HoloLens, 287–290
    interactive audio workstation, 276–282
    mobile, 284–287
    Ossic headphones, 290–292
    reality versus fun, 306–307
    tools enhancing workflow, 275–282
    user experience (device
        conundrum), 283
    wise use of technology, 300–302
Playstation VR
    How We Soar, 109–113
    *Star Wars Battlefront: Episode One
        X-Wing Mission*, 113–116
Prerendering, 10
Procedural audio, 217–218

r

Randomized chaos, 66
Raw source assets, *see* Assets
Ray tracing, 80
Real-time parameter control (RTPC), 125
Real-time rendering, 10
Reverb
    VR clock, 168–172
    working with the new realities, 149–151
Rode NTG3 microphone, 221

s

Sanken CS1e microphone, 222–223
Sennheiser Ambeo microphone,
    235–236
Sennheiser MKH60 microphone, 220
Shotgun mics, 219
Shure SM 57 microphone, 224–225
Shure SM7B microphone, 224
Sonic parallax, 252
Sound; *see also* Assets
    creation, 216–217
    libraries, 208–210
Soundblaster Live, 41
Source spectra, impact of, 316–319
Spatial audio, thinking differently
    about, 15–24
    new realities, spatialization in, 20–23

stereo, spatialization in, 17–19
surround sound, spatialization in, 19–20
VR and 360 video, spatial audio in, 23–24
Spatialized plugins, 78
Speaker
    array, 20, 21
    crosstalk, 229
    emitters, 287
    HoloLens, 288
    mixes, 45
    output, 18, 95
Star Wars Battlefront: Episode One X-Wing Mission, 113–116, 116–119

t

Teamwork, 263–273
    communication with non-audio team members and clients, 269–270
    consistency of environment, 264–273
    emotional mapping, 270–273
    team workflow, 273
360 video, 25–26
    questions, 87–89
    spatial audio in, 23–24
    working with, 181–182
Transcoding, 33
Transfer function, 29
Triangulation challenge, 73–81
    delivery, 78
    human problem, 74–77
    localization and spatialization, 74
    physics, expensiveness of, 79–81
    spatialization, 78–79

u

Uncanny valley, 57–58
Underscore, 122
User experience (UX), 55
User interface (UI), 55, 104

v

Virtual environment, creation of, 195–203
    example (wind and water), 199–200
    footsteps, 202–203
    forest creation, 196–199
    ocean waves, 200–202
Virtual reality (VR), 25–26
    audio, development of, 52–55
    challenges, 83–84
    clock, *see* VR clock, creation of
    opportunities, 320
    project analysis, 99–100
    replacing the world, 25
    spatial audio in, 23–24
    storytelling, interactive audio workstation and, 280–282
    360 video, 25–26
Vive, 102–105
Vocabulary, learning, 313–314
Voice-over (VO) content, 116
VR, *see* Virtual reality
VR clock, creation of, 164–172
    accuracy and detail, 165–166
    actual sound of a clock, 164–165
    physical placement, 168
    reverb, 168–172
    sidebar, 166–168
    simulating sound wave properties, 168–172
    smoke and mirrors, 172

w

Wavefront curvature, 69–70
WAV files, 277
Weather system, building of, 191–194
"Wild West of technology," 3
Wind-up clock, 165
Working together, *see* Teamwork
World building with audio, 191–195
    applications for immersive audio, 194
    building a weather system, 191–194
    getting the details right, 194–195
Wwise, 46, 81, 293

x

Xbox, 41, 287

y

Yonder: The Cloud Catcher Chronicles, 191

z

Zero plane, 33–34